Madness and Modernity

Mental Illness and the Visual Arts in Vienna 1900

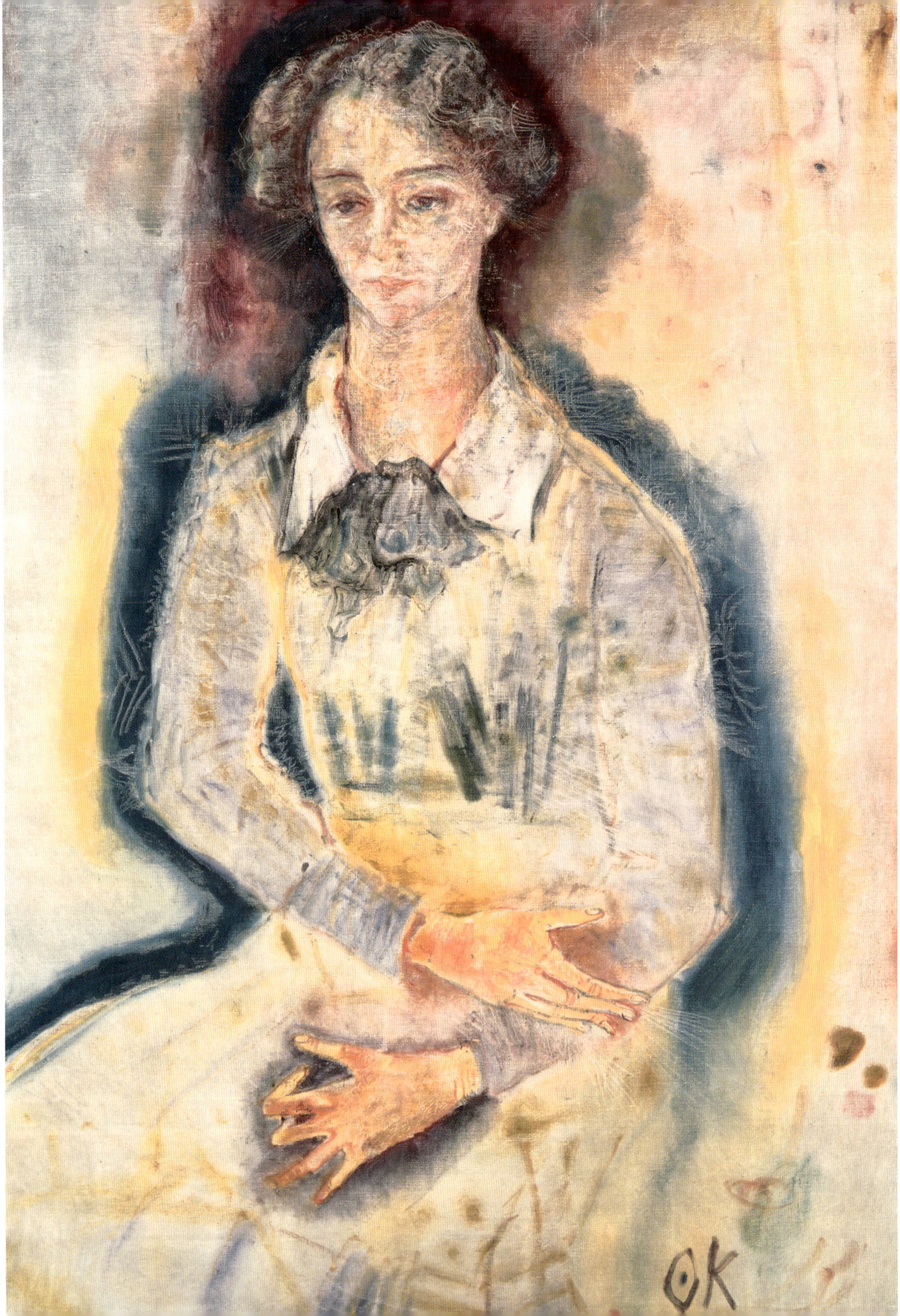
OK

Madness and Modernity

Mental Illness and the Visual Arts in Vienna 1900

EDITED BY GEMMA BLACKSHAW
& LESLIE TOPP

Published on the occasion of the exhibition
Madness and Modernity: Mental Illness and the Visual Arts in Vienna 1900, Wellcome Collection, London,
1 April–28 June 2009

LUND HUMPHRIES

First published in 2009 by Lund Humphries, in association with the Wellcome Collection

Lund Humphries
Wey Court East
Union Road
Farnham
Surrey
GU9 7PT
UK

and

Suite 420
101 Cherry Street
Burlington
VT 05401-4405
USA

www.lundhumphries.com

Lund Humphries is part of Ashgate Publishing

We gratefully acknowledge the support of the Arts and Humanities Research Council and the Wellcome Trust for the production of this book.

British Library Cataloguing-in-Publication Data

A catalogue record for this book is available from the British Library

Library of Congress Control Number: 2008938783

ISBN: 978-1-84822-020-1

Edited by Alison Hill
Designed by Mick Keates
Set in Weiss
Originated by Altaimage
Printed in the UK by Butler Tanner & Dennis Ltd, Frome, Somerset

Frontispiece: Oskar Kokoschka, *Portrait of Lotte Franzos*, 1909, oil on canvas, 115 × 79.5 cm (45¼ × 31⅜ in) Phillips Collection, Washington D. C.

CONTENTS

Foreword

James Peto, Senior Curator, Wellcome Collection

The newly restored marble facing of Otto Wagner's St Leopold Church gleams so cleanly that, in the sunlight, it is almost too bright to look at. The figures that stand above the portico look down on an extraordinary site: the 60 buildings of the Otto Wagner Spital (formerly 'am Steinhof') spread out beneath them to form a neat arrangement of pavilions and green spaces, woven together by a network of roadways. The trees that have grown tall in the 100 years since the hospital was built now partially obscure the sweeping view down to the city of Vienna below.

The church stands at the apex of the hospital's extensive complex, designed by Wagner in collaboration with urban planners and psychiatrists as an Institution for the Care and Cure of the Mentally Ill and for Nervous Disorders. The first patients to arrive at Steinhof when it opened in 1907 must have marvelled at the scale of it all, at the sense of freedom implied by the open spaces and extended vistas – whether along corridors opening onto gardens, or down the hill from the church towards the city. Among those early patients was Ludwig Ritter von Janikowski, a literary figure widely admired in Viennese circles. Among the many visitors – welcomed to Steinhof to help promote a sense of openness as opposed to confinement – was the young Austrian Expressionist painter, Oskar Kokoschka.

Kokoschka came to Steinhof to paint Janikowski's portrait. Clearly fascinated by his subject's mental state, he depicts Janikowski with an intense but detached expression, the yellows and greens of his palate and the nervous scratches in the paint adding to the sense of disorder, anguish and ill-health. As detailed in this book, the exhibition in which this painting first appeared drew an extraordinary critical reception. One critic, looking into the eyes of Janikowski's portrait, writes of 'the horror which calls out from the lacklustre gaze of a ruined intellect'. Another describes Kokoschka's subjects as 'care-worn citizens of the metropolis' who 'gape and scream' at the visitor, while a third says of his experience of the exhibition: 'After this virulence, clean air is necessary'.

Clean air was exactly what Otto Wagner wanted to give the patients at Steinhof. The abundance of greenery, the well-ventilated pavilions and light-filled rooms aimed to offer a re-invigorating freshness and a sense of order and purpose which would counter the 'virulent', nerve-jangling chaos of modern urban life.

While Wagner and his advisors from the world of psychiatry were working on a design for Steinhof that would give as much consideration to physical well-being as to the inner workings of the patients' minds, down below in the city Sigmund Freud was sitting at his desk in Berggasse, writing his *Essays on the Theory of Sexuality*. It is with Freud and his consulting room that the Viennese interest in mental illness at the turn of the century is most commonly associated. There could hardly be a sharper contrast, however, than that between Freud's book-lined, antique-filled and heavily draped consulting room, where all is concentrated inside the head, and the white-tiled, light-filled, outward-looking spaces of Steinhof.

These contrasting places and very different characters – Freud, Wagner, von Janikowski, Kokoschka, and many more besides – are brought together in this book, united by their presence in the city of Vienna in the first ten years of the twentieth century, and by their interest in mental illness – in its expression and in its treatment.

Madness and Modernity is published to accompany the exhibition of the same name, curated by Gemma Blackshaw and Leslie Topp for Wellcome Collection, London, in spring 2009. At Wellcome Collection, our programme of exhibitions, events and publications combines the perspectives of those working in the arts and humanities with those of scientists. We want science to be understood as part of culture, not as somehow separate from it. Scientific exploration and understanding – especially in the fields of physical and mental health – is therefore central to our exhibition programme. Both the fine arts and the exploration of the mind in fin-de-siècle Vienna have been much studied in recent books and exhibitions. But Gemma Blackshaw, Leslie Topp and their colleagues, Sabine Wieber, Luke Heighton and Nicola Imrie, have brought a fresh approach to the place, the period and the people, with original research prompting new ideas and arguments.

In enquiring about the extent to which the study of mental illness may have influenced leading modernists, they also raise intriguing questions about how modernism might have influenced our attitudes to the mentally ill. This book and the exhibition it accompanies shed light on some fascinating correspondences, hitherto little explored, between psychiatrists, artists, architects, designers and patients, and on modernism's determined belief in the transformative power of scientific understanding allied to artistic expression.

Introduction and Acknowledgements

Gemma Blackshaw and Leslie Topp

Vienna 1900 – that highly evocative time and place – has long been considered the birthplace of modernity. The home of such modern giants as Sigmund Freud, Gustav Klimt, Arthur Schnitzler and Otto Wagner, Vienna during the fin-de-siècle period of 1890–1910 continues to capture the attention of scholars, curators and gallery-visitors, keen to explore 'one of the most fertile breeding grounds' of twentieth-century culture.[1] The distinctive intermingling of the city's intelligentsia in such spaces as the coffeehouse, the cabaret, the sanatorium and the Secession building created connections between different spheres of cultural production. These connections – between, for example, literature, psychoanalysis and painting – have facilitated the development of themes which re-surface again and again in Vienna 1900 exhibitions: sex and death; dream and reality; inertia and revolt.[2] Moreover, the cross-fertilization of ideas that defined the city's cultural activity and – in the case of the visual arts – characterised the Secession group exhibitions has provided subsequent curators with the opportunity to draw objects and individuals together from a broad base. The exhibition and book *Madness and Modernity: Mental Illness and the Visual Arts in Vienna 1900* both continue this legacy and offer a departure from it.

When Freud published his first writings on psychoanalysis the revolution in the visual arts was well underway. Indeed, Vienna's artists, designers and architects were already interested and involved in the issues surrounding mental illness. Freud's status in the twentieth century has led to his domination of accounts of psychiatry in Vienna 1900 and its impact on the visual arts, but this has concealed the multiple connections that existed between the dominant psychiatry of the day and the city's modern art practice. *Madness and Modernity* presents – for the first time – this interdisciplinary activity, where modernist architects and designers collaborated with leading psychiatrists to create state psychiatric hospitals and nervous sanatoria as total artworks, where artists visited institutions seeking inspiration from the 'expressionist' attitudes of the patients, and where psychiatric theories and terminologies permeated both social criticism and the reception of the progressive

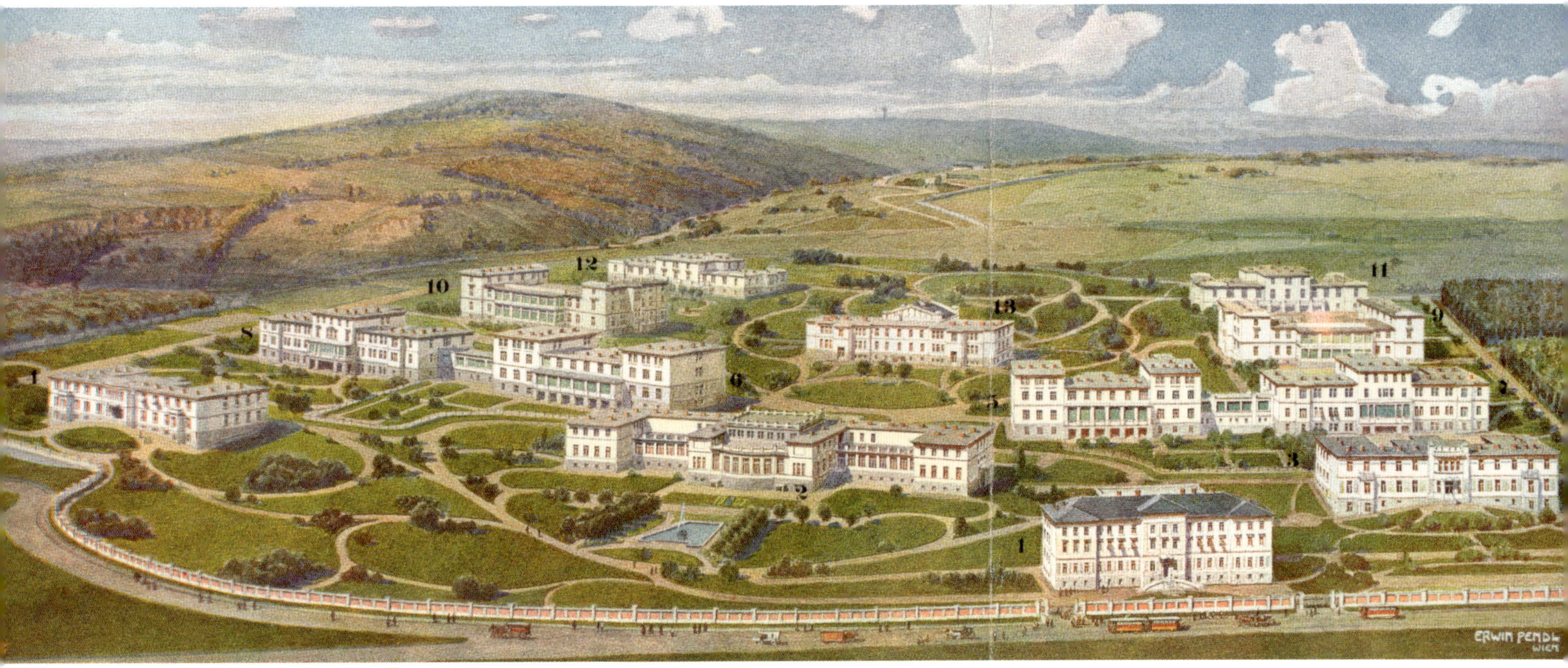

1 Erwin Pendl, view of the Provincial Sanatorium at Steinhof, from *The Provincial Sanatorium of 'Steinhof' in Vienna (Austria) XIII Prospectus* (Vienna: Province of Lower Austria, [1907]). Reproduced by permission of the Nieder-Österreichisches Landesbibliothek

visual arts. The objects that embody this activity are wide-ranging: architectural renderings of hospital buildings (fig.1); portraits of the city's intelligentsia (fig.2); electro-therapeutic equipment (fig.3); drawings by patients confined in institutions (fig.4); drawings by artists of the nervous body (fig.5) and dining room chairs (fig.6) designed for plush sanatoriums, to give but a few examples. This richness of both familiar and unfamiliar objects continues the spirit of Vienna 1900 exhibitions, such as the recent *Gustav Klimt: Painting, Design and Modern Life* at Tate Liverpool.[3] But it also departs from such shows by maintaining a tight focus on two inextricably linked questions about how psychiatry influenced early modernism in the visual arts, and how modernism has since influenced our attitudes to the mentally ill. These questions are not posed within those thematic paradigms of Vienna 1900 exhibitions briefly outlined above. Rather, they are explored through a presentation of a live yet uncharted context where psychiatrists, visual art practitioners and patients encountered and engaged with each other, often purposefully seeking each other out.

This context was raised as a new research area by Leslie Topp (Birkbeck, University of London) and Gemma Blackshaw (University of Plymouth) in a successful bid to the UK's Arts and Humanities Research Council (AHRC). Having met at the Association of Art Historians annual conference, aptly titled 'Making Connections', at Oxford Brookes University in 2001, we saw the potential of combining our shared interests in the impact of psychiatry on Austrian modern architecture and art practice. The grant, awarded in

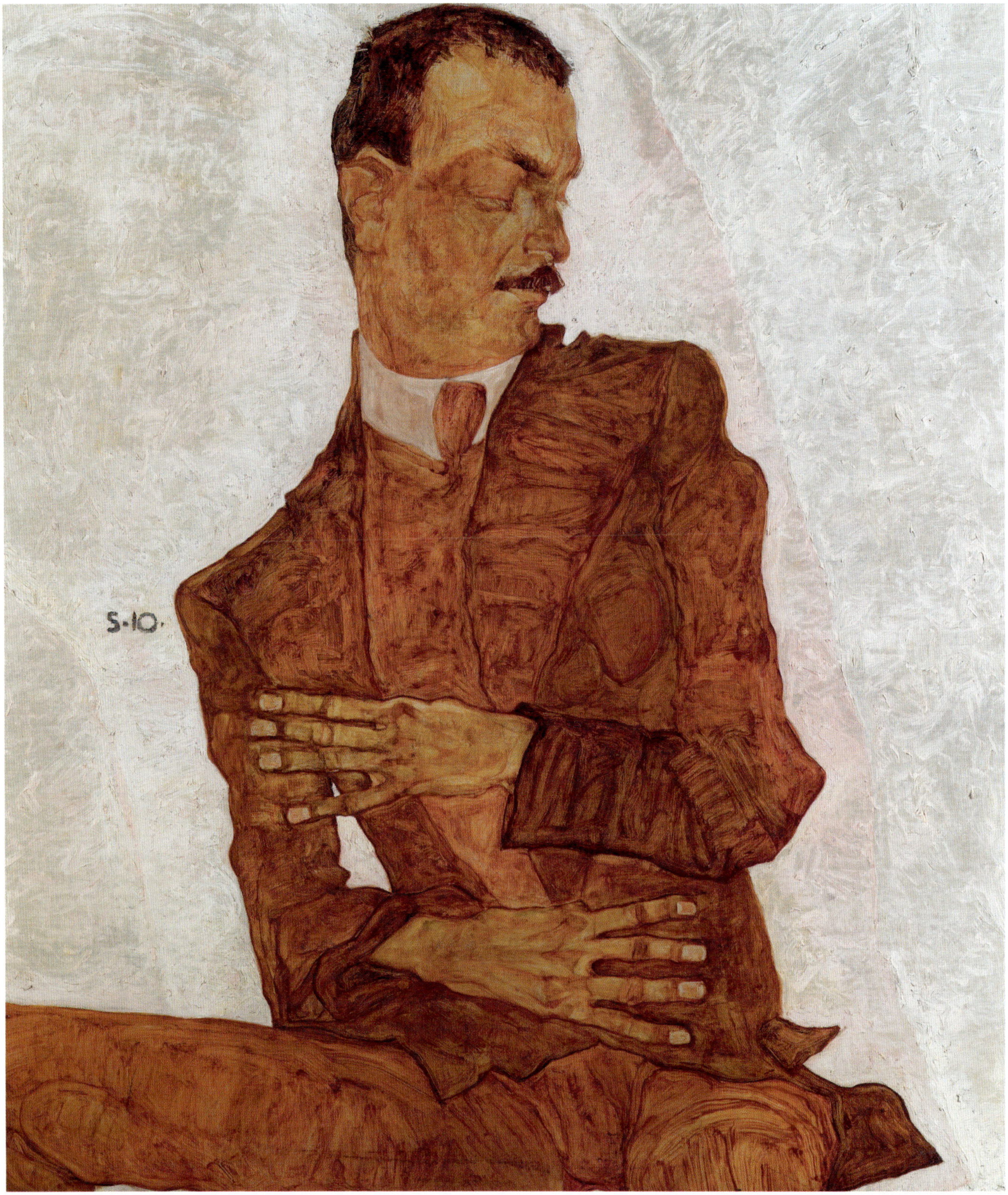
S·10·

Opposite:
2 Egon Schiele,
Portrait of Arthur Roessler, 1910,
oil on canvas, 99.6 × 99.8 cm
(39¼ × 39¼ in).
Wien Museum

2003, heralded the start of a four-year project which sought to consider the interaction of psychiatry and the visual arts in Vienna and the Habsburg Empire from 1890 to 1914 as a context for understanding the themes of sickness and health, freedom and enclosure, utopia and dystopia, which defined both fields in the period. The goals of this project were to engage in original primary research to widen and deepen our understanding of this interaction; and to reconsider assumptions about mental illness and the visual arts in Vienna 1900 studies, in light of this research. Project members also included Sabine Wieber, the post-doctoral research-associate who has made such a significant contribution to the research and energy of the project, and Nicola Imrie and Luke Heighton, the project's two PhD students. Our heartfelt thanks go to them all for their dedication; from extended field-trips to distant sanatoriums and train journeys through the snowy Austrian Alps to conferences and reading groups on more familiar ground.

We also owe thanks to the AHRC for financing the research and aspects of the production of this book and the anonymous reviewers who wrote in support of the grant application, as well as to our host institutions, Birkbeck College and the University of Plymouth (and to Oxford Brookes University, where the project was originally based). The project culminates in this book and the exhibition held at Wellcome Collection, the public exhibition venue of the Wellcome Trust. The Wellcome Trust has supported the project on many levels, such as in their contribution of funds towards the related 'Journeys into Madness' conference, co-organised by Blackshaw and Wieber in 2007 at the Wellcome Collection Conference Centre. In particular we would like to acknowledge the unwavering commitment of James Peto, Senior Curator at Wellcome Collection and Ken Arnold, Head of Public Programmes to realising the exhibition. Jane Holmes at Wellcome Collection, the exhibition designers Calum Storrie and Lucienne Roberts, and the filmmaker David Bickerstaff have all played crucial roles in shaping the exhibition and helping to make it happen. We would also like to thank our institutions and colleagues for the periods of research leave and funding we have been able to secure in writing the book and preparing the exhibition.

The business of securing loans for exhibitions on Vienna 1900 is, we discovered, a fraught one. The exhibition could not have been realised without the generous support of our British and international lenders including: Ida Fairbain; Freud Museum, London; Graphische Sammlung Albertina, Vienna; Jane Kallir, Galerie St Etienne, New York; Richard Nagy, London; Neue Galerie, New York; The New York Psychoanalytical Society and Institute; Österreichische Galerie Belvedere, Vienna; Otto-Wagner-Spital, Vienna; Christian M. Nebehay Antiquariat

3 Rossel, Schwarz & Company of Wiesbaden, Germany, exercise (mechanotherapy) chair, c.1901–5, 180 × 70 × 108 cm (70⅞ × 27½ × 42½ in). Science Museum, London

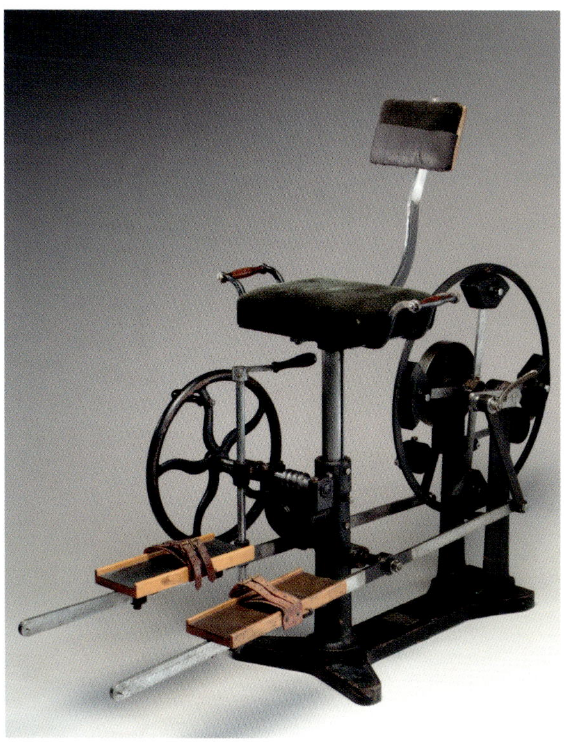

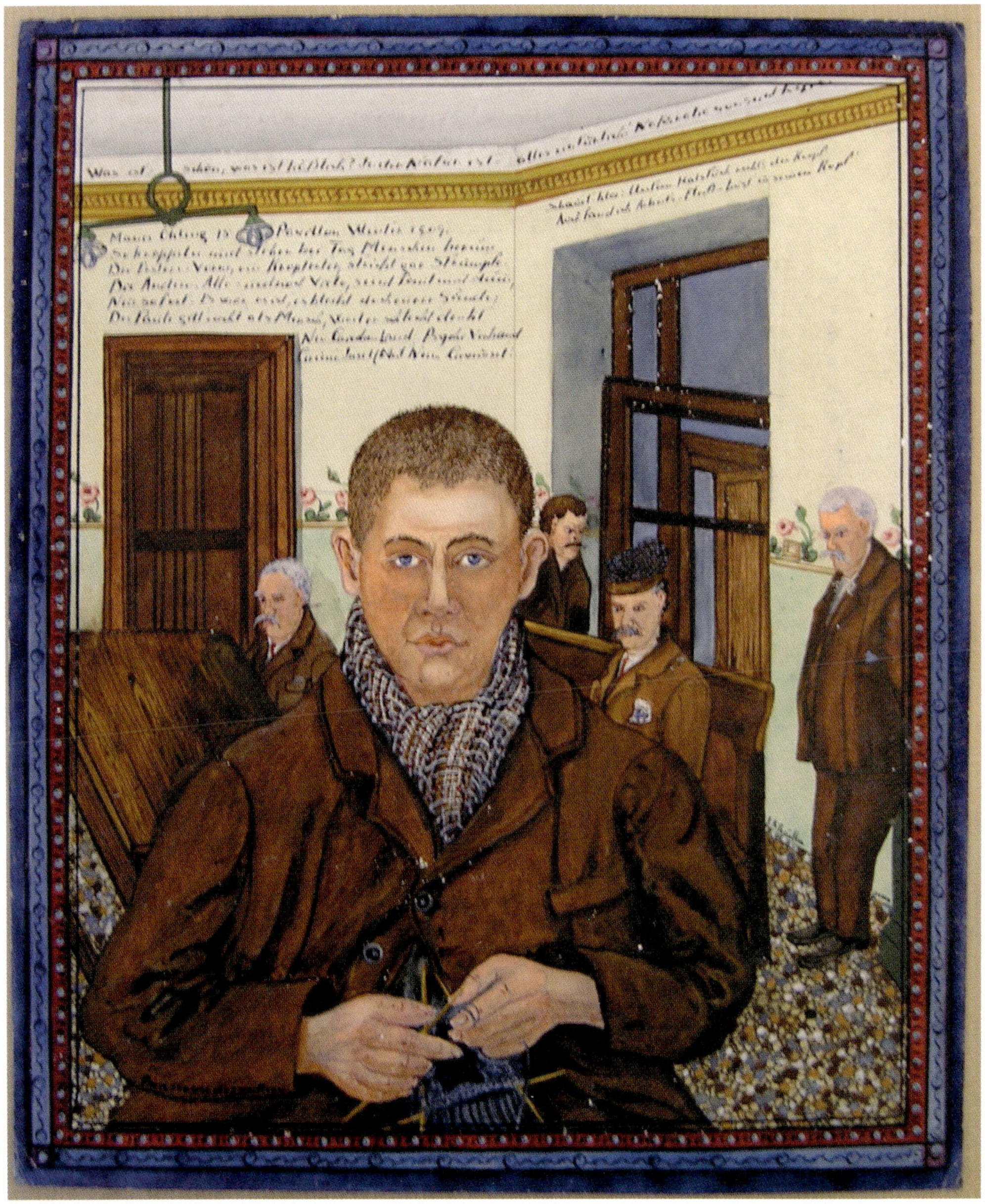

Left:
4 Josef Karl Rädler, *Untitled* (Portrait of a patient knitting), 1909, watercolour and gouache, with inscriptions, 32 × 25.7 cm ($12\frac{5}{8} \times 10\frac{1}{4}$ in). Christian M. Nebehay Antiquariat & Kunsthandlung

Opposite, top:
5 Egon Schiele, *Male Torso (Body and Arm)*, 1911, gouache, watercolour and crayon, 43.2 × 29.2 cm ($17 \times 11\frac{1}{2}$ in). Private Collection courtesy of Richard Nagy Ltd, London

Opposite, below:
6 Josef Hoffmann, dining room chair for the Purkersdorf Sanatorium, 1904, Bentwood, beech with replacement upholstery, 99 × 43 × 44.5 cm ($39 \times 17 \times 17\frac{1}{2}$ in). Victoria and Albert Museum

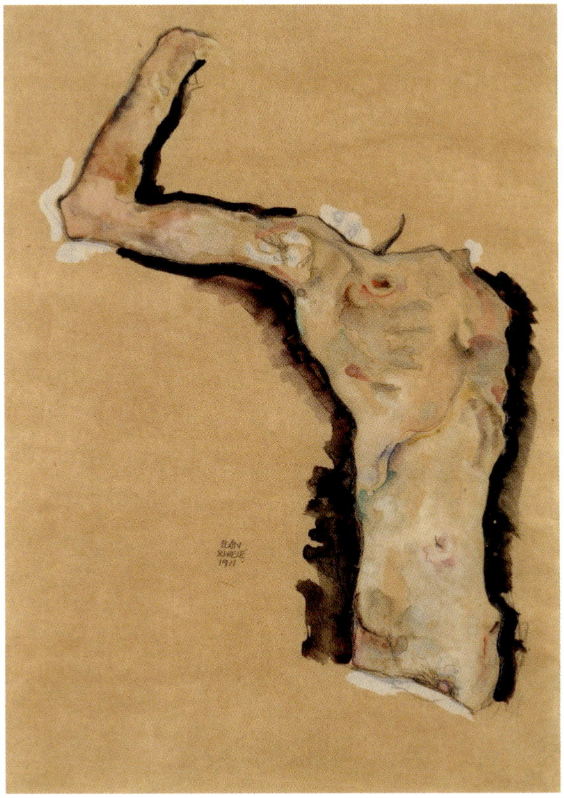

& Kunsthandlung; Pathologisch-anatomisches Bundesmuseum, Vienna; Phillips Collection, Washington DC; Dr Ernst Ploil, Vienna; Prinzhorn Sammlung, University of Heidelberg; Raiffeisenbank, Schladming, Austria; Science Museum, London; Technisches Museum Wien, Vienna; and Wien Museum, Vienna.

We would also like to thank the following people for their generous assistance in the preparation of the exhibition and of this book: Katharina Baier, Ewald Bilonoha, Eve Blau, Tim Boon, Bettina Brand-Claussen, Marie Carty, Sheron Das Neves, Keith Davies, Isabelle Exinger, Johann Freilacher, Eberhard Gabriel, Ferdinand Gutschi, Reinhold Heller, John Hoole, Sonia Horn, Robert Hutfless, Rüdiger Joppien, Jane Kallir, Renata Kassal-Mikula, Paul Keiblinger, Hans-Jörg Krug, Helmut Lackner, Gertrude Langer-Ostrawsky, Ronald Lauder, Katharine Lochnan, Yves Macaux, Michael Molnar, Richard Nagy, Tobias Natter, Peter Nisbet, Beatrix Patzak, Ernst Ploil, Renée Price, Sean Rainbird, Christiane Rainer, Thomas Roeske, Janis Staggs, Ursula Storch, Nellie Thompson and especially Christian Witt-Dörring. Lucy Clark, Miranda Harrison and Alex Hitchins at Lund Humphries, the copy editor Alison Hill and the designer Mick Keates deserve our thanks for their commitment and contributions to this book. And finally, but very significantly, we would like to thank those closest to us for their enduring patience, support and love during the preparation for *Madness and Modernity*: Annemarie and Michael Blackshaw, Michael Lawson-Smith, Neil Kenny, Elizabeth Kenny, and Elizabeth and Bob Topp.

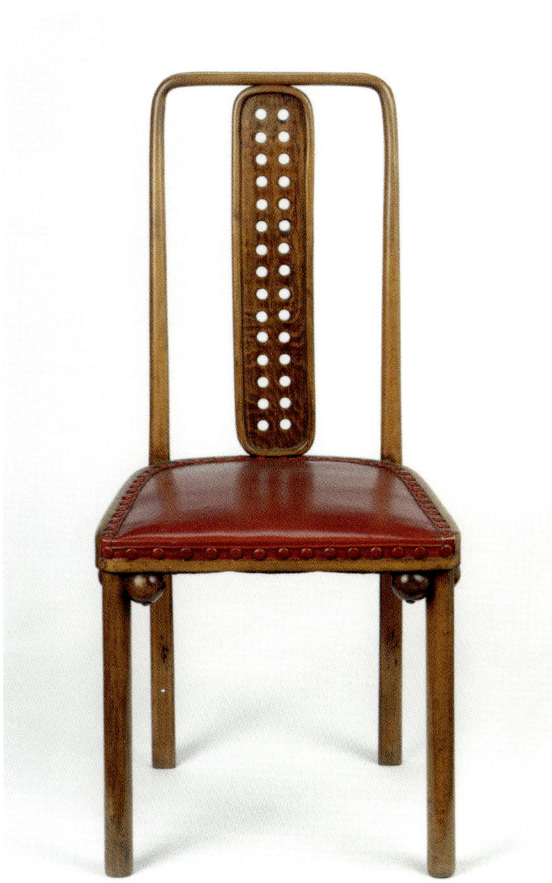

NOTES

1. Carl E. Schorske, *Fin-de-Siècle Vienna: Politics and Culture* (New York: Vintage Books, 1981), p. xviii.
2. *Traum und Wirklichkeit: Wien 1870–1930*, Wien Museum, Vienna, 1985; *Vienne 1880-1938: L'Apocalypse Joyeuse*, Centre Pompidou, Paris, 1986; The Naked Truth, Schirn Kunsthalle, Frankfurt and Leopold Museum, Vienna, 2005.
3. Curated by Tobias G. Natter and Christoph Grunenberg, May–August 2008.

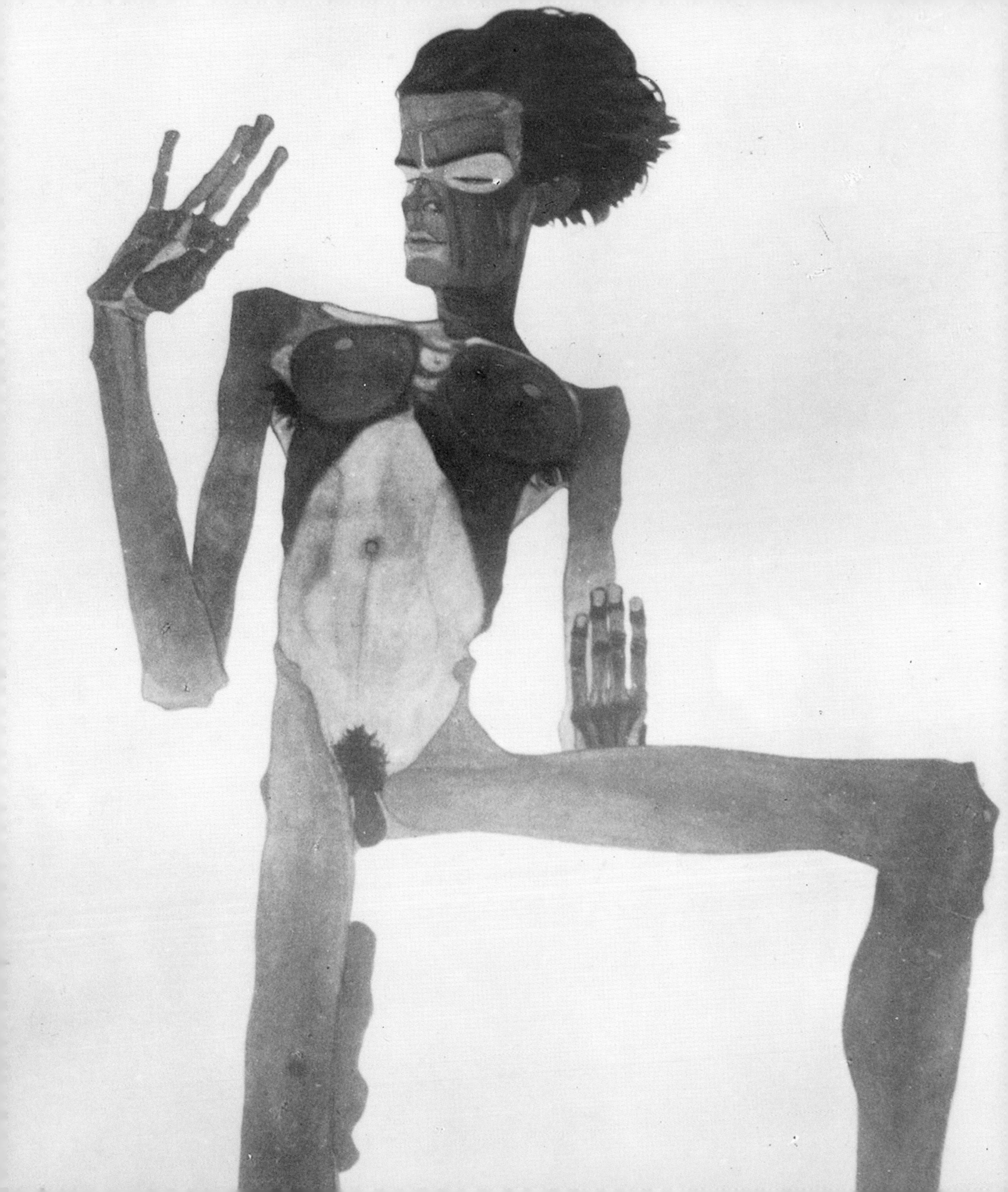

Chapter 1

Scrutinised Bodies and Lunatic Utopias: Mental illness, psychiatry and the visual arts in Vienna, 1898–1914

LESLIE TOPP AND GEMMA BLACKSHAW

Mental illness and psychiatry had enormous cultural resonance in Vienna around 1900. Madness had been a favourite theme of artists and writers for centuries. But in Vienna, it was not only 'madness' but also psychiatry, and the ways it thought about and treated mental illness, that resonated with artists as they sought new modes of expression and social relevance. The products of this interdisciplinary meeting are many and various, ranging in the visual arts from modernist self-portraiture, to designs for asylums and sanatoria, to allegorical sculpture and exhibitions of patient art. This chapter proposes a framework for understanding the many different ways in which the visual arts, mental illness and psychiatry affected one another in fin-de-siècle Vienna.

23 Egon Schiele, *Male Nude Kneeling, with Raised Hands (Self-Portrait)* (detail), 1910, oil on canvas, 150 × 150 cm (59 × 59 in) (approx), present whereabouts unknown

The mutual fascination that existed between psychiatry and the visual arts stems from the fact that both fields shared a preoccupation with two issues: the link between body and mind; and the notion that modern urban capitalist society is simultaneously in decline, and offers the cure for its own ailments. This chapter surveys the two fields, unpacking the pertinent ideas and practices at play in each. It also traces a spectrum of moments in which psychiatry and the visual arts come together, with starkly different end points and more ambivalent middle areas. Finally this chapter proposes a new way of thinking about the importance of Sigmund Freud (1856-1939) within this context.

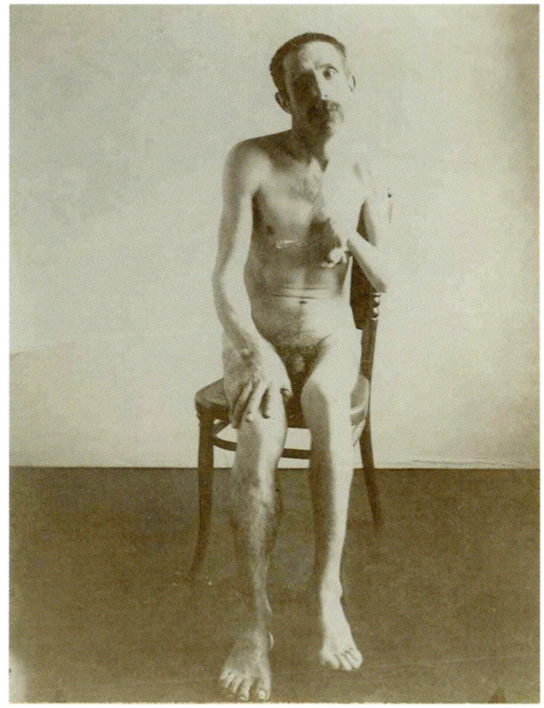

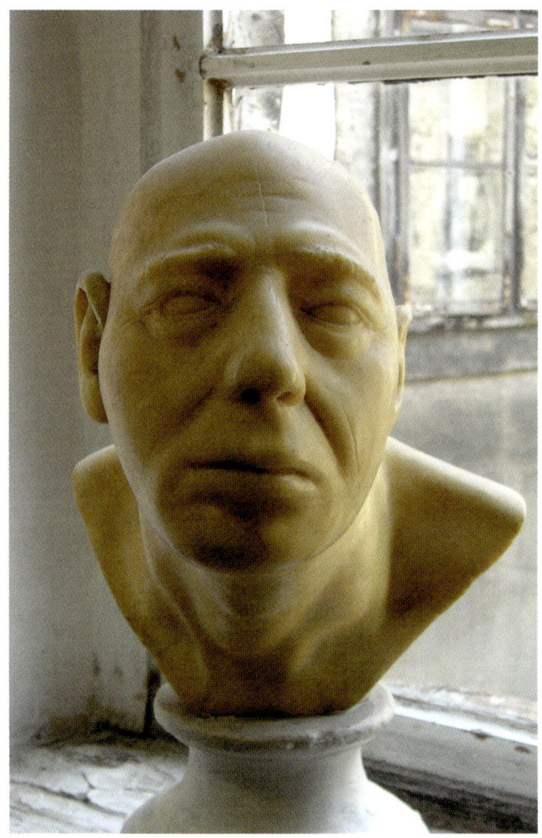

PSYCHIATRY AND THE EXPERIENCE OF MADNESS IN VIENNA, 1900

Viennese psychiatry had three branches.[1] Most prestigious was clinical psychiatry, which was based at the university and investigated the causes of mental illness. In the 1860s, 1870s and 1880s, Viennese clinical psychiatrists were leaders in the area of brain pathology – the search for the seat of mental illness in the brain's anatomy, undertaken via autopsies of deceased asylum patients and the microscopic analysis of brain tissue. By the turn of the century, psychiatrists, while remaining convinced that the roots of mental illness were in bodily phenomena, were more interested in the clinical observation of living patients, including the meticulous description of their facial and bodily characteristics and gestures. As Heinrich Schlöss wrote in his *Introduction to Psychiatry* of 1919, the 'stigmata' of mental illness could be easily recognised: 'In the face: the unequal enervation of the cranial hemispheres. In the limbs: congenitally flat feet; a greater than usual number of fingers or toes. Further indications: curvature of the spine, abnormal body hair.'[2] (fig.7) This passage shows the increasing presence of a descriptive, analytical, cataloguing impulse in psychiatry, the tools for which included drawing, modelling and photography.[3] Visual depictions of patients and their bodies were both tools for research and effective means of publicising that research. The work of Jean-Martin Charcot (fig.8), who championed the diagnostic value of the image of the patient at La Salpêtrière hospital in Paris, was readily available in publication[4] and was formative for Viennese psychiatrists (Freud opted to study under Charcot in 1885). The image, he claimed, was the means by which categories of neurological disease could be constructed, offering doctors the opportunity to freeze a moment in a medical examination and study it repeatedly. The image of the patient's body – modelled in wax (fig.9), captured in a sketch, caught by the camera – was easily disseminated and thus scrutinised collectively.

The second branch of psychiatry in Vienna focused on the planning

Opposite, top:
7 Photograph of unknown patient, probably from a collection made by Dr Heinrich Schlöss at the Lower Austrian Asylum at Kierling-Gugging, Otto-Wagner-Spital, Vienna

Right:
8 Photographic portrait of Jean Martin Charcot. A copy of this portrait was inscribed to Freud and presented to him in 1886

Opposite, below:
9 Karl Henning, one of a pair of wax heads depicting the Koller brothers, 1897–8, 40 cm (15¾ in) high (approx). Pathologisches-Anatomisches Bundesmuseum, Vienna

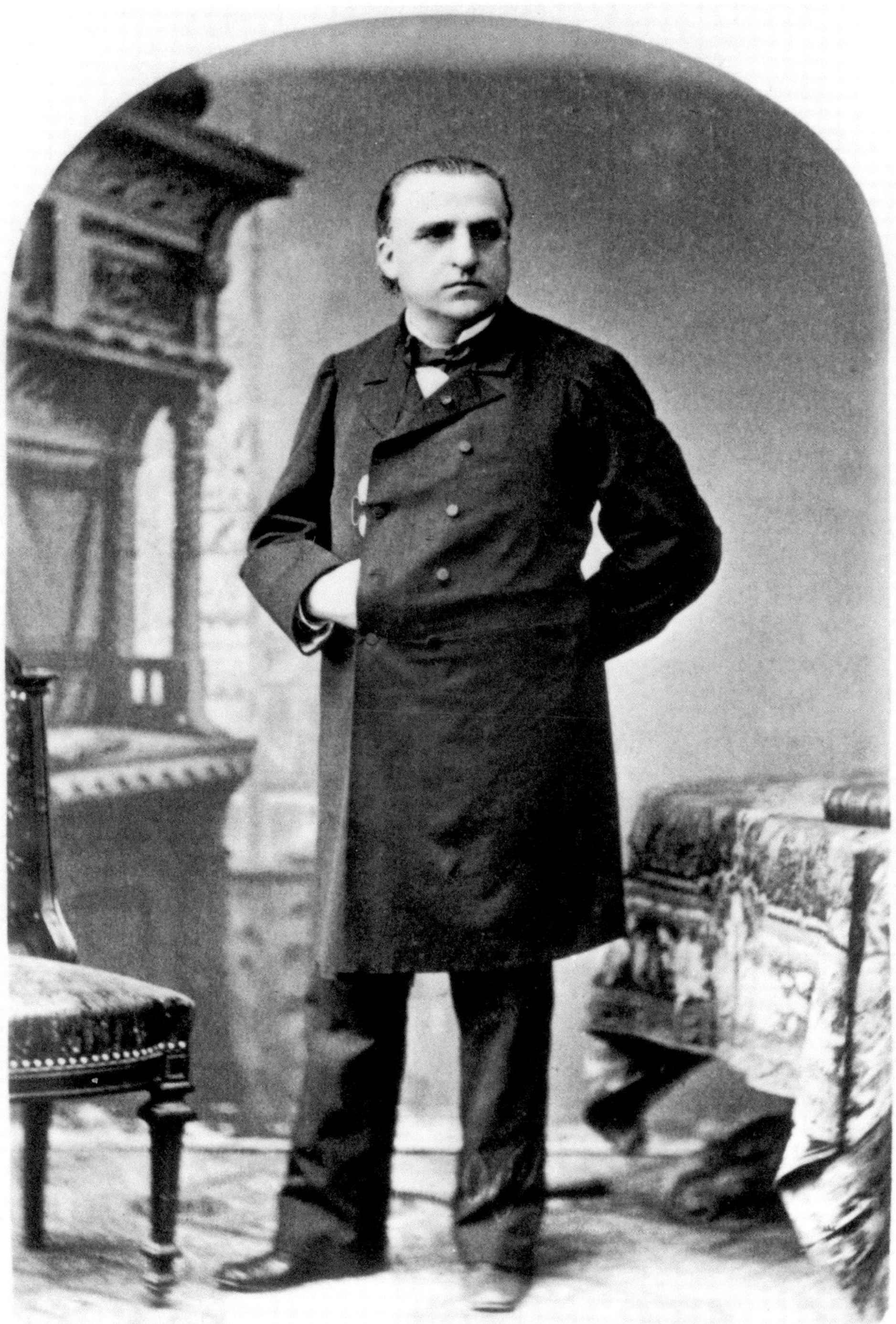

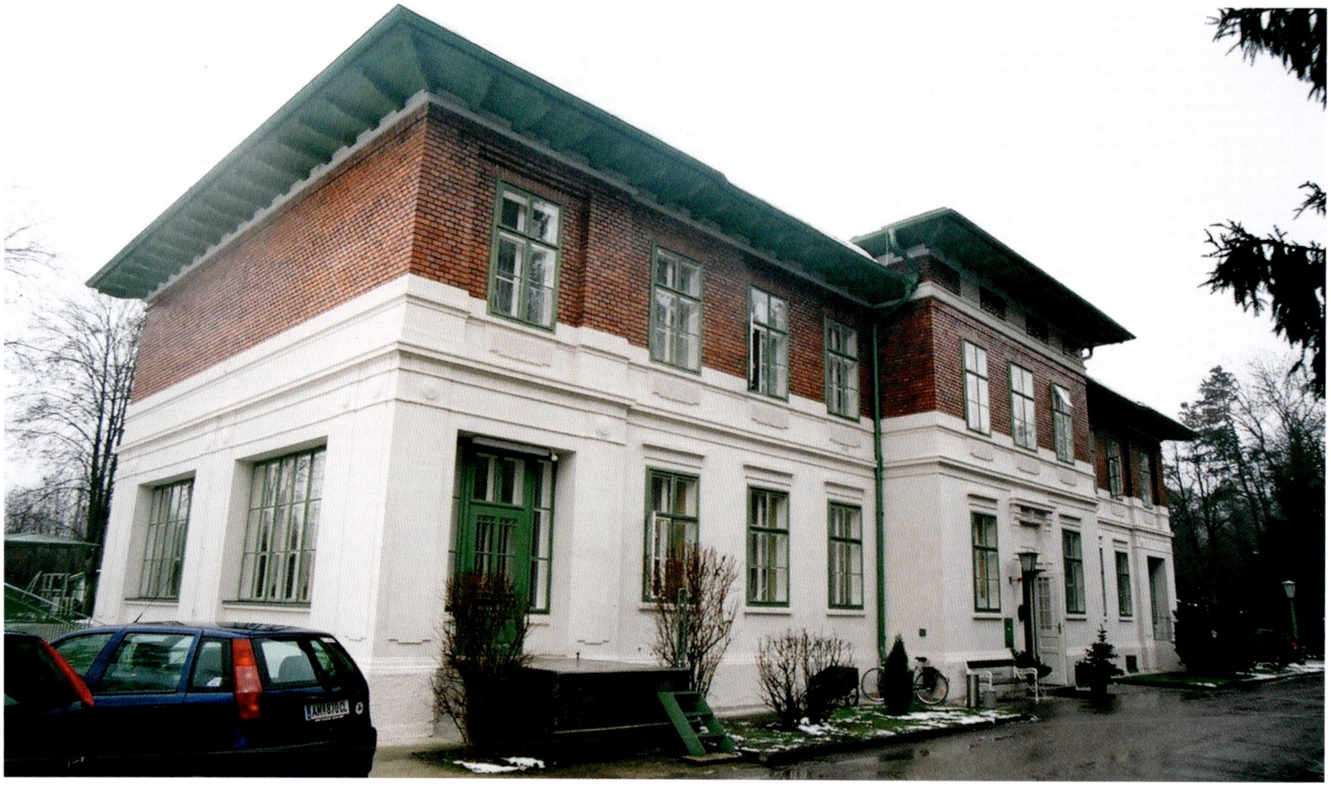

10 Pavilion for quiet female pauper patients, The Emperor Franz Josef I Lower Austrian Provincial Asylum at Mauer-Öhling, built 1898–1902, architect Carlo von Boog

of psychiatric institutions and the management of patients inside them.[5] Psychiatrists thought that an institution of confinement could itself, if carefully designed and administered, act as an essential tool in the patient's cure. Implicit in this notion was a critique of the world beyond the walls of the asylum. Mental illness was caused, triggered or exacerbated (depending on the school of thought one subscribed to) by the stresses of civilisation; the asylum represented a world put to right, in which patients would live a simple life in harmony with nature. In Vienna around 1900, the idea of the therapeutic asylum was made current by the building of two new state-of-the-art psychiatric institutions, Mauer-Öhling (built 1898–1902 west of Vienna, fig.10) and Steinhof (built 1903–07 on the edge of the city, see figs 64 and 87). In the rhetoric surrounding these two institutions, they became small utopian settlements, models of modern rational living in deliberate contrast to the chaotic conditions of the metropolis.

The critique of modern civilisation and the vision of a therapeutic environment were also central to the third branch of Viennese psychiatry, which was concerned with nervous disorders.[6] These included conditions such as hysteria, hypochondria and neurasthenia (involving symptoms we now associate with depression, anxiety and stress) and were both less severe and more widespread than full-blown mental illness. A lively psychiatric discourse identified modern urban life as the main enemy of the nerves, with the educated middle and upper classes being particularly vulnerable. Like the asylum psychiatrists, the nerve doctors advocated the removal of the patient from their usual surroundings to a purpose-designed institution, in this case a sanatorium for nervous ailments, many of which flourished in this period across Central Europe (see fig.82). Freud's psychoanalytic approach to the causes and treatment of nervous ailments, initiated in Vienna around 1900, rejected these mainstream tendencies in favour of attention to patients' dreams and memories and what was known as the 'talking cure'.

While psychiatry in Vienna had considerable public prestige, there also existed a concerted resistance to it (in the form of an embryonic anti-psychiatry movement) which was in turn rejected by psychiatrists who became concerned with their public image.[7] The anti-psychiatry movement publicised accounts of individuals who claimed to be wrongly confined and, in some cases, abused in public and private psychiatric institutions. These are rare glimpses into the lives of the 'subjects' of psychiatry. There are also brief moments of access to the voices of those suffering from mental illness through letters, writings, objects and images preserved in archives and ephemeral publications (figs 11 and 12). But progressive visual artists did not engage in a critique of psychiatry; nor were they drawn, it seems, to the voices of the mentally ill. Rather, they identified with the *imaging* of the mentally ill. The distinctive representation of the patient as an object without agency, overcome with disease, could be brought effectively into the imaging of the artist and his supporters, contributing to a distinctly Viennese modernist rhetoric of anguish and alienation.

PROGRESSIVE VISUAL ARTS

Practices and world views were similarly diverse among Vienna's progressive visual artists in the period 1898 to 1914. There were important changes in art practice (particularly in painting) over the course of this period, and art historians have tended to resort to the labels 'Secessionist' and 'Expressionist' to distinguish the artists around Gustav Klimt (1862–1918), pre-eminent in the first half of the period, from the younger painters, including Egon Schiele (1890–1918) and Oskar Kokoschka (1886–1980), who came to the fore around 1909. 'Secessionists' were concerned with exploring the possibilities of art outside the confines of academic tradition, while 'Expressionists' sought to depict subjective emotions and responses that objects and events aroused in them. Despite these different art historical labels, there was a good deal of continuity between the two practices, especially apparent in the dominance throughout of the human body as the preferred subject of art (in marked contrast, for example, to progressive practice in the same period in Paris.) This was not the balanced, beautiful body of the classical tradition, but a body highly sexualised, often abnormally thin, and ugly by traditional standards (fig.13). It was also often a diseased body, the subject of medical discourse. Artists deliberately flouted conservative bourgeois sensibilities with their depiction of the human body, and scandal often surrounded their exhibitions.

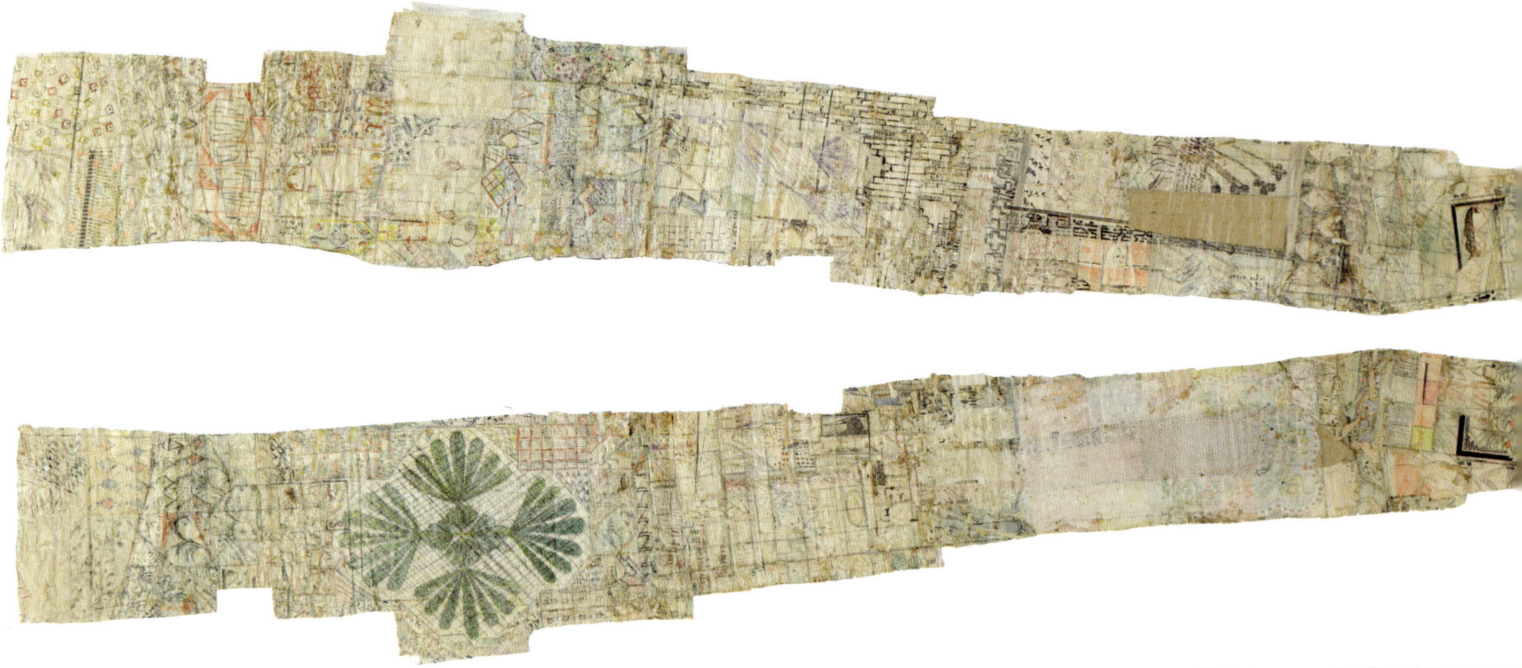

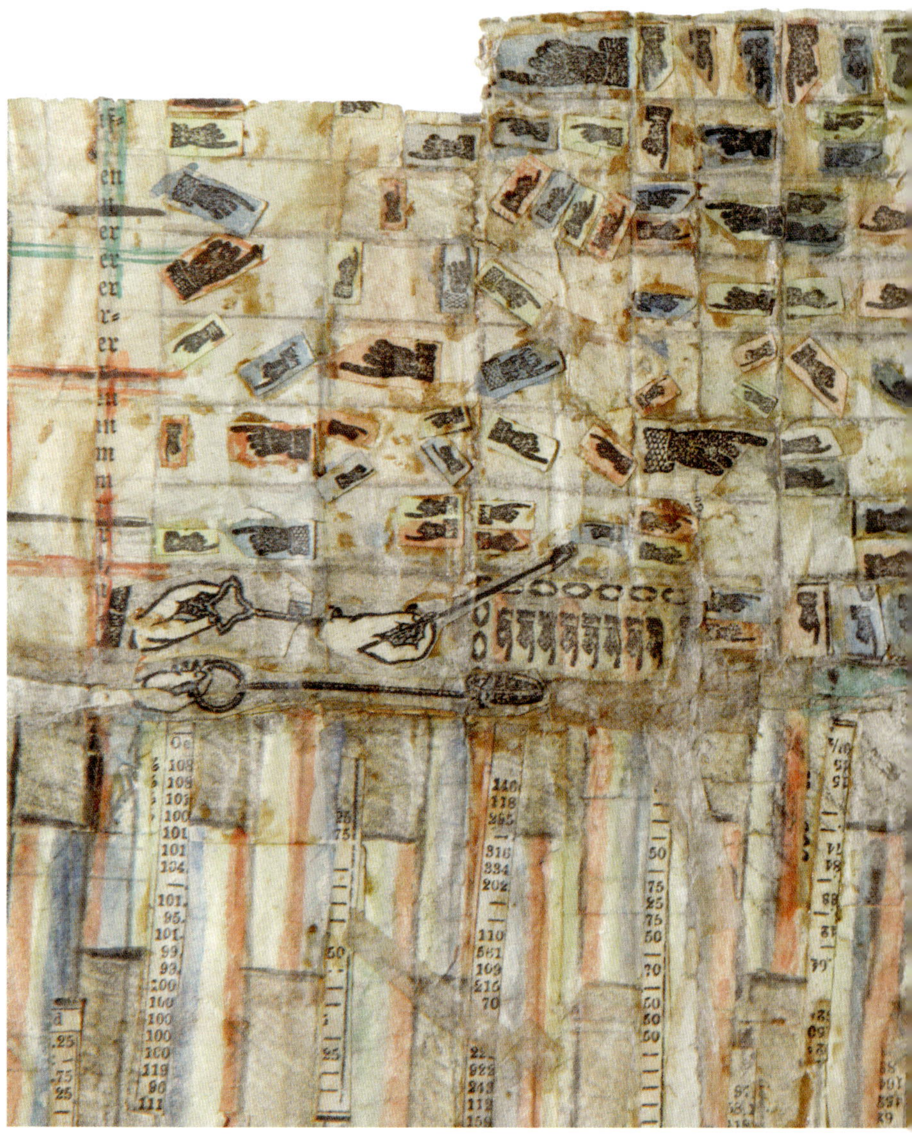

Above:
11 Frau St, collage made in Ober-Döbling clinic, Vienna, c.1890, newspaper scraps, 25 × 270 cm (9⅞ × 106⅜ in) shown recto and verso. Sammlung Prinzhorn, University of Heidelberg

Right:
12 Frau St, Collage, (detail)

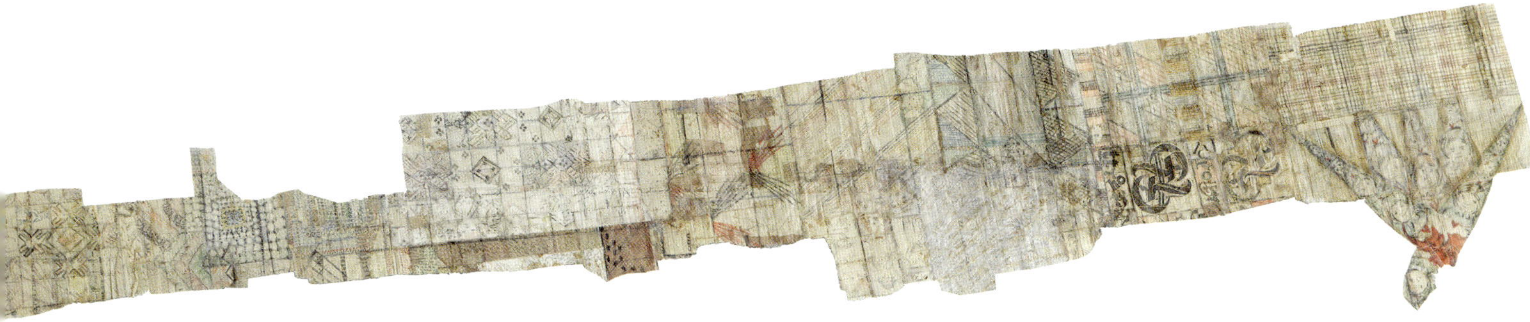

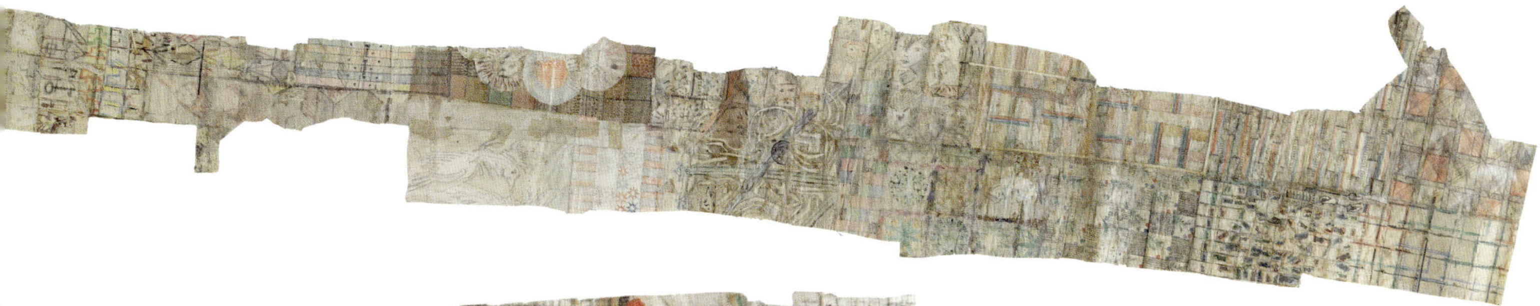

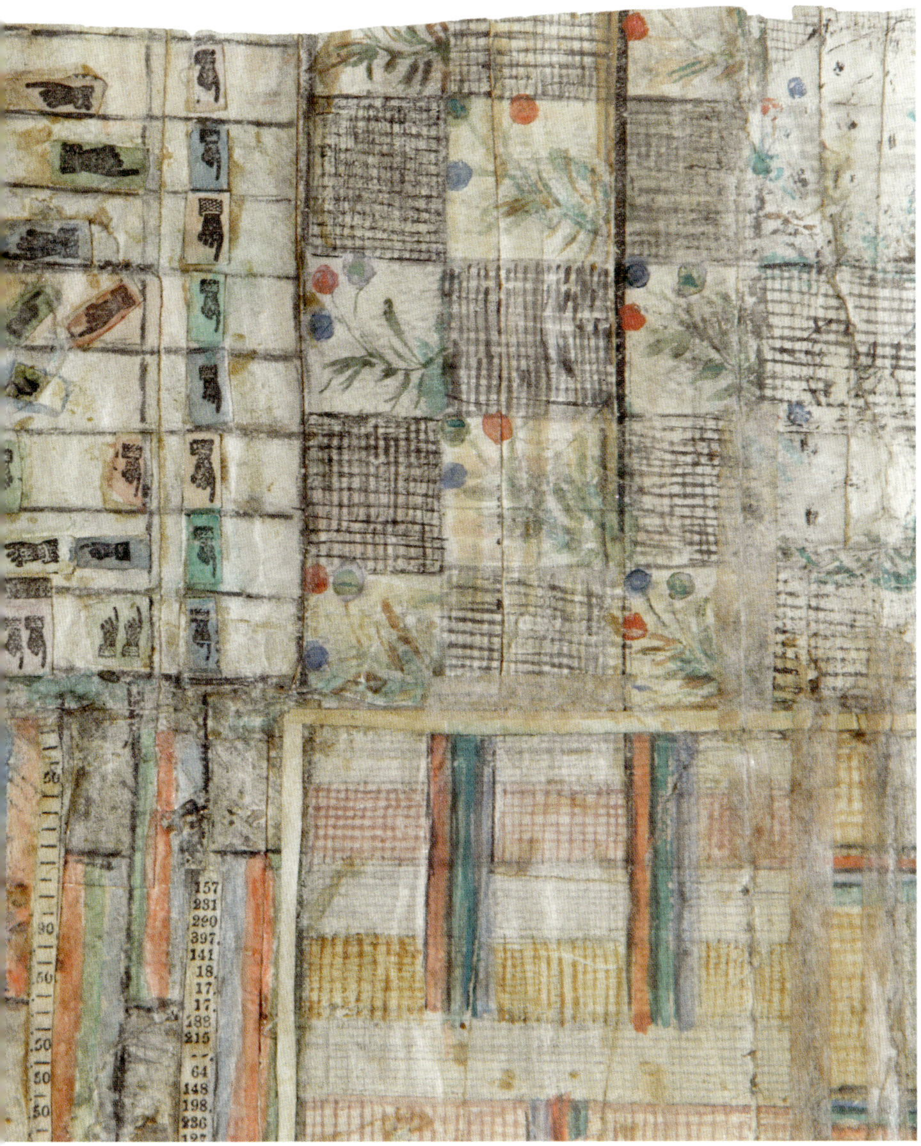

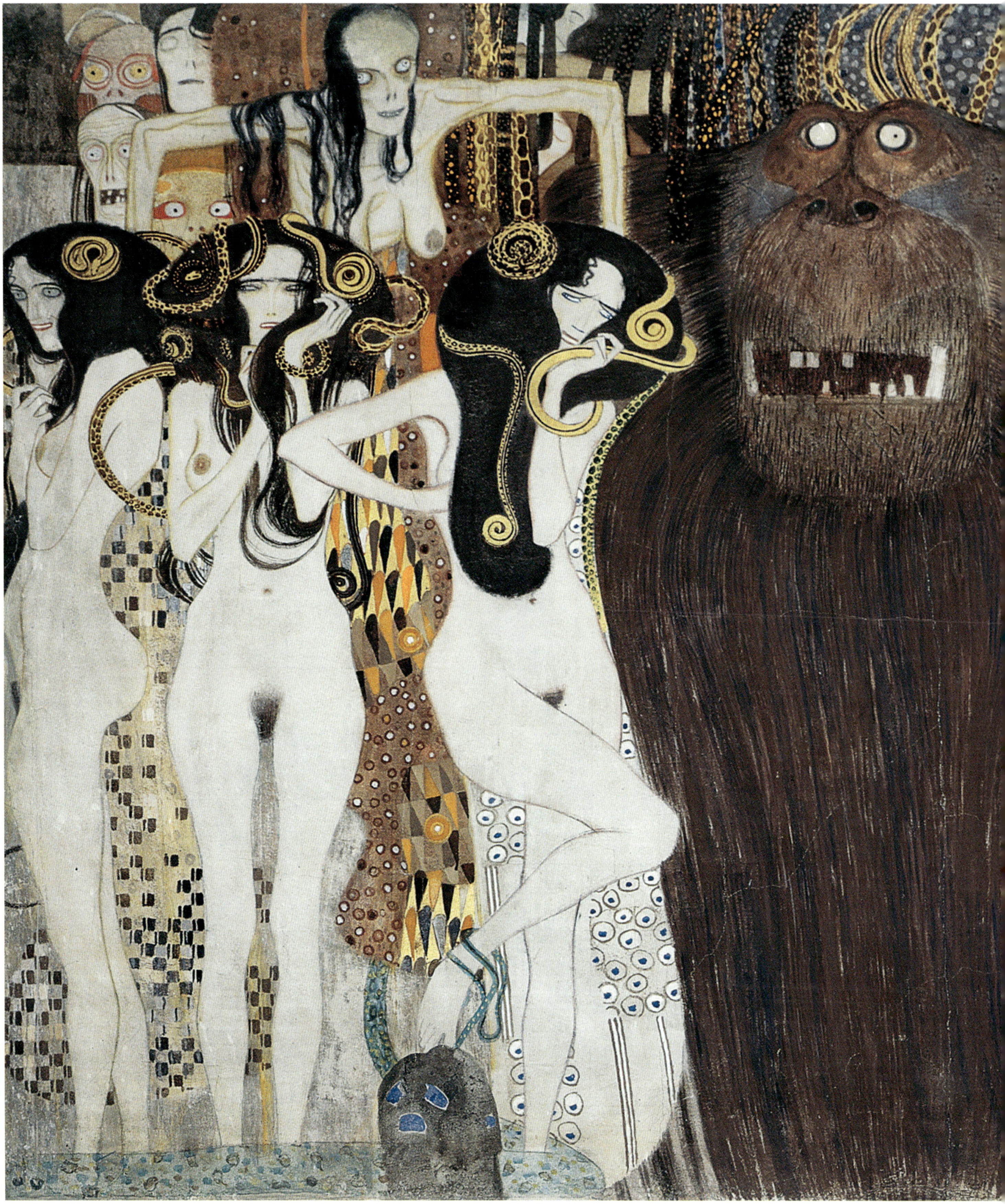

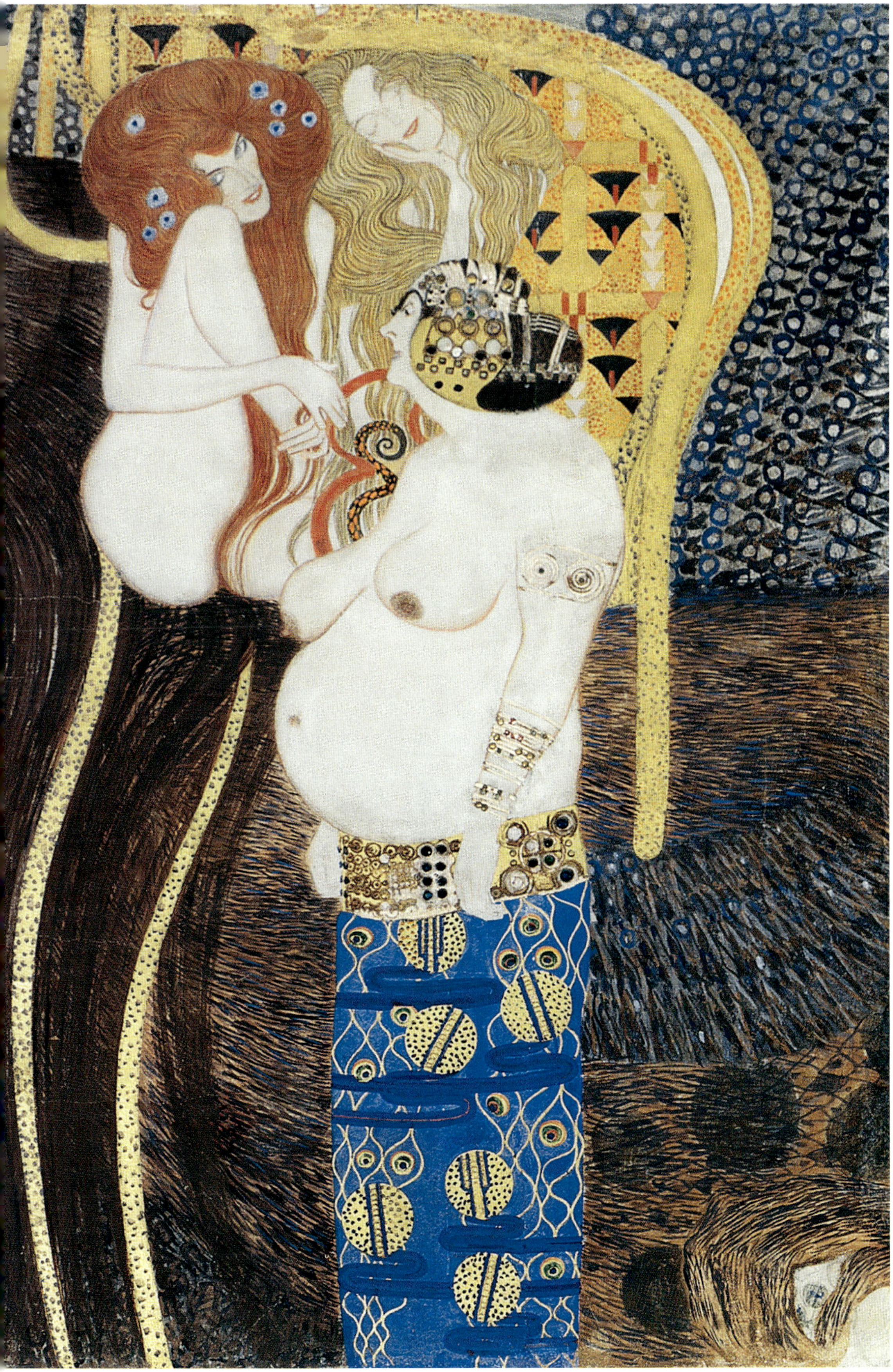

13 Gustav Klimt, *Beethoven Frieze* (detail), 1901–2, various materials. Belvedere, Vienna

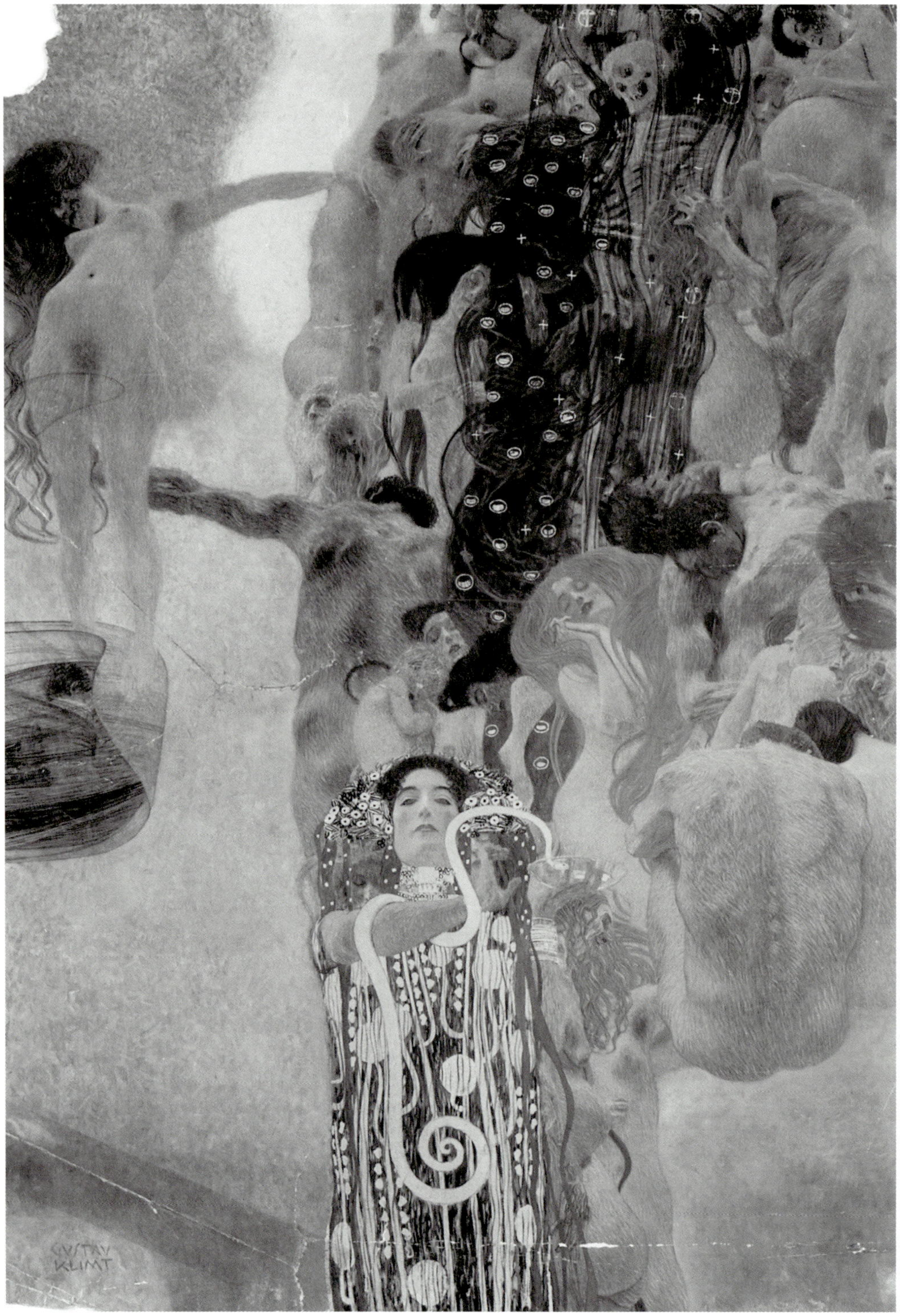

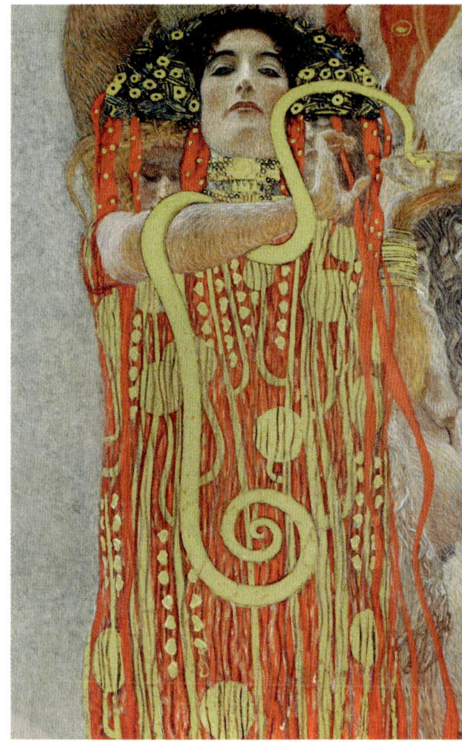

Left:
14 Gustav Klimt, *Medicine*, 1901, oil on canvas, 430 × 300 cm (169¼ × 118¼ in). Exhibited at the 10th Secession exhibition of 1901. Ceiling painting for the University of Vienna, destroyed 1945. Albertina, Vienna

Above:
15 Klimt, *Medicine* (detail). The only surviving colour photograph of any of the three university paintings

An important early moment in the Viennese cult of the diseased body was Klimt's *Medicine* (fig.14), one of three major paintings intended for the main auditorium of the University of Vienna. Exhibited in 1901, it caused a furore for its pessimistic interpretation of the University's celebrated medical school. Klimt's preference for the motifs of mortal combat, sexual excess, and submission to the forces of Schopenhauerian struggle was well-known through his work exhibited at the Secession from 1898 onwards, but the delirious and diseased bodies of *Medicine* still made for a public sensation. The inability of *Hygeia* (fig.15), the personification of Health, to intervene in the suffering column of figures represented in all stages from birth to death, staged Klimt's rejection of the progress of modern medicine and formalised the identification of the progressive visual arts with a sickened modernity. Klimt's laying claim to the representation of disease was to have a profound effect on the subsequent characterisation of modern art in Vienna as pathological. As the German art historian Julius Meier-Graefe wrote in his seminal *Modern Art* of 1904, in anticipation of the new generation: 'This young Vienna was like a lad who has grown too quickly, tremendously tall but shockingly thin, weak of bone and precociously diseased.'[8]

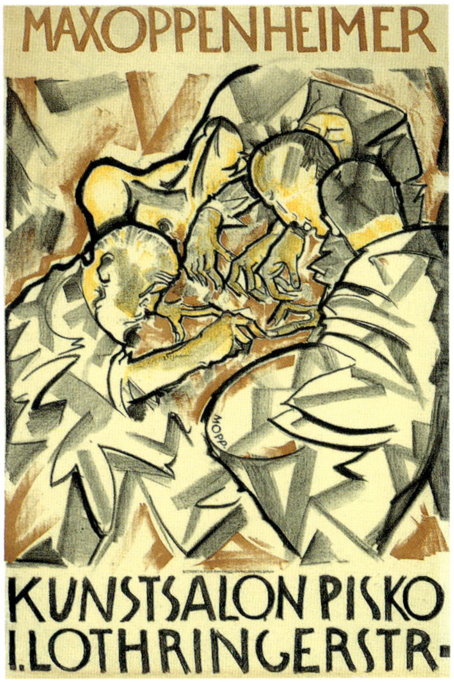

Below:
16 Anatomical wax model, c.1780, made in Florence. Now in the collections of the Medical University of Vienna

Right:
17 Max Oppenheimer, poster for his one-man-show at the Kunstsalon Pisko, Vienna, 1913. Museum für Kunst und Gewerbe, Hamburg

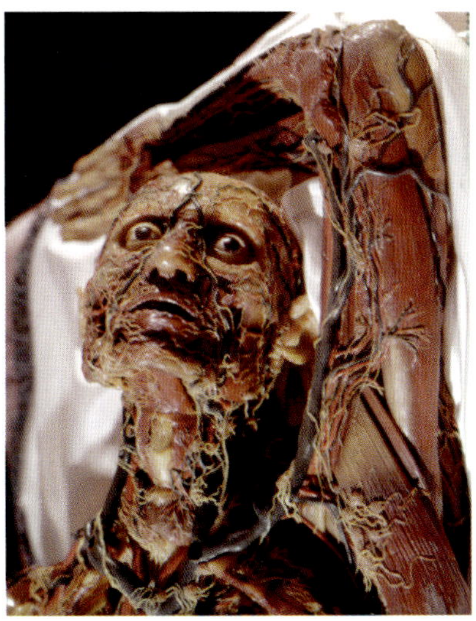

Meier-Graefe's description was fully realised in Oskar Kokoschka's early portraits.[9] The bodies in Klimt's *Medicine* were considered by one critic to be more suited for an anatomical museum than a University Great Hall,[10] but Kokoschka's representation of the bones, muscles, veins and arteries of his sitters was closer to the eighteenth century anatomical wax models of Vienna's Josephinum (fig.16). In keeping with the discourse of clinical psychiatry, Vienna's critics responded to these portraits of diseased bodies as images of mental illness, claiming that Kokoschka's tool was not the artist's brush, but the surgeon's scalpel. This characterisation of the artist was most vividly re-interpreted by Max Oppenheimer (1885–1954) in his painting *The Operation* of 1912 (fig.18), where the artist – recently attacked in the press by Kokoschka's supporters – depicts himself writhing on the operating table whilst his stomach is opened up by a cast of doctors, so vividly realised that they could well be portraits of Oppenheimer's enemies. This vivisection scene (which was reworked into a poster advertising Oppenheimer's one-man-show at Vienna's Kunstsalon Pisko in 1913 (fig.17), represents Oppenheimer's protest against Kokoschka's bid for supremacy in the

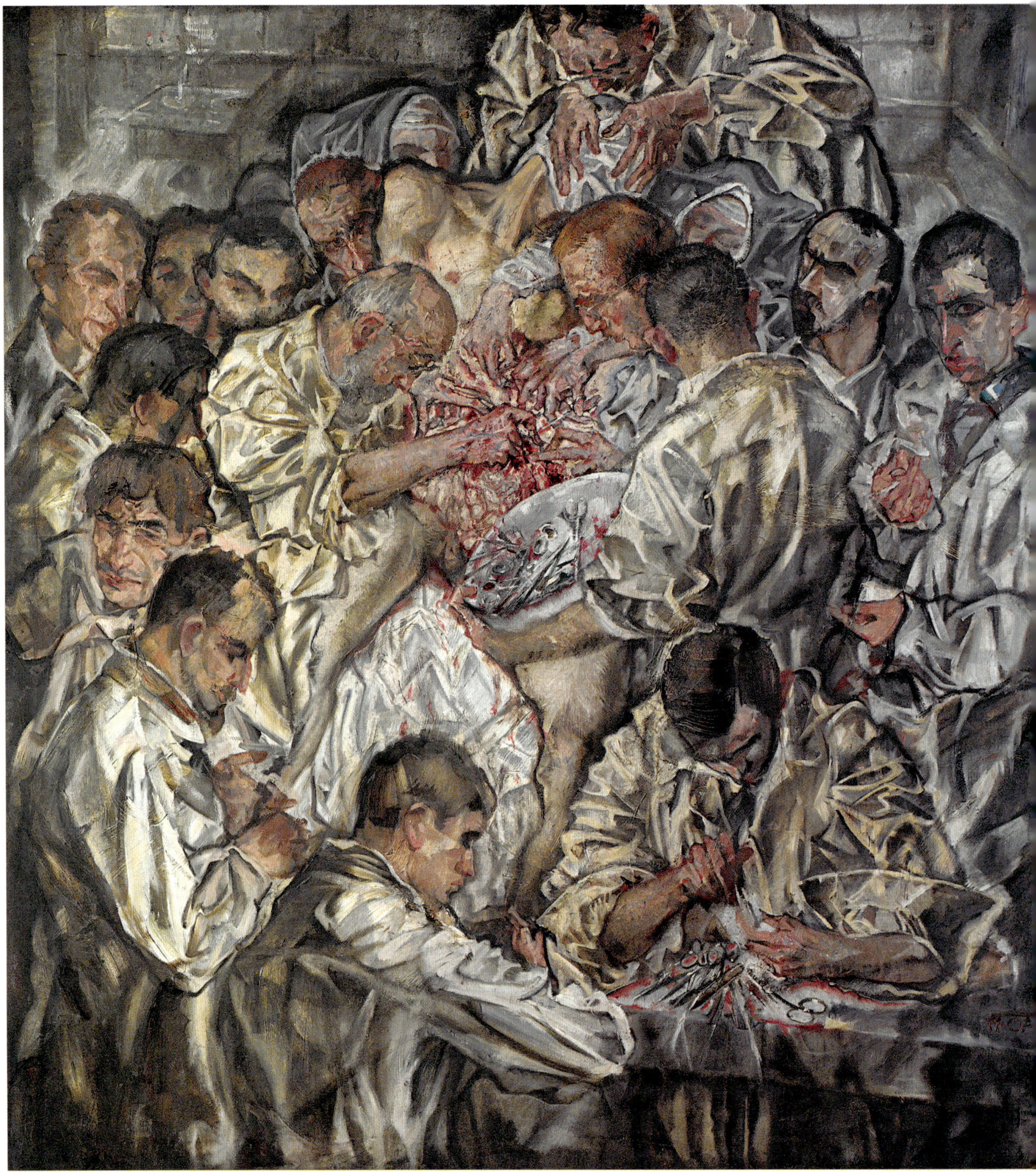

Opposite:
18 Max Oppenheimer, *The Operation*, 1912, oil on canvas, 165 × 150 cm (65 × 59 in). Národní Galerie, Prague

city's art market. But Kokoschka's position was secured through a rhetoric which defined his portraits as revealing psychological 'truth' through the vivisection of the sitter's body. One sitter described her portrait as a skin-peel: 'He had captured my likeness by lifting off the top layer revealing the face of a fairly desperate convict underneath.'[11]

Architecture and design were also central to the culture of artistic experimentation in Vienna in 1900. Otto Wagner (1841–1918) and the young architects and designers around him initiated a thorough rethinking of the built environment, interior and exterior.[12] Historical revivalism was rejected in favour of immersion in present needs and the technological achievements of modern society. 'Truth' was the rallying cry: architects and designers should be true to modern life, use materials honestly, and reject anything sham or inauthentic.[13] The aesthetic was one of bold simple forms, clean lines, and rationality in plan (fig.19). The leaders of the modern approach to architecture and design were also beholden to current medical thinking, though it was not the anatomist, but the public health expert, with his attention to hygiene and the reform of the urban environment, who inspired them. Most of these figures were also utopianists, believing that the transformation of the built environment would bring about the transformation of society.

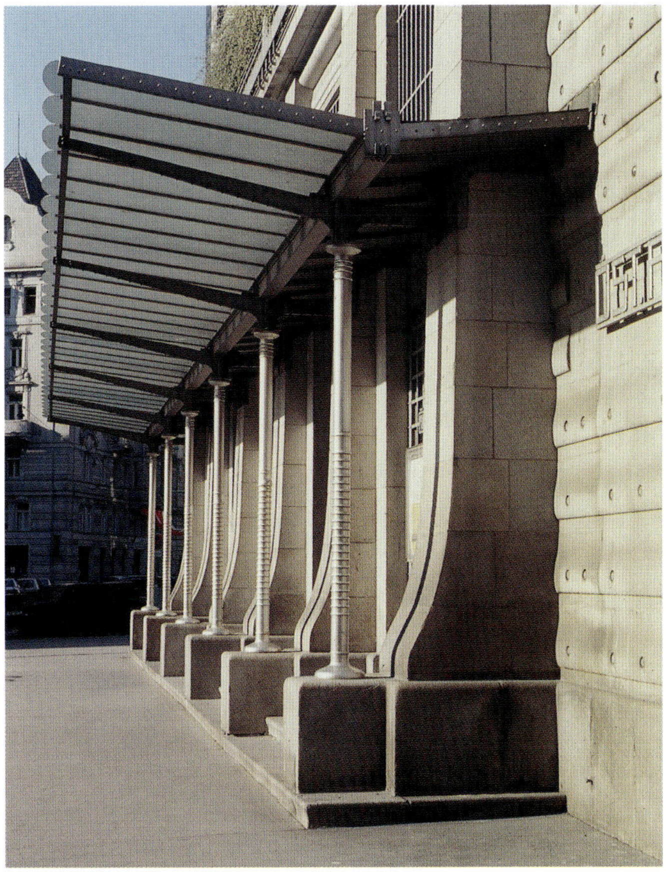

19 Otto Wagner, Postal Savings Bank, detail of entrance, 1905–7

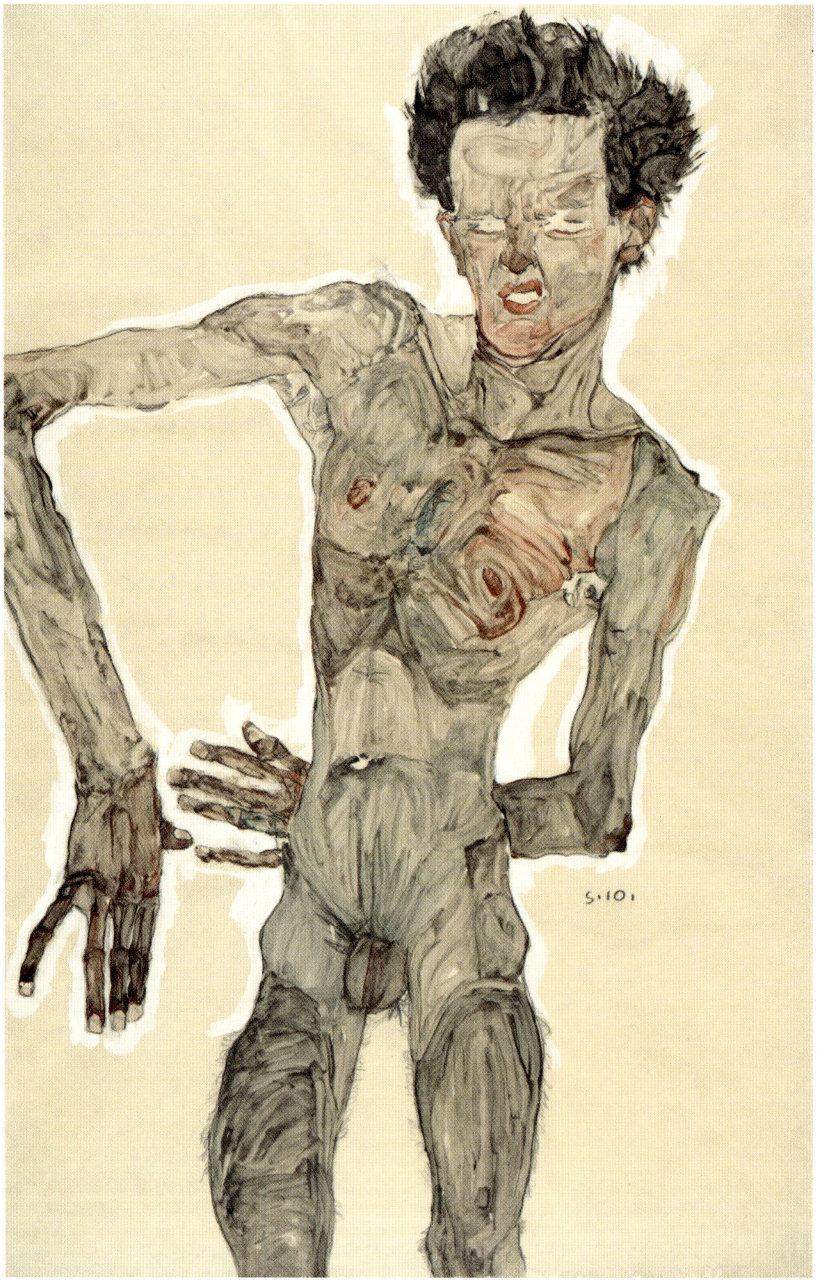

Left:
20 Egon Schiele, *Nude Self-Portrait Grimacing*, 1910, gouache, watercolour and pencil with white heightening, 55.8 × 36.9 cm (22 × 14½ in). Albertina, Vienna

Far right:
21 *Macrodactylie*, Nouvelle Iconographie de la Salpêtrière: Clinique du système nerveux

Right:
22 *Gigantisme et Infantilisme*, Nouvelle Iconographie de la Salpêtrière: Clinique du système nerveux

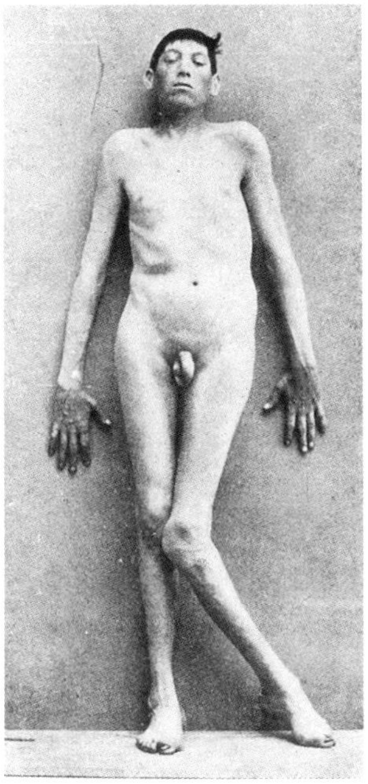

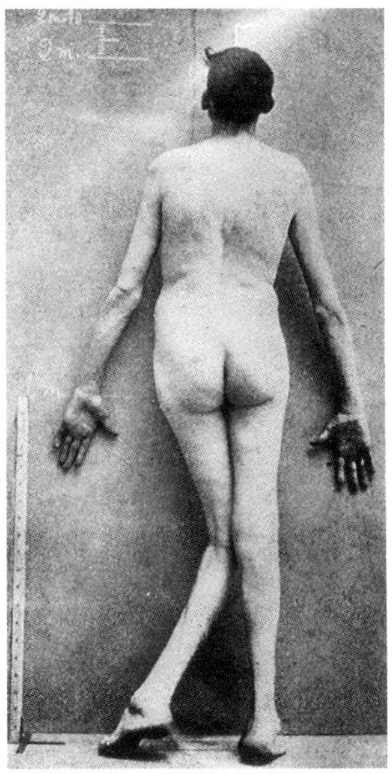

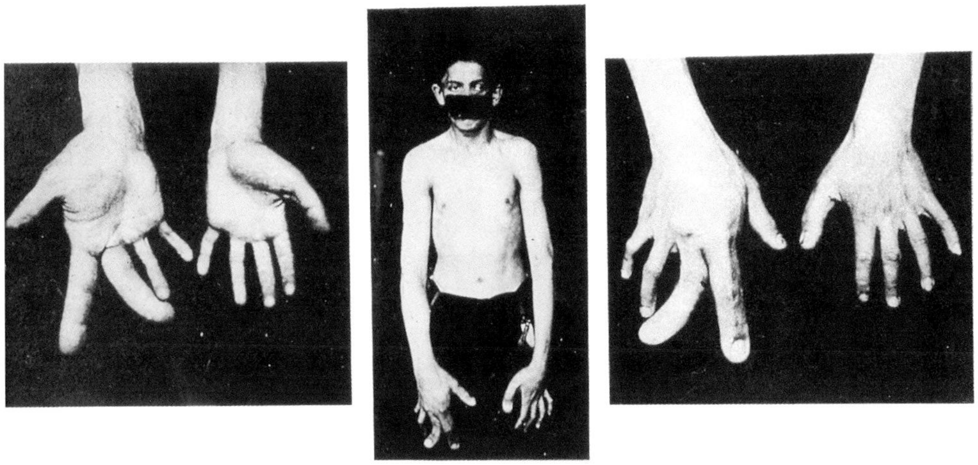

SCRUTINISED BODIES AND LUNATIC UTOPIAS – A SPECTRUM

When two fields contain such various and seemingly contradictory impulses within them, their interaction will not be straightforward. In fact psychiatry and the visual arts in Vienna seemed to interact in two starkly different ways. On the one hand, the search for and visualisation of causes and signs of mental illness in bodily phenomena, coming out of clinical psychiatry, fed modernism in painting and the creation of the visual language of the outsider. On the other, the search for and visualisation of treatment, coming out of asylum psychiatry fed utopian architecture and design. This chapter describes both ends of the spectrum and goes on to examine what lies between them.

In contrast to Kokoschka and Oppenheimer, Schiele's engagement with the imaging of mental illness was tied into his self-portraiture. Schiele attracted the attention of the Viennese patron Carl Reininghaus with a series of self-portraits on canvas completed in 1910. From this moment onwards, he became absorbed in the pathological representation of his body, pushing it to the limits of the 'abnormal', 'ugly' and 'irrational' in harrowing images on canvas and paper which have become the leitmotifs of his practice (figs 20, 23). We argue that one of the influences on this practice was the photographs of male patients produced at La Salpêtrière (fig.21), which were readily available in publication and were circulated around Vienna.[14] Charcot's belief in the diagnostic value of the image of the patient went hand in hand with his belief that the gaze of the doctor had to be fused with the gaze of the artist. Moreover, he considered the photographs to make an important contribution to the representation of the human body in the history of art, gearing his journal – aptly titled *Nouvelle* Iconographie *de la Salpêtrière* [our emphasis] – to artists as much as to psychiatrists. The photographs in this journal (fig.22), with their obsessive framing and repetition of the fragmented and distorted body, provided Schiele with a new vocabulary of the body which could be used powerfully to support his image as the artist-outsider.

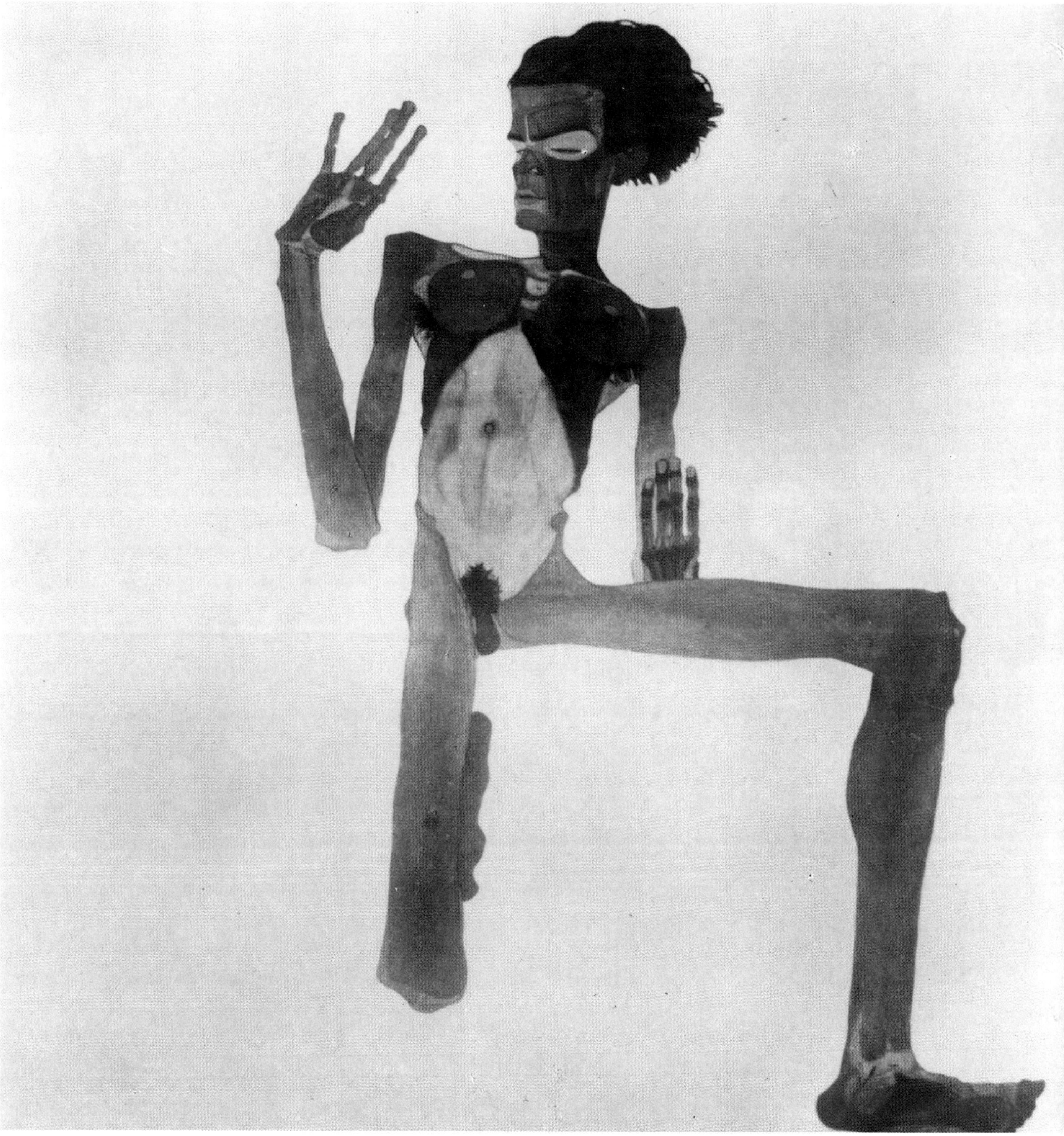

Opposite:
23 Egon Schiele, *Male Nude Kneeling, with Raised Hands (Self-Portrait)*, 1910, oil on canvas, 150 × 150 cm (59 × 59 in) (approx), present whereabouts unknown

While Schiele drew on the imagery coming out of clinical research into the many and various signs of mental illness inscribed on the body, the leader of the modern tendency in Viennese architecture, Otto Wagner, gained a commission that brought him into contact with asylum psychiatry, with its very different goals and impulses. Asylum psychiatry, as we have seen, embraced a rhetoric that elevated the institution to the position of model for the flawed world beyond its walls, a place that in its clarity, healthfulness and unity with nature, contained an implicit critique of the chaotic, overcrowded modern metropolis. This confidence in the transformative potential of a redesigned built environment resonated with Otto Wagner's goals for the 'modern architecture' he called for. He was dogged in his pursuit of the commission for the site plan and church of the new state-of-the-art Viennese psychiatric hospital 'am Steinhof'; the planners of the institution negotiated significant budget increases to make his plans possible. Steinhof was conceived by psychiatrists and government officials as a small city in itself, containing 60 separate buildings in a beautiful, natural setting overlooking Vienna from the west (fig.24). Wagner's urban plan for the institution, with his gold-domed modern church as its focal point, heightened its visual rhetoric by associating Steinhof with the latest in utopian planning.[15]

Another way of understanding the difference between these two ends of the spectrum is by examining how the power relationship between medicine and the lay public is refracted through the visual arts in each case. Schiele, Kokoschka and Oppenheimer draw on psychiatric images for the power inherent in the unflinching and critical medical gaze upon the abnormal. They co-opt (and complicate) the critical diagnostic gaze, unphased in its cool analysis of the ugly, misshapen and mad. Part of what is being claimed by the artists and circulated among the 'in' group of patrons and critics is the powerful position of the doctor (and this comes through in the medical language of the critics, representing the viewers of the works). The twist is that that critical gaze is not directed at a voiceless and

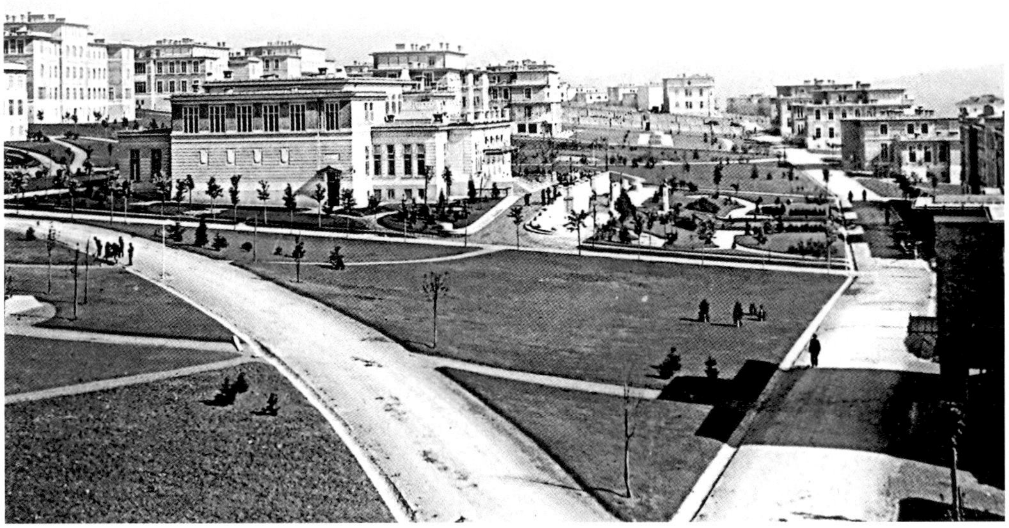

24 Photograph of the Lower Austrian Provincial Institution for the Cure and Care of the Mentally and Nervously Ill 'am Steinhof', c.1907

powerless object, but is turned back upon themselves: Schiele in his self-portraits and Kokoschka's and Schiele's intellectual and empowered sitters who are simultaneously in the positions of powerful gazer and passive gazed upon. There is a very different operation of power at play in the design of Steinhof. The public for asylum design is a passive one and the operation is one of seduction and control – not only of the actual asylum patients (who do not need to be seduced by the architecture) but also, more importantly, of the general public, who are supposed to be awed by a vision of a totally designed healthy life, and of the power of architecture to transform (the assumption being that they are ripe for transformation).

Between these two ends of the spectrum there is a range of other, more ambivalent moments in which psychiatry and the visual arts come together in Vienna. One of these is the Purkersdorf Sanatorium, an important monument of both the progressive visual arts in Vienna and of the psychiatry of nervous disorders. It was established in 1890 by the pre-eminent Viennese psychiatrist of the time, Richard von Krafft-Ebing, as a place to which affluent sufferers from nervous ailments could check themselves in and experience an extended period of simple, regimented living in an idyllic Vienna Woods setting, removed from the stresses of family and the city (see fig.62). In 1904, Wagner's student Josef Hoffmann was commissioned to build a new central medical and residential building for the sanatorium complex, and he involved his recently established design workshop, the

25 Photograph of Mechanotherapy Room, Purkersdorf Sanatorium, Purkersdorf, Austria, 1904–5

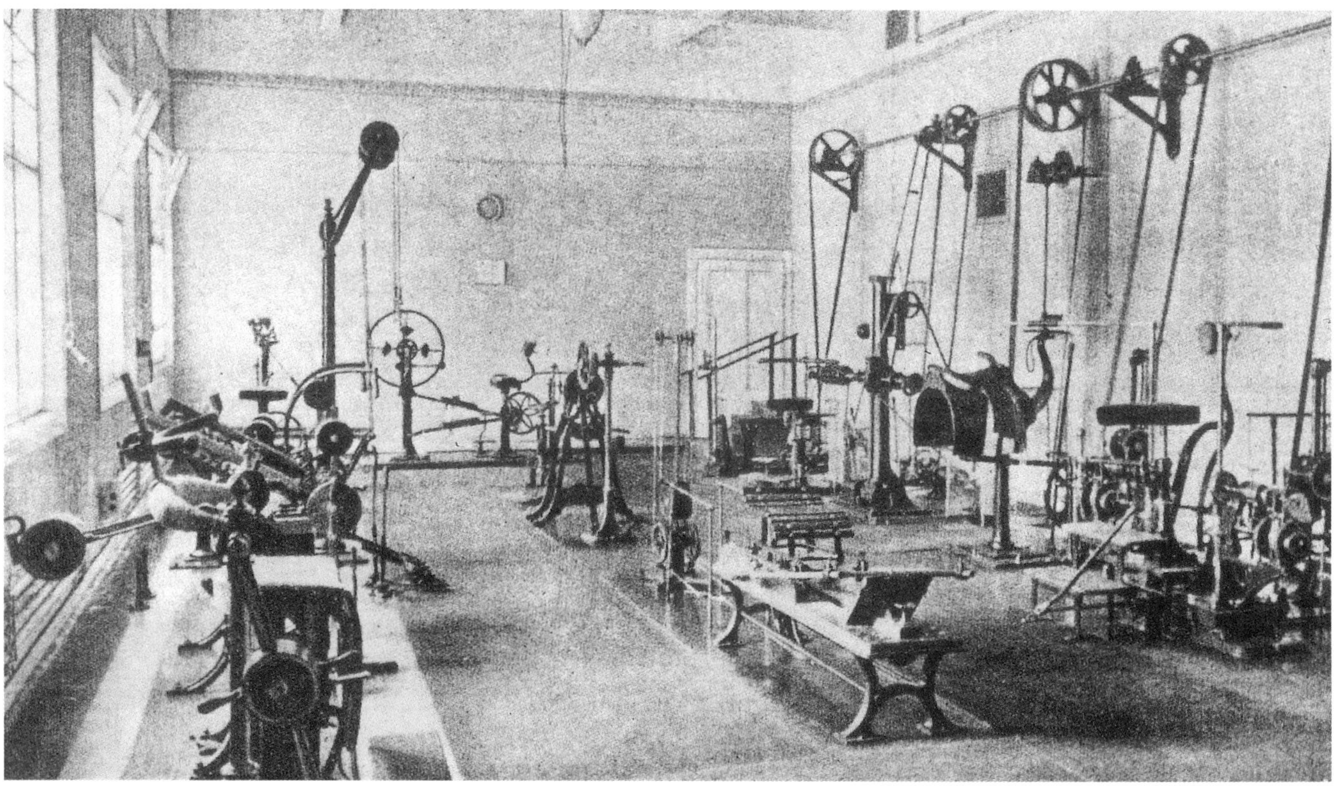

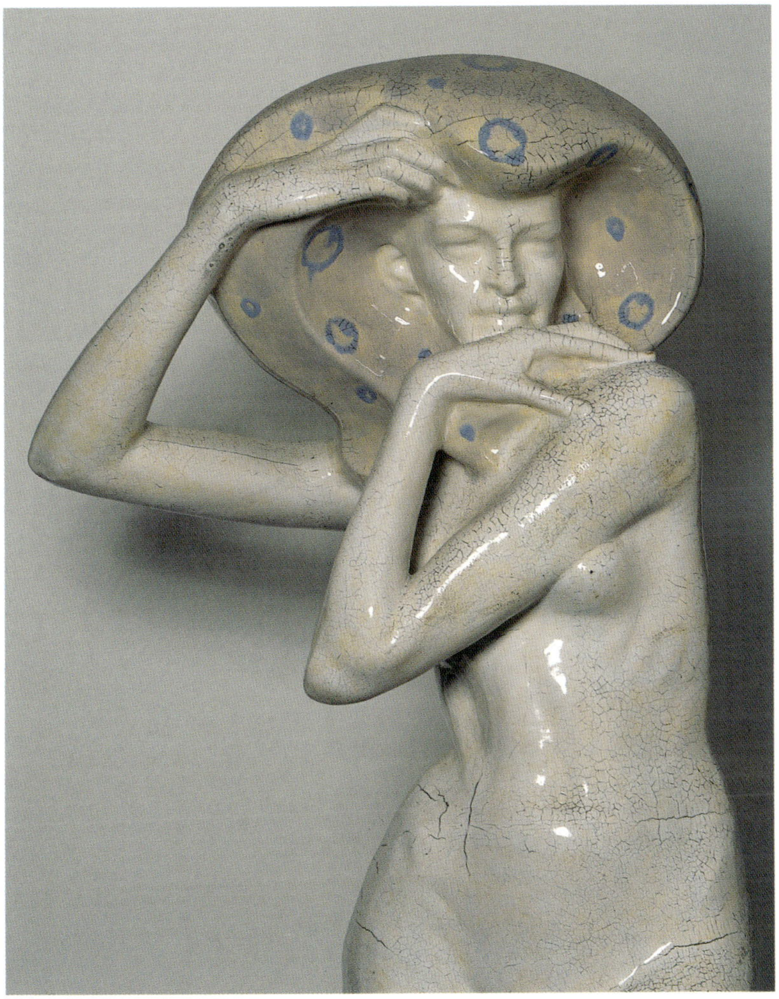

26 Richard Luksch, entrance figure for the Purkersdorf Sanatorium (detail), 1905, Faience Ceramic, 202 × 64 cm (79½ × 25¼ in). Museum für Kunst und Gewerbe, Hamburg

Wiener Werkstätte, in the overall design he conceived. The designers translated the vision of a simple, controlled life in nature into a white, box-like volume with uncluttered, rectilinear and carefully proportioned interiors and furnishings; the state-of-the-art therapeutic machinery that filled the 'mechanotherapy' room was matched by an overall image of the building as a smoothly functioning machine (fig.25).[16] The totalising vision of bodily control and regularity presented by the architecture and interiors of the Purkersdorf Sanatorium again differs starkly from the extreme contortions and abnormality embraced by Schiele and Kokoschka. But our project has brought to the forefront another aspect of the original design for Purkersdorf, two ceramic female figures (fig.26) designed by the Secessionist sculptor Richard Luksch and intended for one of the building's façades (see chapter 9). Sabine Wieber has demonstrated that Luksch's figures draw on a type familiar from the literature of nervous ailments, the 'wasting' woman, whose over-refined life has led to bodily denial and fragility.[17] The gauntness of the women's bodies and their contorted poses could be seen as an earlier and less extreme version of the devices in Egon Schiele's nudes (though without the model being party to the dissecting gaze.) What kind of relationship between power and looking do we see, then, at Purkersdorf? A passive public seduced by visions of therapeutic control, but also a sophisticated and financially empowered one, appealed to in the Luksch figures by being put in the position of diagnostic observer of disease.

Returning to Steinhof, the project has also revealed moments in which a critical artistic gaze was brought to bear within the utopian asylum. Kokoschka was commissioned by Adolf Loos (1870–1933) to paint the portrait of Ludwig Ritter von Janikowski, a writer closely affiliated to Karl Kraus, whilst he was receiving treatment at Steinhof (fig.27).[18] In this portrait, Kokoschka turned to scratching the painted surface to animate the space surrounding the sitter's head, which is so highly worked and coloured with thick paint that it appears almost disembodied, looming out of the darkness. These techniques, developed during the sitting in Steinhof, were quickly transferred to Kokoschka's sitters outside the hospital walls, such as in his portrait of Lotte Franzos (see fig.45), thus collapsing the

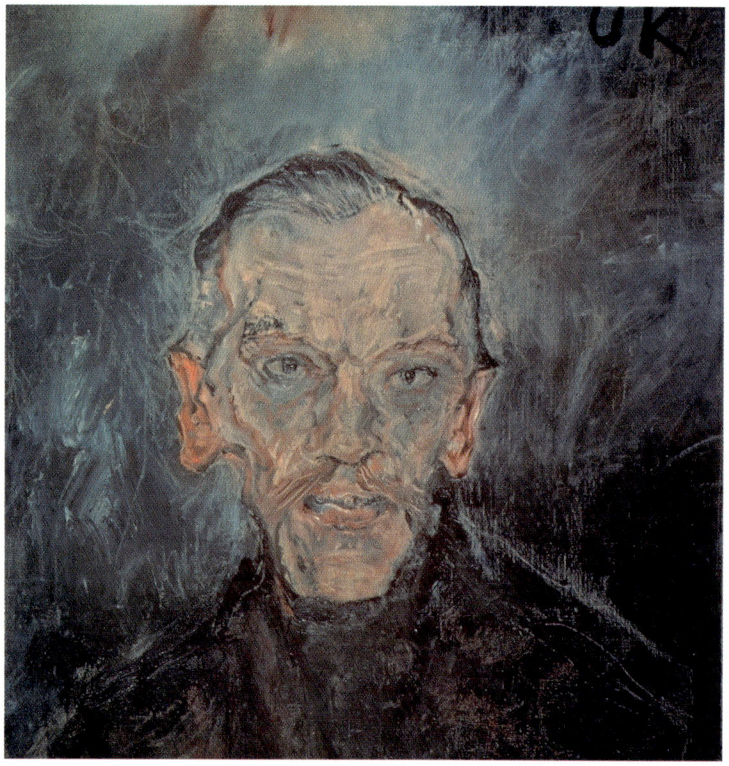

27 Oskar Kokoschka, *Portrait of Ludwig Ritter von Janikowski*, 1909, oil on canvas, 60.2 × 55.2 cm (23¾ × 21¾ in). Private Collection

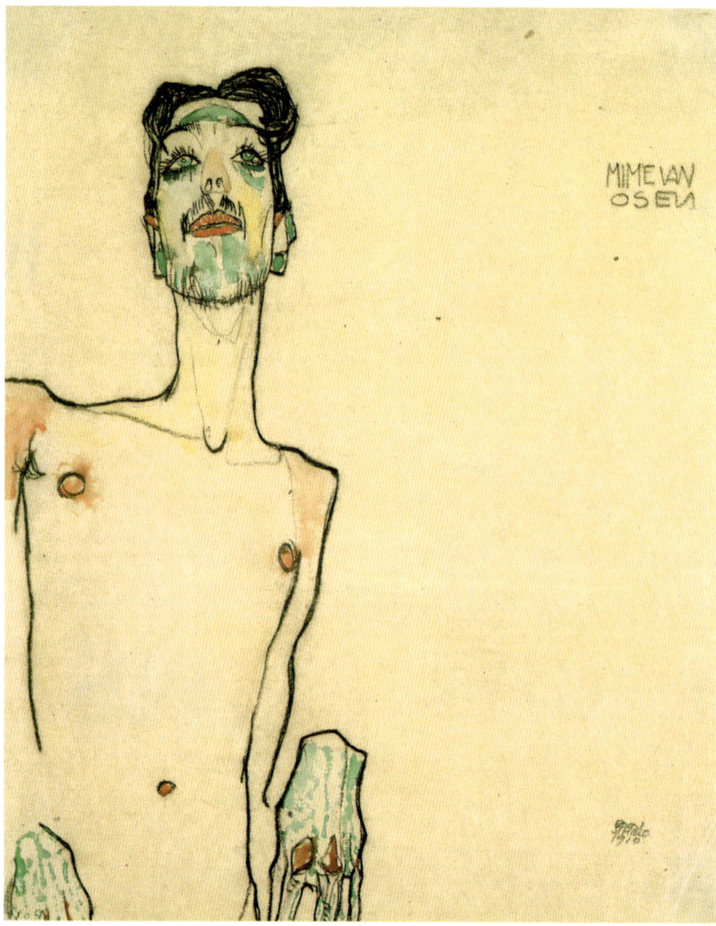

28 Egon Schiele, *Portrait of Mime van Osen*, 1910, charcoal and watercolour, 37.8 × 29.7 cm (14⅞ × 11¾ in). Neue Galerie Graz am Landesmuseum Joanneum

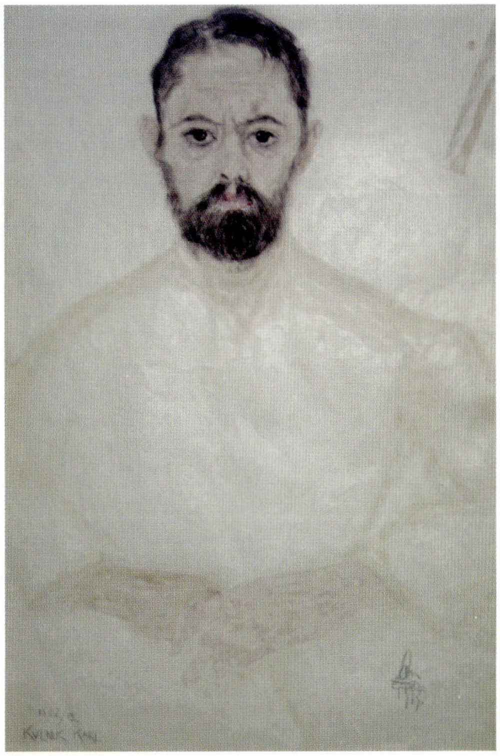

29 Erwin dom Osen, *Portrait of patient (Karl Kalnik)*, 1913, pencil and pastel on paper, 45 × 65 cm (17¾ × 25⅝ in) (approx). Raiffeisenbank Schladming, Austria

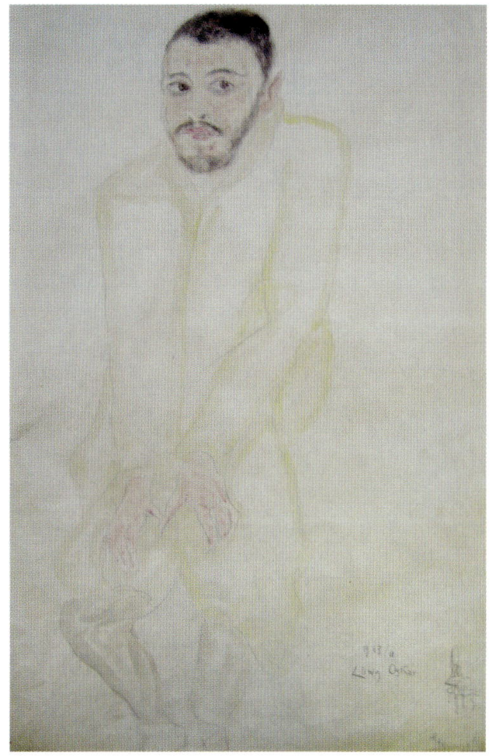

30 Erwin dom Osen, *Portrait of patient (Oskar Löwg)*, 1913, pencil and pastel on paper, 40 × 60 cm (15¾ × 23⅝ in) (approx). Raiffeisenbank Schladming, Austria

boundary between 'insane' and 'sane'. Erwin dom Osen (fig.28) was another artist selected to work inside Steinhof. In a letter to his friend Schiele, he writes: 'I still have to finish... a few drawings at Steinhof for the "Science Day" where Dr. Kronfeld will be speaking on pathological (!) expression in portraiture... I am already simulating all kinds of diseases so that I can get away sooner.'[19] As a result of research for this project, three of these portraits produced in 1913 to illustrate Kronfeld's lecture have been identified for the first time. The two displayed in this exhibition, of Karl Kalnik (fig.29) and Oskar Löwg (fig.30), include patient numbers inscribed by Osen that match the Steinhof records and enable us to identify the date of their admission to Steinhof –1913 and 1911 respectively – and their medical history. These portraits are precious examples of encounters between artists and the 'subjects' of psychiatry in Vienna.

The presence of artists within the asylum should be seen in the context of a concerted effort to welcome interested observers as well as the general public to visit the new, model institution. Shortly after Steinhof opened, some 800 visitors flowed through on a single Sunday morning, significantly disrupting the institution's routine and in some cases mocking the patients.[20] Did Steinhof operate not only as a model utopian settlement but also as a kind of exhibition? In 1898, the Viennese were presented with an exhibition on the care of the insane as part of a larger exhibition marking the Emperor's Jubilee. Alongside models of the latest plans for the asylum at Mauer-Öhling were photographs of psychiatric patients and objects made by patients 'in the grip of hallucinations'.[21] This kind of multifarious display may have presaged a situation in which a state-of-the-art psychiatric institution, recast as a utopian city by its modernist architect, played host to the clinical gaze of avant-garde painters, the clean lines of the architecture serving as a neutral background against which the bodily signs of the mental disturbance of its residents stood out starkly to artists attuned to such signs.

WHAT ABOUT FREUD?

In contrast to the aspects of psychiatry discussed so far, Sigmund Freud's psychoanalysis, the main tenets of which were established in Vienna in the same period, had only a very faint resonance with the progressive visual arts. The interpretive framework set out here helps to explain why this was the case. Mainstream psychiatry and the progressive visual arts shared two preoccupations: with the study of mental illness through an attention to bodily abnormality, and with the utopian notion that Western urban culture was both in decline and offered the solution for its own transformation. Freud's radical rethinking of the nature and treatment of mental disorders rejected both of these ways of thinking. He turned away from the analysis of the visible body as a psychiatric tool and focus of analysis, and towards hidden psychological forces (observed via words rather than images). His approach was also anti-utopian in that it rejected a static vision of a new perfected society in favour of the notion that all people were flawed and neurotic, and that this was part of the human condition. These anti-visual and anti-architectural stances are not taken up seriously by the visual arts until the 1920s. Freud did sit for a portrait by the young Max Oppenheimer in 1907 (fig.31). The result was one of Oppenheimer's most restrained and incommunicative works, lacking the contorted gestures and elongated faces of his 'psychological' portraits: a silent portrait of a man at odds with his time.

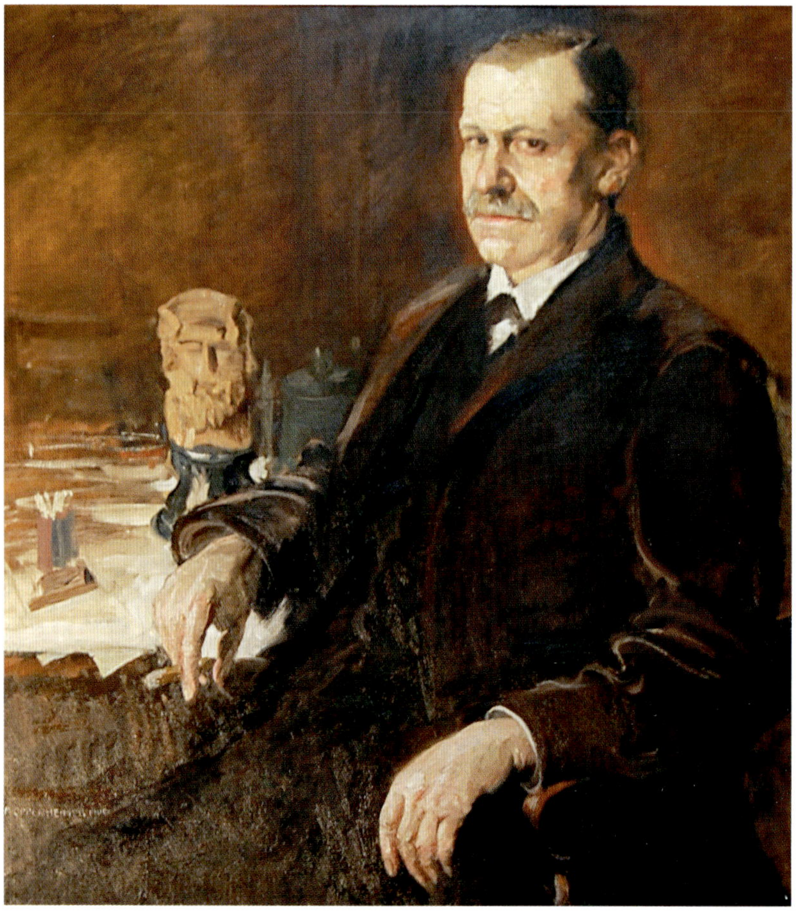

31 Max Oppenheimer, *Portrait of Sigmund Freud*, 1909. The New York Psychoanalytic Society and Institute

NOTES

1. See Erna Lesky, *The Vienna Medical School of the 19th Century* (Baltimore: Johns Hopkins University Press, 1976); Brigitte Keintzel and Eberhard Gabriel, (eds.), *Gründe der Seele: Die Wiener Psychiatrie im 20. Jahrhundert* (Vienna: Picus, 1999).
2. Heinrich Schlöss, *Einführung in die Psychiatrie für weitere Kreise*, second, revised and expanded edition (Berlin: Herdersche Verlagshandlung, 1919), pp 134–5.
3. See chapter 2.
4. See for example the journal *Nouvelle Iconographie de la Salpêtrière: Clinique des Maladies du Système Nerveux*, 1888–1918.
5. See chapter 5.
6. See chapters 5 and 8.
7. Leslie Topp, 'The Modern Mental Hospital in Late Nineteenth-Century Germany and Austria: Psychiatric Space and Images of Freedom and Control', in *Madness, Architecture and the Built Environment: Psychiatric Spaces in Historical Context*, Leslie Topp, James Moran and Jonathan Andrews (eds.) (New York and London: Routledge, 2007), pp 241–3.
8. Julius Meier-Graefe, *Modern Art: being a contribution to a new system of aesthetics* (London: Heinemann, 1908), p. 307. First published in German in 1904.
9. See chapter 3.
10. Hermann Bahr, *Gegen Klimt* (Vienna: Eisenstein, 1903), p. 46.
11. Quoted in P. Raabe (ed.), *The Era of German Expressionism*, trans. by J. M. Ritchie (Woodstock, NY: Overlook Press, 1974), p. 335.
12. It should be noted that Adolf Loos, another key modern architect of Vienna 1900, embraced a very different set of beliefs.
13. Leslie Topp, *Architecture and Truth in Fin-de-Siècle Vienna* (Cambridge: Cambridge University Press, 2004).
14. For a detailed discussion of the dissemination of Charcot's work in Vienna and its impact on Schiele see Gemma Blackshaw, 'The Pathological Body: Modernist Strategising in Egon Schiele's Self-Portraiture', *Oxford Art Journal*, 30 (2007), pp 377–401.
15. See chapters 5 and 6.
16. See chapter 5.
17. See chapter 9 and Sabine Wieber, 'Nervous Bodies and Femmes Fragile: Sculpting the Sanatorium in Vienna 1900', forthcoming.
18. The date of this painting varies from 1909–10. See Tobias Natter, ed., *Oskar Kokoschka: Early Portraits from Vienna and Berlin*, exhibition catalogue (New York: Neue Galerie; New Haven: Yale University Press, 2002), p. 112. Janikowski's death in 1911 was commemorated in an obituary written by Karl Kraus in *Die Fackel*, XIII Jahr, no. 311/312, 30 September 1911.
19. Alessandra Comini, *Egon Schiele's Portraits* (Los Angeles: University of Califormia Press, 1974), pp 203–4, n. 66.
20. Wiener Stadt-und Landesarchiv, MAbt 209 A1/1–5, draft letter from Director Heinrich Schlöss, 18.5.1908.
21. Luke Heighton, 'Exhibiting Madness, Art and the Asylum: The Creation and Exhibition of Images by Psychiatric Hospital Patients in Vienna, 1890–1914' (unpublished doctoral thesis, University of London, Birkbeck College, 2008).

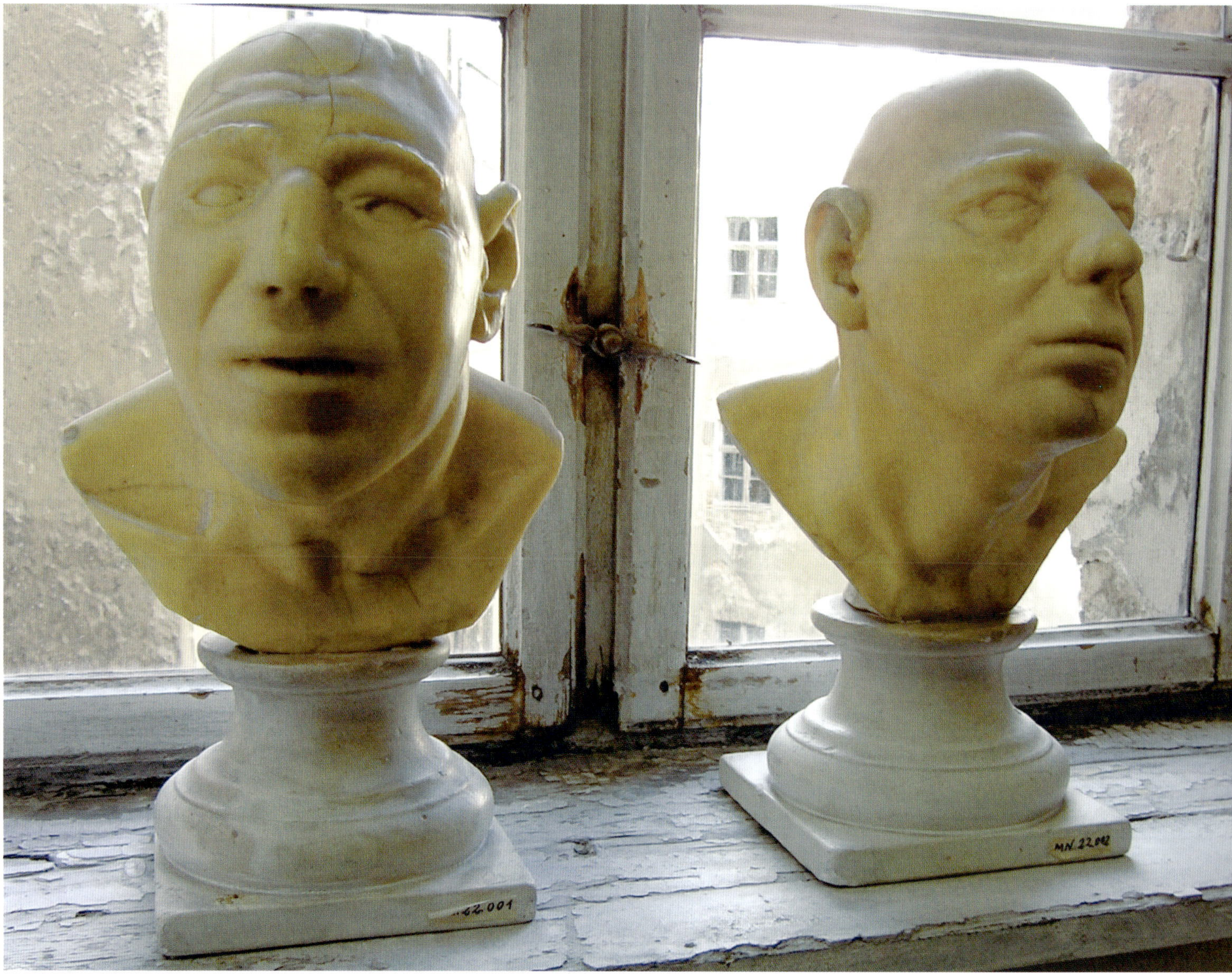

Chapter 2

Karl Henning, Wax Models of Two Male Heads, 1897–98, Federal Pathological-Anatomical Museum, Vienna

NICOLA IMRIE

Academic research is often like detective work; it is very much about conducting investigations and making connections. This chapter recounts research into two life-size wax models of male heads, shedding light on two asylum patients' lives and a doctor's preoccupation with their accurate physical representation.

An image in a book[1] led to the Federal Pathological-Anatomical Museum in Vienna, housed in the Narrenturm (see chapter 5.) It contains the two heads; honey-coloured portraits of two almost identical men with sloping foreheads and searching expressions (fig.32). Among over 2,000 wax casts (moulages) of a limited area surrounding an injury, a surgical intervention or deformity (figs 33, 34), the heads are unique in showing an all-around view of a body part modelled in wax.

32 Karl Henning, portrait busts of brothers with microcephaly, 1897–8, wax, 40 cm (15¾ in) high (approx), Pathologisch-Anatomisches Bundesmuseum, Vienna

Who made these models? Who were the two men? The engraved signature 'Dr Henning' (fig.35) appears on each plinth. Entries in the museum catalogue explained that Karl Henning modelled the heads of two 'idiotic brothers' suffering from microcephaly, a neurological-developmental disorder which effects the growth of the brain causing

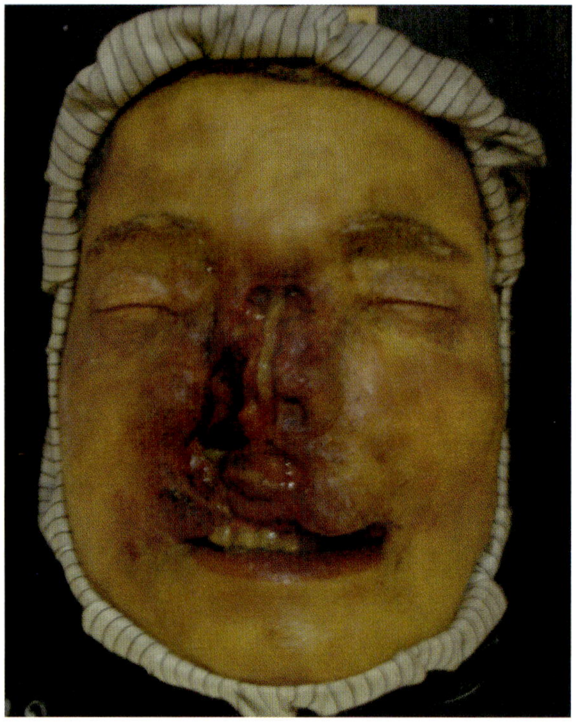

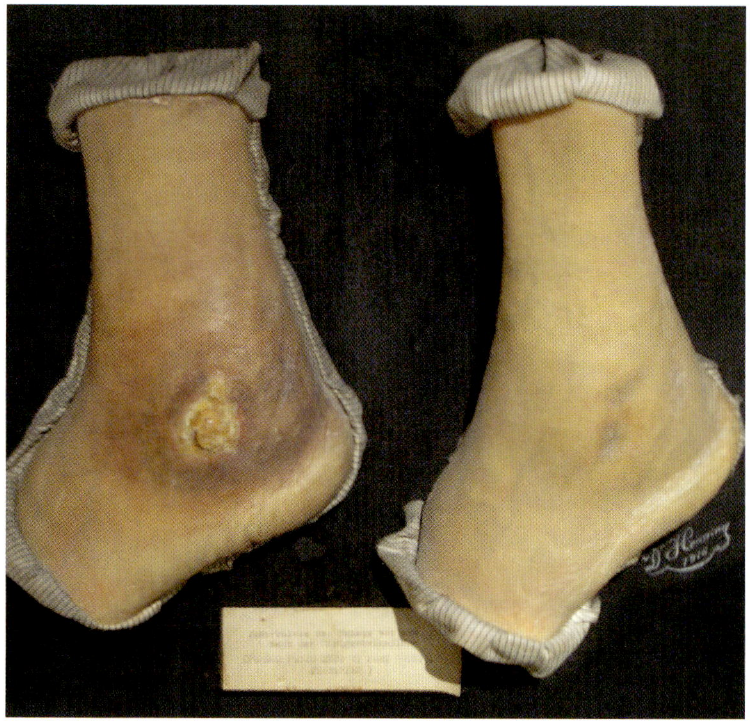

mental disablement.[2] The heads were presented to the museum in 1984 by the prosector at the Vienna Psychiatric Hospital (formerly known as 'Steinhof'). The Steinhof connection was reinforced by rough inscriptions on the underside of each plinth: 'Eigentum Anstalt Steinhof' (Property of the Steinhof Institution) (fig.36). The question of who the two men were remained. Furthermore, who was Henning and why did he make these models?

33 Karl Henning, moulage of facial carcinoma (MN 17.052), Pathologisch-Anatomisches Bundesmuseum, Vienna

34 Karl Henning, moulage of a tubercular ankle before and after x-ray irradiation, 1916 (MN 16.344), Pathologisch-Anatomisches Bundesmuseum, Vienna

Henning was a physician by training but also a talented artist. By the time he graduated from medical school in 1888, he had already illustrated a six-volume anatomical teaching manual.[3] How and when he moved into three dimensions is unknown. However, it is likely that when Henning became an assistant to the dermatologist Moritz Kaposi in 1890, the production of moulages to illustrate disease and damage had become increasingly important.[4] Like the anatomy manual, the moulages served teaching and demonstration purposes.[5]

Over the course of the 1890s, Henning's skill and reputation grew. He exhibited his work internationally to wide acclaim, producing moulages not only for colleagues in Vienna, but across the Austro-Hungarian Empire and in Germany.[6] In April 1897, after five probationary years, Henning's *Atelier for Moulage* was granted permanent status at Vienna General Hospital and Henning became head of department.[7] When precisely did he model the two heads and for what reason?

The psychiatric hospital at Steinhof opened in 1907 and its first director was Heinrich Schlöss. Eberhard Gabriel, former medical director at the hospital, drew our attention

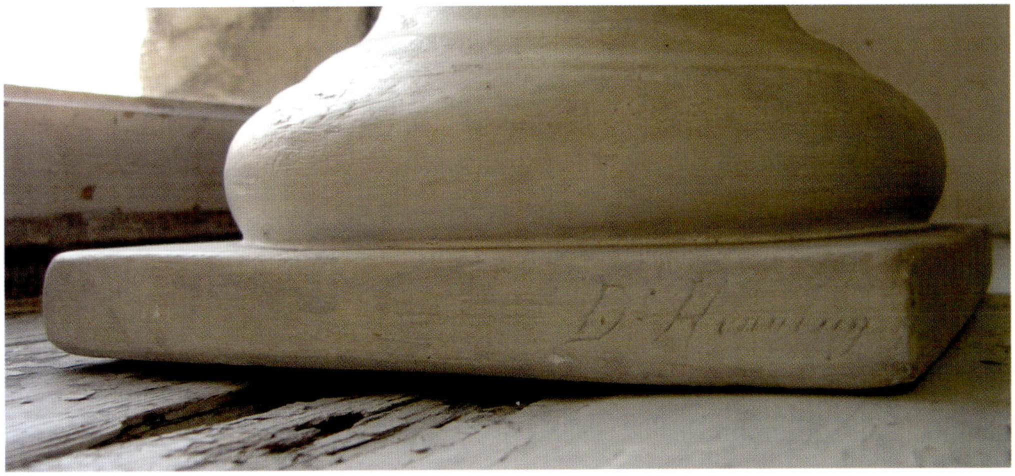

35 Karl Henning, portrait busts; the signature 'Dr Henning' appears on the base of the plinth of both wax heads

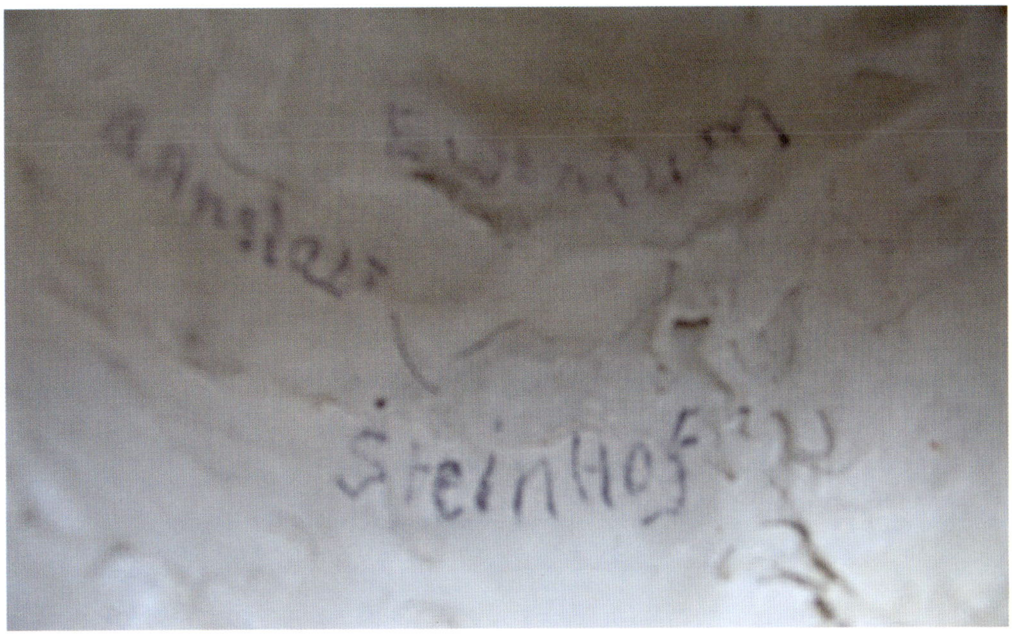

36 Inscription 'Eigentum Anstalt Steinhof' (Property of Steinhof Institution) on the underside of the plinth of both wax heads

to a series of photographs of patients which had, he assumed, belonged to Schlöss. The reverse of many photographs was marked with the stamp of the Lower Austrian Asylum at Kierling-Gugging, where Schlöss was a senior physician until 1899. Among the photographs was one of two men facing away from the camera (fig.37). The pairing of the two men, their posture and distinctive folds of skin on the backs of their heads suggested that they were Henning's models (figs 38, 39). But more evidence was required to identify them securely.

Dr Gabriel took up the thread, finding records of two brothers with microcephaly, who were patients at Kierling-Gugging during Schlöss' employment in the 1890s.[8] On account of disturbed and even violent behaviour resulting from their disorder,

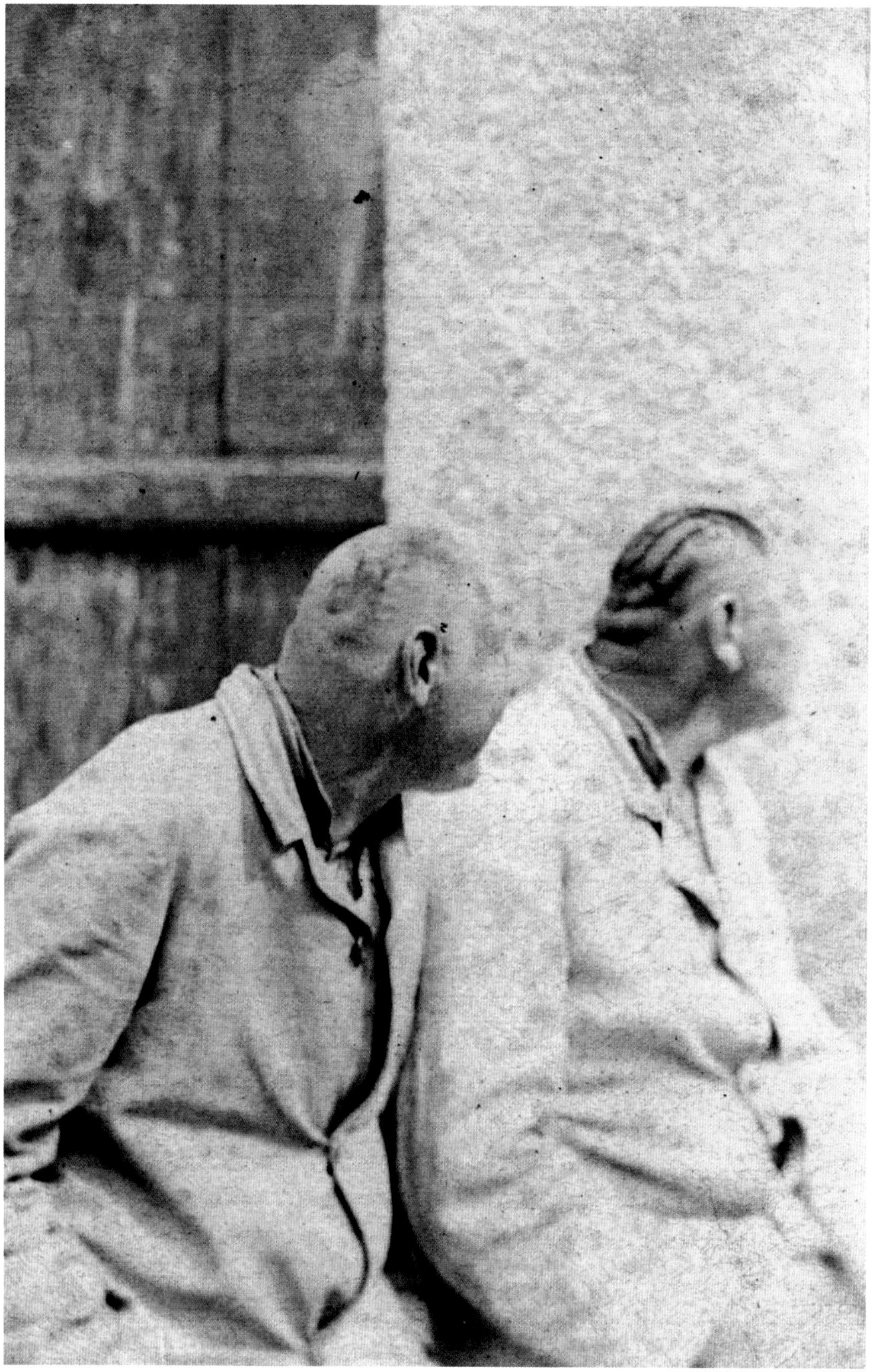

37 Photograph of two male patients at the Lower Austrian Asylum Kierling-Gugging, mid 1890s. Otto-Wagner-Spital, Vienna

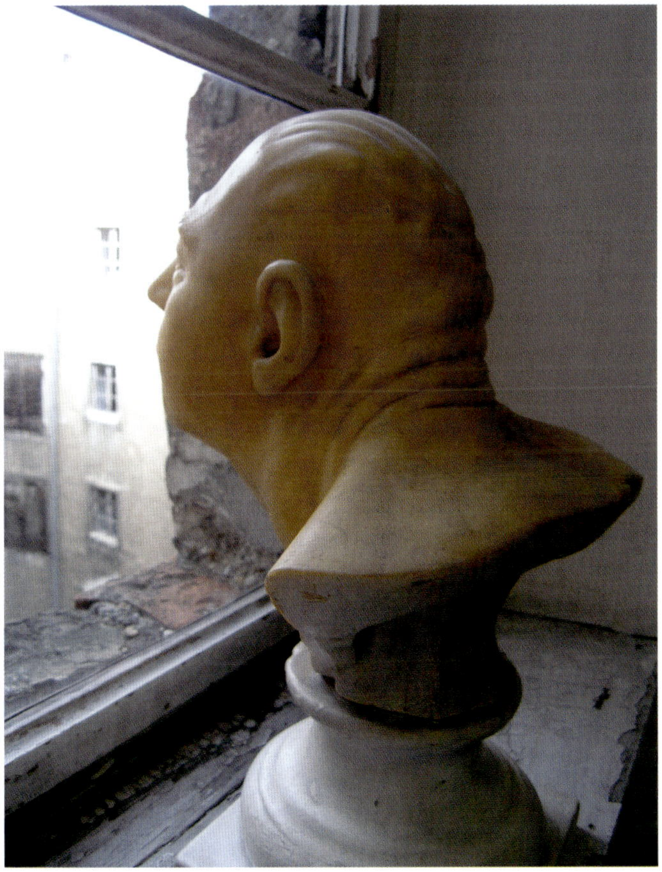

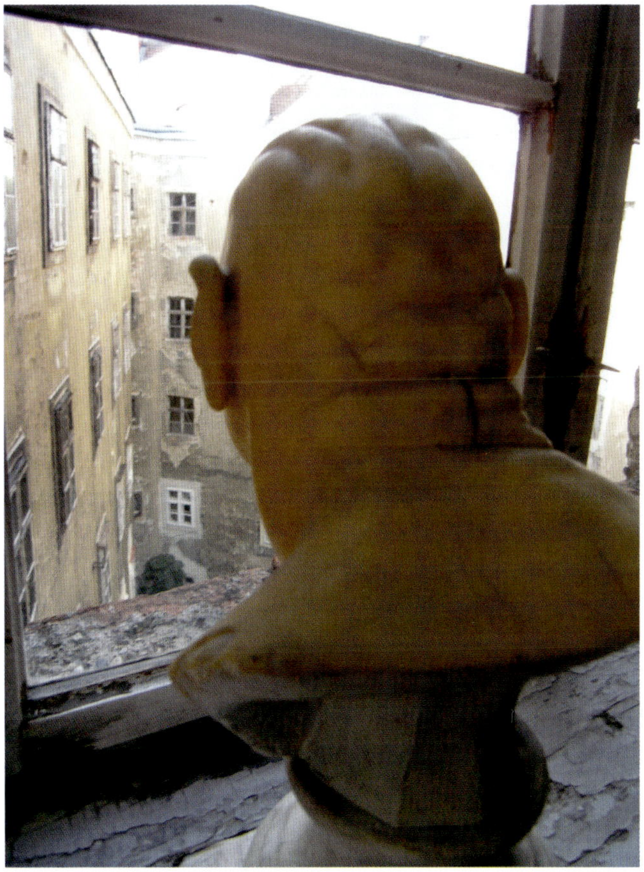

Left:
38 Rear of wax head
(on the right in fig.32)

Right:
39 Rear of wax head
(on the left in fig.32)

Leopold (*b.*1852) and Anton Koller (*b.*1856) were both admitted to Kierling-Gugging in 1892. In the 1890s, asylums treated patients with both psychiatric and neurological disorders and research focused on heredity. The fact that both brothers, along with eight of their siblings, were born with a neurological-developmental disorder attracted academic attention. Schlöss presented the brothers to neurology colleagues in Vienna in November 1894. He discussed the family history (including an alcoholic father), the severe restrictions they experienced in everyday life and communication and drew attention t o their physical characteristics, particularly the way the skin fell in folds on the backs of their heads.[9] Schlöss seems to have been determined to capture these heads in the most lifelike manner then possible; in May 1897 the brothers were transferred to the Vienna state asylum (Steinhof's predecessor) in order to sit for Henning.[10] Anton Koller never returned to Kierling-Gugging; he died of tuberculosis in September 1898 in the Vienna asylum. His brother, Leopold, returned alone in August 1898 and died at Kierling-Gugging in 1910.

While it is difficult now to determine exactly why, the two brothers and their distinctive heads made a strong medical impression at the time. No other similar life-sized models in the round are known among Henning's work. They must have been of significant value, for when Schlöss moved to the new hospital at Steinhof in 1907, he made sure the heads accompanied him.

NOTES

1. Alfred Stohl, *Der Narrenturm oder die dunkle Seite der Wissenschaft* (Vienna: Böhlau, 2000), pp 248–9.
2. At that time, the word 'idiotic' was used to describe the mentally disabled.
3. Thomas Schalke, *Diseases in Wax*, trans. by Kathy Spatschek (Chicago: Quintessence Publishing, 1995), p. 93; 'Karl Henning' in *Historisches Lexikon Wien*, ed by Felix Czeike (Vienna: Kremayr and Scheriau/Orac, 2004), iii, p. 143.
4. Schalke, p. 93, Karl A. Portele, *Die Moulagensammlung des Pathologisch-anatomischen Museums in Wien*, 1 (1977), p. 7.
5. Portele, p. 12, 'Atelier für Moulage (Provisorisch)', *Jahrbuch der Wiener K. k. Krankenanstalten*, 2 (1893), 474–5.
6. Schalke, p. 94, Portele, pp 7–9.
7. Portele, p. 8, 'Henning', p. 143.
8. The patient records of brothers Leopold Koller (AZ 24/1897) and Anton Koller (AZ 221/1910) were discovered in the archive of the Lower Austrian Asylum at Gugging, held today at the Lower Austrian Provincial Archive at St Pölten.
9. Heinrich Schlöss, 'Demonstration zweier mikrocephaler Idioten', *Wiener klinische Wochenschrift*, 23 (1895), 425.
10. Entries detailing the transfer of the brothers from Gugging to Vienna can be found on the fifth page of each brother's patient record.

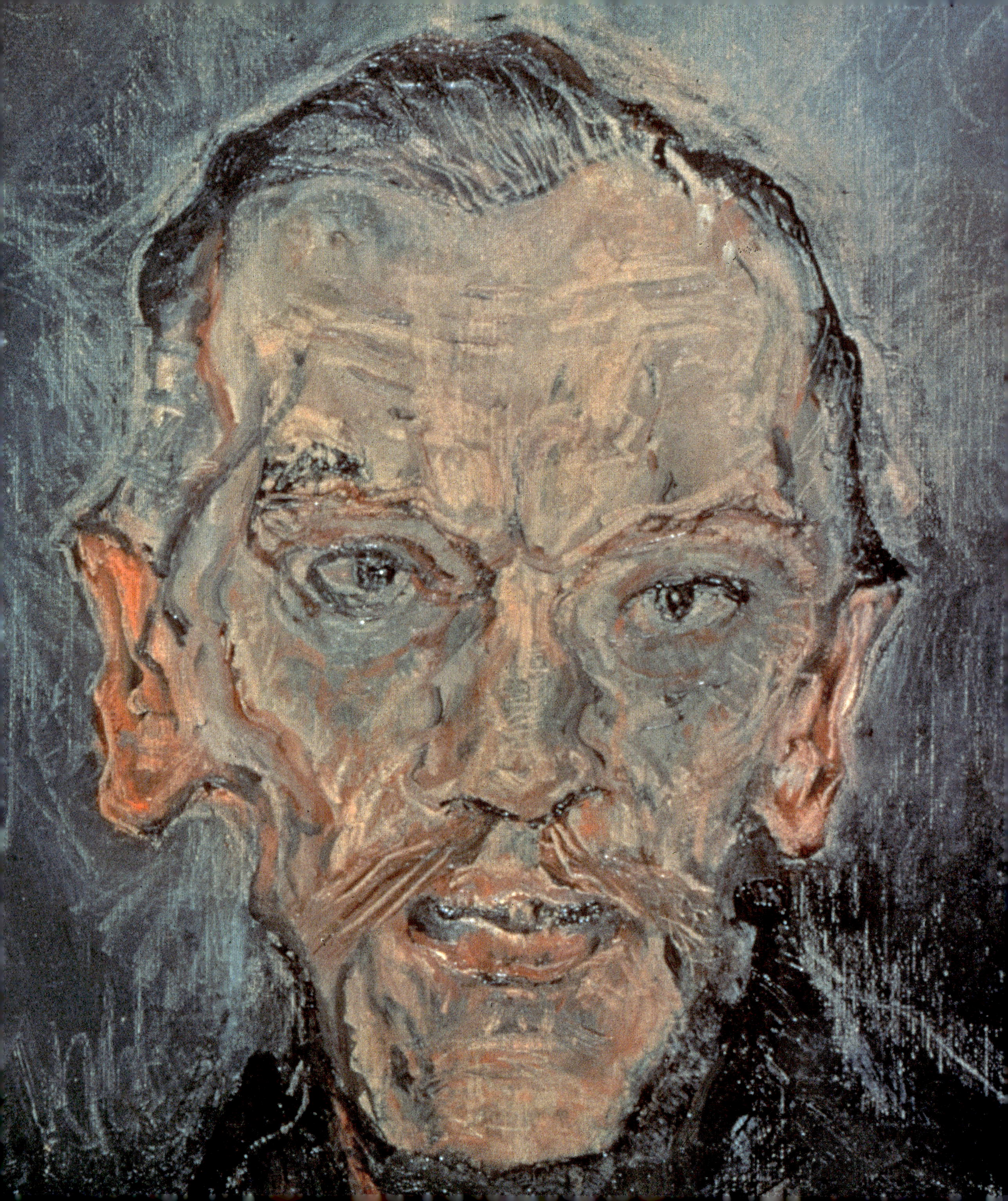

Chapter 3

'Mad' Modernists: Imaging mental illness in Viennese portraits

GEMMA BLACKSHAW

47 Oskar Kokoschka, *Portrait of Ludwig Ritter von Janikowski*, (detail) 1909, oil on canvas, 60.2 × 55.2 cm (23¾ × 21¾ in). Private Collection

In February 1911, the young Oskar Kokoschka (fig.40) returned to Vienna from Berlin to exhibit 25 oil paintings at the Hagenbund (fig.41).[1] An astonishing 23 of these works were portraits of well-known individuals living in Vienna or connected to the city's intellectual circles. This whiff of celebrity, combined with the 'foul smells' of rotting flesh that reputedly wafted from the portraits to repel exhibition-visitors, made for a sensational show. As a reviewer for the *Österreichische Volks-Zeitung* exclaimed, Kokoschka 'sometimes even divulges the names of those portrayed whose physiognomies leer, gawp and caper out from the sullied canvases with all the signs of quiet or raving madness.'[2] Though divided in their appreciation of Kokoschka, the critics were united in their interpretation of his portraits as images of mental illness. The sickened modernity signalled in the vacant stares and rancid bodies of Kokoschka's sitters certainly made for exciting journalism. Twelve other artists were represented at the Hagenbund, but as far as the reception history reads, it was – without doubt – a one-man-show.[3]

Kokoschka's portrait of the Viennese writer Peter Altenberg (1859–1919) was included

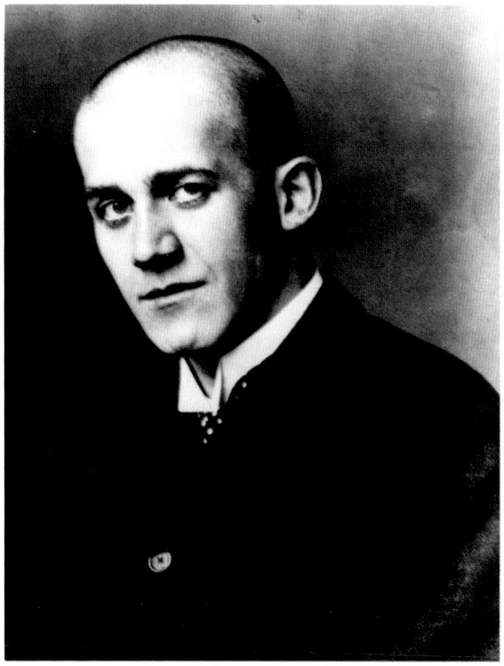

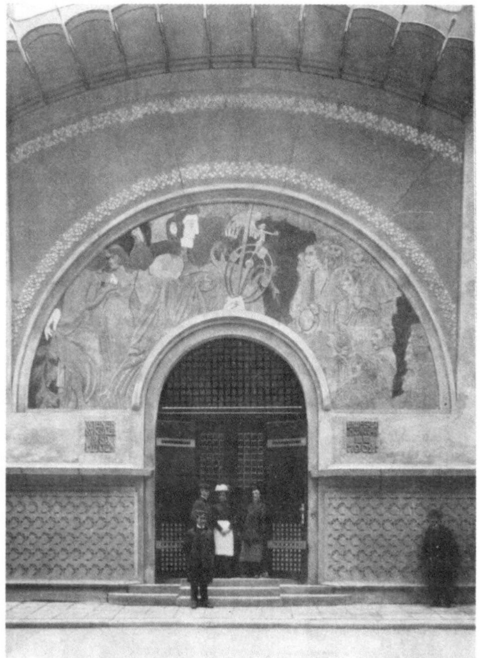

Far left:
40 Photograph of Oskar Kokoschka, 1909

Left:
41 Joseph Urban, exhibition building for the Hagenbund, Vienna, from *Wiener Bau-Industrie Zeitung*, Supplement (*Wiener Bauten-Album*), vol. XIX, plate 67

in the exhibition (fig.42). But Altenberg, whose various addictions and spells in nervous sanatoriums and psychiatric hospitals were an intrinsic part of his highly crafted public persona, was strangely ambivalent about the show. In a cryptic review entitled 'Authentic' for the German satirical magazine *Simplicissimus*, the famed 'coffeehouse wit'[4] remarked:

> In the H...b... [Hagenbund] there was a collective exhibition by a young person who had capitalised on the genuine madness of a van Gogh, etc., etc. by adding in a quantity of his own miserable nature and talents – granted him by the mercy of fate, or rather by the mercilessness of fate – as was necessary and appropriate for his patrons...[5]

Kokoschka is not ever named in the article, although the portraits of 'naked and clothed devastations' that comprise his art leaves the reader in no doubt that he is the artist in question. Unusually, Altenberg – who rarely failed to grasp an opportunity for self-promotion – does not single his own portrait out for comment either. The real content of the review is encapsulated in a lengthy postscript which reads:

> P.S. Van Gogh was a famous painter who was nevertheless interned in an asylum seven times. But those who run around free are by no means 'van Goghs' for that reason... Madness is a chance additional extra, like a pimple or a bad cold. My dear sirs, whether normal or abnormal, it is all a question of 'original genius'. Just because you think you are the 'Emperor of China' is of limited importance for humanity and is significant only for the one

Opposite:
42 Oskar Kokoschka, *Portrait of Peter Altenberg*, 1909, oil on canvas, 76 × 71.5 cm (30 × 28⅛ in). Private Collection

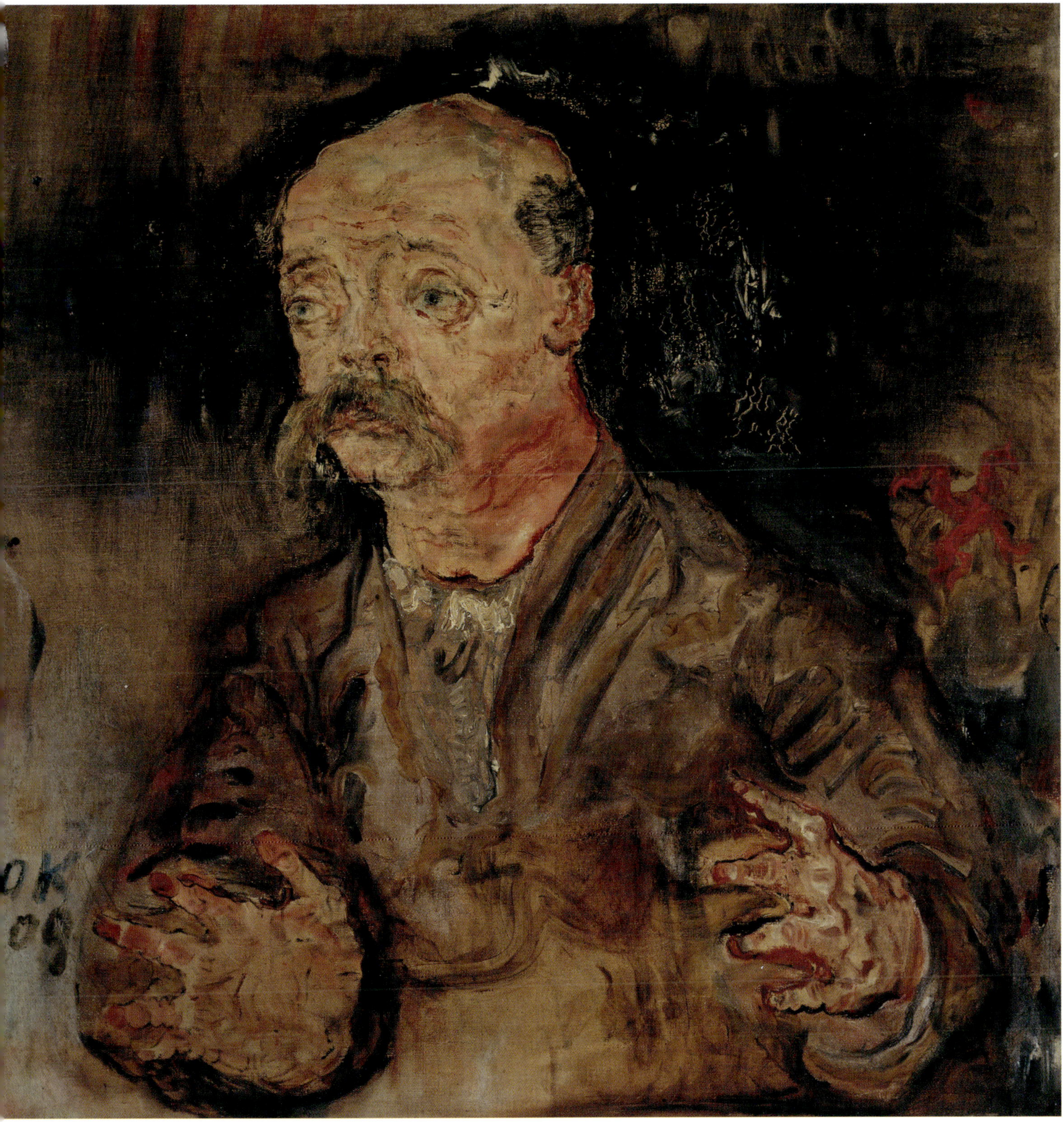
OK
09

> sanatorium in which this worthless idiot, thanks to money paid by his relatives, terminates his days, that is to say years. Nowadays people have a colossal concern for madmen who are nothing but madmen. Just because there have been some who, besides this remarkable performance of the brain, are also able to show evidence of other, more important achievements![6]

In this P.S. Altenberg both celebrates the genius of Vincent van Gogh (1853–1890) – whose authentic madness is nothing more than an 'additional extra'– and despairs of those who take this to mean that *all* madmen are geniuses. He criticises Kokoschka for capitalising on this mistaken relationship between madness and genius by strategically representing himself and his patrons as 'mad'. In doing so, Altenberg exposes key themes that defined Vienna's early twentieth-century avant-garde: the economy of madness in modernist circles; the construction of modernist genealogies based on claims to mental illness; the centrality of the portrait in the display and dissemination of modernism's 'mad' identity; and the use of the portrait in an aggressive art market to muster avant-garde communities. It is these themes, so cogently identified by Altenberg back in 1911, that this chapter will explore with reference to Kokoschka's portraits of Vienna's 'mad' modernists and – in the author's own 'P.S.'– the challenge posed by his competitor, the equally prolific though largely forgotten Viennese portrait painter, Max Oppenheimer.

'MAD' PORTRAITS: KOKOSCHKA AT THE HAGENBUND

The success of the Hagenbund show must have come as a relief to Kokoschka's patron, the architect and cultural critic, Adolf Loos (fig.43). Loos had invested heavily in Kokoschka since first encountering his work at the Kunstschau of 1909, funding the artist on an 18-month trip across Europe to paint the portraits of Loos's friends and contacts. Any work rejected by the client was bought by Loos. Guaranteed sales sealed Kokoschka's dedication to the project, despite being bored by it. In December 1910 he wrote to Loos: 'I've done four pictures in the last few days, and I'm now practically being pursued by grinning human heads, so that I'm sick to death with the whole business of portrait painting.'[7]

Monotony aside, Kokoschka was given the freedom to work outside the usual constraints of commissioned work and develop his own, distinctive aesthetic. In this aesthetic, the debilitated human body, often represented in a state of physical decay, is used to signify the psychological degeneration or enervation of the sitter. The coherence and consistency of this aesthetic meant that it operated powerfully at a market level. Kokoschka's portraits of Altenberg and Loos (fig.44), typical of this body of portraiture, could be used strategically with others to develop a unified group identity for what was in reality a fractured community of individuals with varied interests, spread across

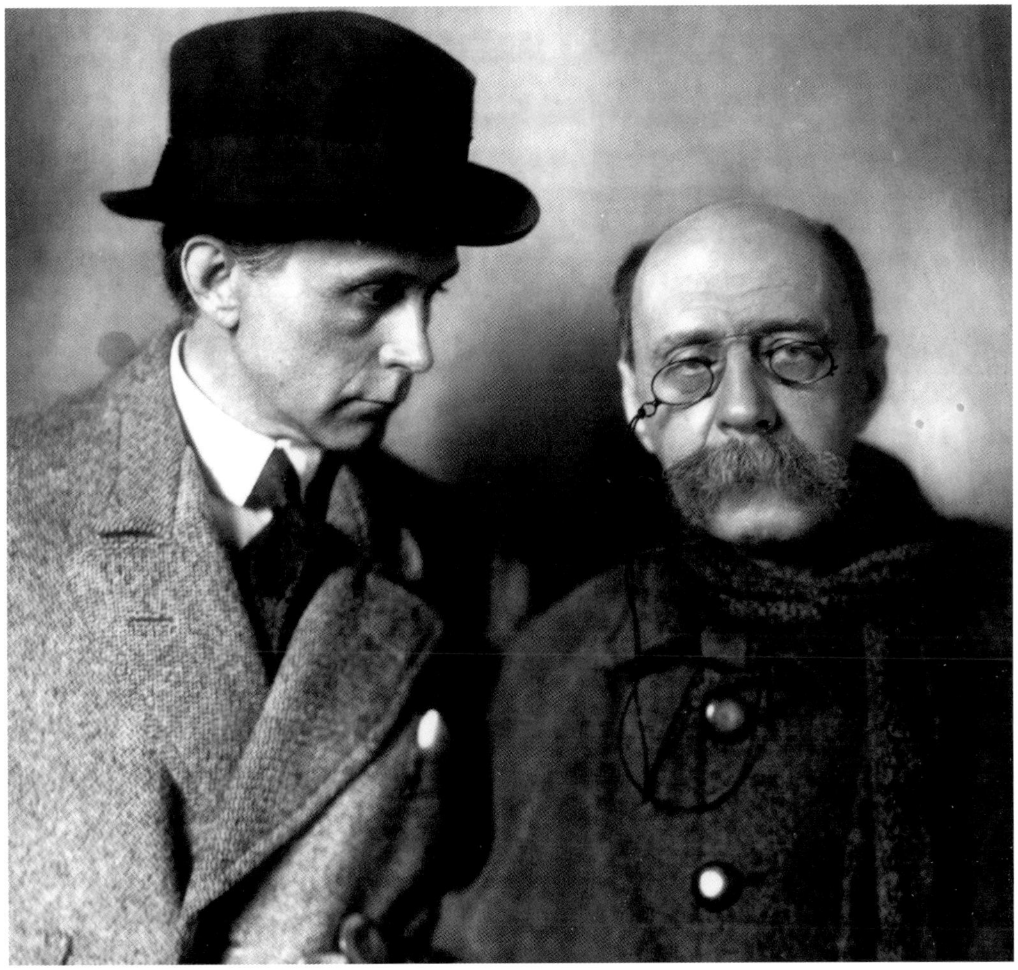

43 Photograph of Adolf Loos (left) and Peter Altenberg, *c.*1918. Austrian National Library Vienna, Picture Archive

different European cities. Moreover, the portraits served to stress this community as a resistance-group, challenging bourgeois conventions and mores through their shared 'disease'.

Loos, ever the strategist, first organised for the portraits to be exhibited in Berlin at the Galerie Paul Cassirer from June to July 1910. The show went virtually unnoticed, with only two reviews appearing in *Der Sturm*, the journal edited by Loos and Kokoschka's friend Herwarth Walden.[8] Kurt Hiller foreshadowed the Viennese reception by characterising Kokoschka's portraits as 'bursting with psychology': 'visages of care-worn citizens of the metropolis, hyper-sophisticated, grotesque faces of the famous crowd around to gape and scream at the exhibition-visitor.'[9] However, the otherwise muted response in Berlin in no way prepared Kokoschka and Loos for the sensational reception of the near-identical show in Vienna.

Publicity was sparked in part by the cast of recognisable figures in Kokoschka's two rooms, many of whom were named in the catalogue for the show and in the reviews.

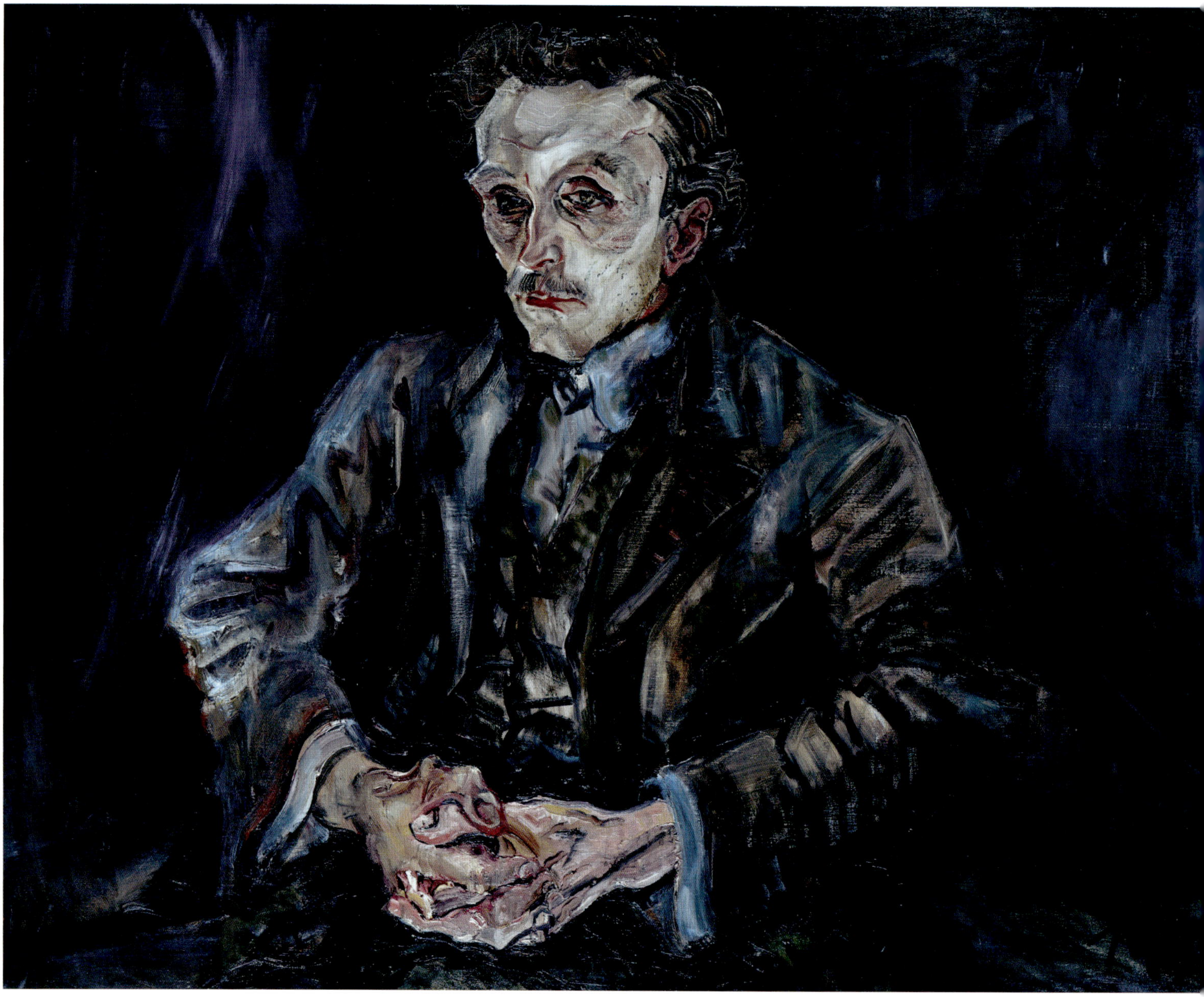

44 Oskar Kokoschka,
Portrait of Adolf Loos,
1909, oil on canvas,
74 × 91 cm ($29\frac{1}{4} \times 35\frac{7}{8}$ in).
Nationalgalerie, Staatliche
Museen zu Berlin/A11 448/

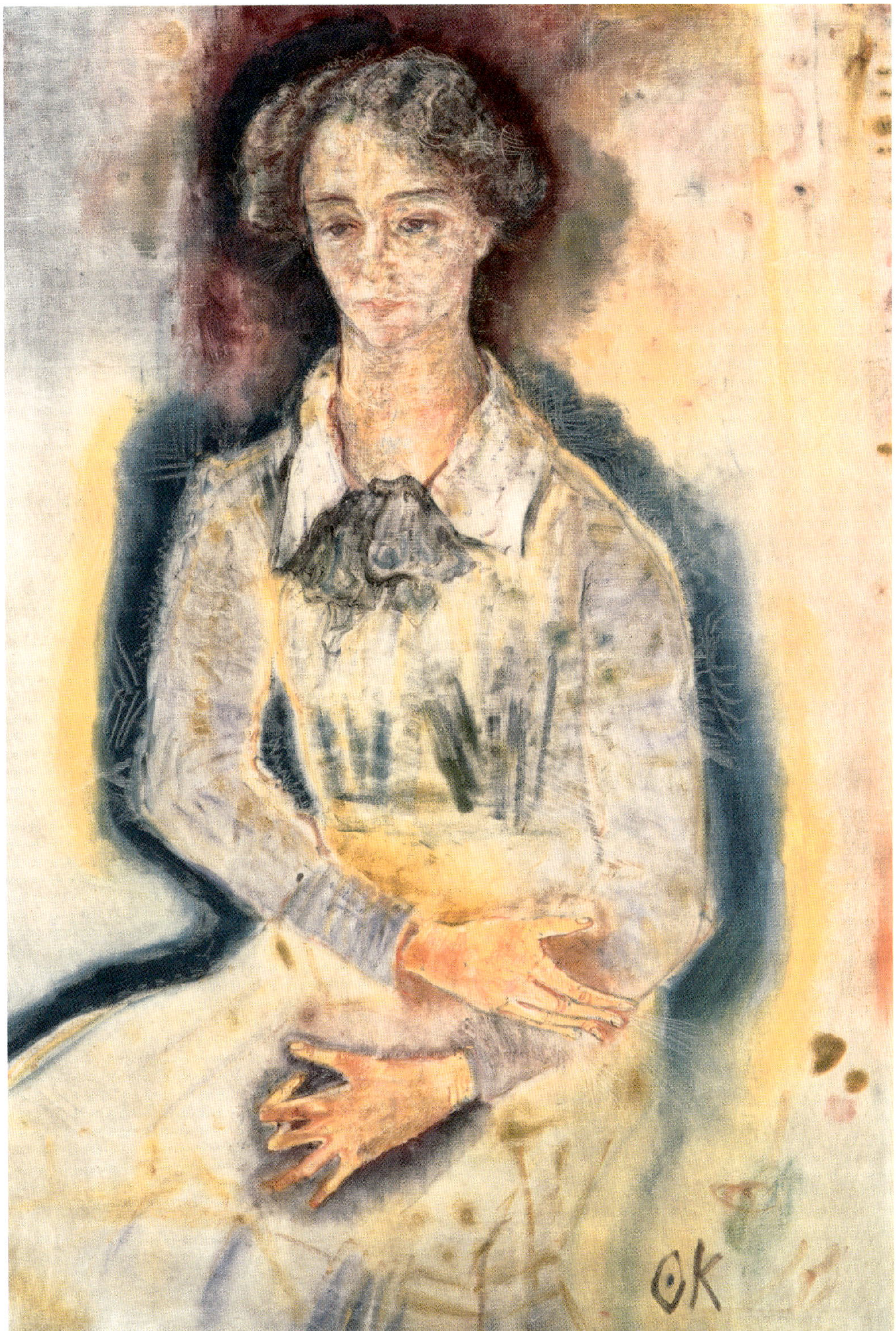

45 Oskar Kokoschka, *Portrait of Lotte Franzos*, 1909, oil on canvas, 115 × 79.5 cm (45¼ × 31⅜ in). Phillips Collection, Washington, D.C.

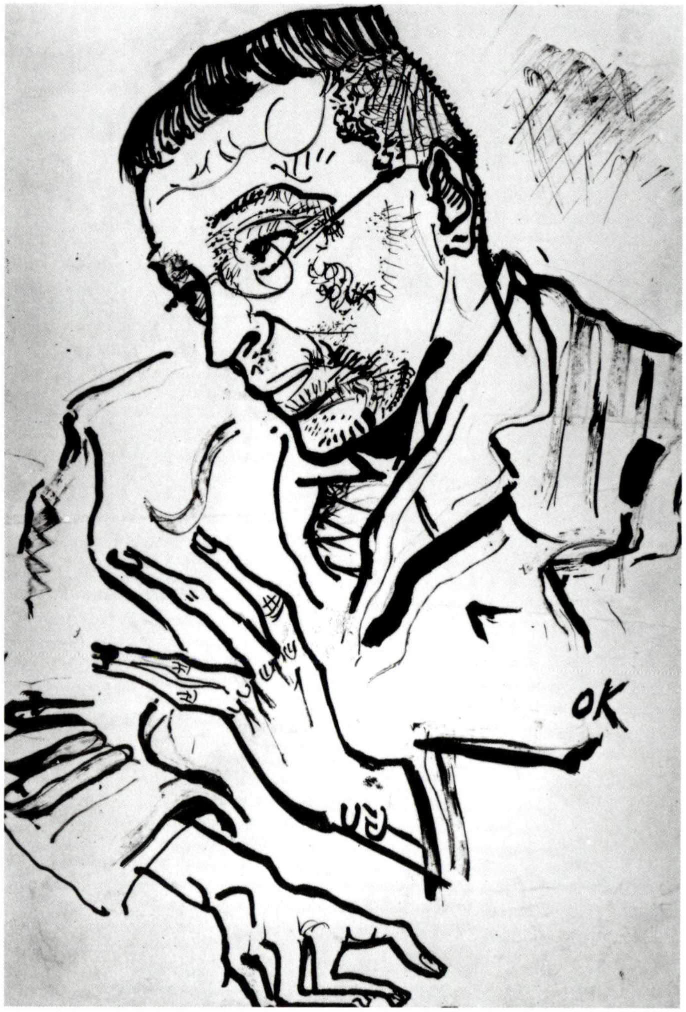

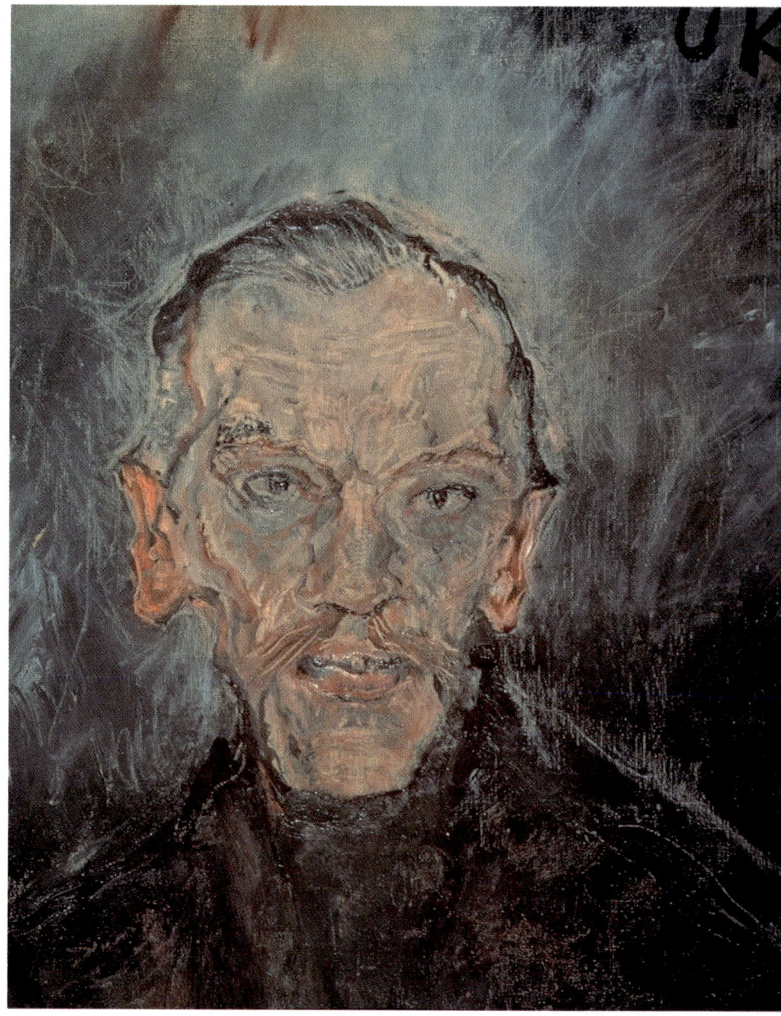

Two major Viennese newspapers sent leading art historians and critics to review the show, and they only had eyes for Kokoschka's portraits. Josef Strzygowski, writing for *Die Zeit* exclaimed: 'What a foul smell emanates from the picture of Frau Dr. Franzos! (fig.45) What disgusting plague-spots the painter shows us in this Karl Kraus! (fig.46)'[10] Hans Tietze wrote for the *Fremdenblatt*: 'Try looking into the eyes of the portrait of J. for one minute. Try to defy the horror which calls out from the lacklustre gaze of a ruined intellect.'[11] Tietze's focus on Kokoschka's portrait of Janikowski (fig.47) is significant. Vienna's narrowly circumscribed intellectual circles meant that Tietze, along with others, knew of Janikowski's recent move into the Steinhof psychiatric hospital, where Kokoschka had painted the portrait. The recognition of this portrait was, it can be argued, central to the experience of the Hagenbund show. It signalled to exhibition-visitors Kokoschka's intervention in the representation of the mentally ill, and it reinforced – perhaps even suggested – the distinctive reception of his portraits as images of 'mad' modernists.

46 Oskar Kokoschka, *Portrait of Karl Kraus*, 1910, pen and ink and brush and ink on slightly tinted paper, 29.7 × 20.6 cm (11¾ × 8⅛ in). This is not the portrait exhibited at the Hagenbund

47 Oskar Kokoschka, *Portrait of Ludwig Ritter von Janikowski*, (detail) 1909, oil on canvas, 60.2 × 55.2 cm (23¾ × 21¾ in). Private Collection

THE CRITICAL LANGUAGE OF MENTAL ILLNESS

The critics focused on Kokoschka's representation of his sitters as both physically and mentally diseased. Their reviews demonstrate the currency of the notion in Viennese psychiatry that physical and mental disorder were closely related (a notion explored in chapter 1).[12] In Kraus's *Die Fackel*, the art historian Franz Grüner wrote: 'No viewer steps in front of Kokoschka's portraits without immediately realising that those depicted have been suffering from serious illnesses or have spent many years in prison, afflicted with repellent physical and (it goes without saying) psychological sickness.'[13] In *Kunst und Kunsthandwerk*, Karl Michael Kuzmany protested: 'What all the portraits have in common is the characteristics of physical and psychological contamination... After this virulence, clean air is necessary.'[14]

The critical language developed in the Viennese reviews operated as a heady re-enactment of Kokoschka's own aesthetic. The viscous application of paint, the scraping of the canvas surface with finger-nails and the mottled colouration of flesh was developed in the criticism, with writers revelling in descriptions of decay, rupture and excess. This is particularly the case with Arthur Roessler, art critic for the *Arbeiter Zeitung*, who wrote:

> He brews up his paints from poisonous putrescence, the fermenting juices of disease; they shimmer gall-yellow, fever-green... hectic-red and the substance binding them seems to be penetrating iodide of formyl, carbolic and asafoetida... He smears them on like a salve and allows them to crust scabiously, to form scars... The clumsy portrayal of the disgusting impurity of spongy and porous, leathery and flabby, spotted and speckled, infirm bodies is nothing but the despairing expression of a soul in harrowing disintegration which looks at the world through calcified eyes. Depravity is the attraction of these pictures.[15]

Roessler, who was an ardent supporter of Egon Schiele, attempts here to re-enact the cumulative impact of Kokoschka's portraits. The lack of reproductions in early twentieth-century newspapers made such a re-enactment a key function of the review, with writers having to generate especially vivid descriptions of paintings. But Roessler takes this to the level of performance, developing a language which vies with the work of art. What we see in this particular mode of writing is not only the enthusiasm with which Kokoschka's critics wrote about the portraits, but also the extent to which they were crucial in drawing the portraits into meaning, mobilising their ability to function as signs.

This importance of the critic in determining the reception of Kokoschka's portraits can be seen in another passage in the review by Altenberg, which opened this chapter. Altenberg imagines a scenario where the Archduke Franz Ferdinand, on seeing the shocking works, turns to the exhibition attendant, 'like a child caught committing some naughty act', and – in panic – tries to ensure that his visit is kept a secret. The star-struck attendant, in thick Viennese dialect, reassures his Highness that he would rather be chopped into little bits than reveal the Archduke's identity.[16] But Altenberg points out that the Archduke need not worry. The rooms of the Hagenbund in the morning hours were quite empty: 'which was indeed not at all different from the afternoon hours.' In this witty aside, Altenberg draws attention to how Kokoschka's portraits were not – on their own – the public sensations so implied in the reviews. Or in other words, it took the response of the critics, sniffing the 'putrid' air and matching it with a language of fetid decay to diagnose the 'madness' of modern times, for the portraits to actually *work*.

THE MADNESS OF MODERN TIMES

Critics moved from one alarmist diagnosis to another, but ultimately the bodies of Kokoschka's sitters – whether syphilitic, leprous or plague-spotted – were interpreted as signifying the psychopathology of modern times. As Strzygowski pointed out:

> As disagreeable as Kokoschka's paintings are – rigged up with thumb and knife – I should come to his defence. The group of art-lovers who are happy when their music and literature dissects the afflictions of the age ought to make Kokoschka rich... Others will shun him as a mangy creature and pity the age which finds its reflection in this 'art'.[17]

The readiness with which the critics took the portraits up was due in part to Kokoschka's use of an aesthetic which chimed with anxieties particular to the early twentieth century, and to Vienna – as one of the leading European centres for psychiatry - especially. Kokoschka's representation of the physically depleted bodies of, to use Hiller's term – 'care-worn citizens of the metropolis' – made manifest the Viennese preoccupation with the detrimental effects of the modern urban environment on mental health, the physical and moral degeneration of the species as registered in the increases in crime, and the problem of how to categorise, contain and cure those suffering from a diverse range of conditions from 'nervous disorders' such as hysteria and hypochondria through to full-blown mental illness. The much-publicised writings and practice of Vienna's leading psychiatrist, Richard von Krafft-Ebing, fixed these preoccupations as the defining features of the Viennese cultural landscape: mental health was a quintessentially modern concern.[18]

The distinction between nervous disorders and mental illness was a slippery one, tangible only in whether a patient was self-admitted or involuntarily confined in a sanatorium or hospital. Altenberg, for example, was diagnosed as neurasthenic in his twenties, a term which encompassed a host of nervous conditions including eating disorders, fatigue and depression. In 1913 he was committed to Steinhof by his brother Georg Engländer. Ostensibly interned for alcoholism, aggressive and paranoid letters from Altenberg to his brother seem to show that his condition on entering was psychotic

48 Advertisement for brochure offering advice on how to deal with nerve problems, from *Simplicissimus*, vol. 16, no. 36, 4 December 1911, p. 623

49 Advertisement for brochure on how to prevent the spread of syphilis, from *Simplicissimus*, vol. 16, no. 36, 4 December 1911, p. 632

enough for the doctors to be unable to release him without Engländer's permission. He rails:

> You rotten sod! Despite my spending the last five months explaining to you that the Superintendant has it in for me and wants to ensure my physical, spiritual and intellectual ruin, you have nevertheless collaborated with him... although he *had* declared to me of his own free will: 'You are of course released by us doctors as fully cured. It requires only the simple formality that the person who brought you here contacts us and fetches you'... Since this message of redemption you have allowed days to pass, brother-murderer![19]

Altenberg's experiences of sliding up and down the scale of mental health give important insights into the diagnosis and treatment of the nervous individual in modern Vienna. But these experiences, dramatised in his feuilletons – those witty reflections on contemporary culture published in newspapers – are also interesting for the way that they contributed to Altenberg's identity as a chronicler of modern times.

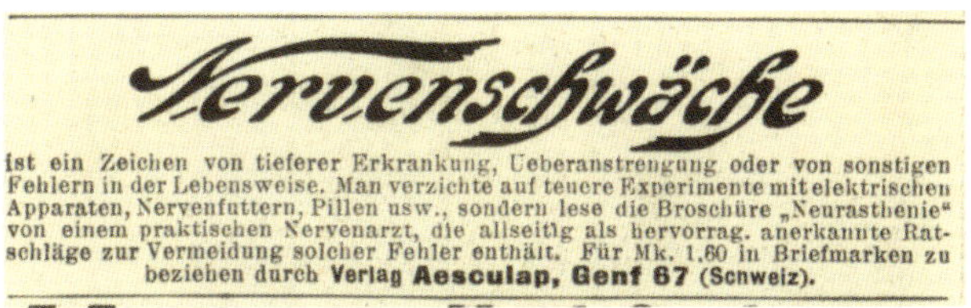

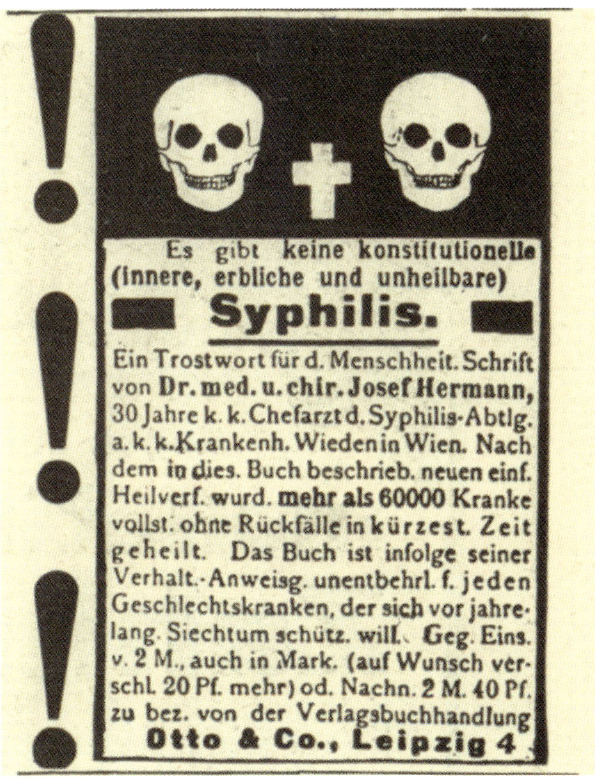

In 'Sanatorium for Nervous Disorders', also published in *Simplicissimus*, he describes bribing an orderly to bring him alcohol, despite the watchful eye of the doctor trying to restore his mental equilibrium with regular breakfasts of tea and buttered rolls.[20] The feuilleton is a typical example of Altenberg sharing his mental health history with his readers – readers who, on turning the pages of *Simplicissimus*, could find adverts for brochures offering advice on how to calm their own frazzled, city-dweller nerves (fig.48) and prevent the spread of syphilis (fig.49). But Altenberg's reflection on his time in the sanatorium is also about his search for the creative, generative potential in his various addictions, anxieties and ailments. He may have criticised Kokoschka for capitalising on the 'genuine madness' of a van Gogh, but in the same review Altenberg admits that he is also implicated and indeed that 'it is perhaps preferable that the "van Goghs" of each profession stick together'. Though disparaging of Kokoschka's attempts to mimic the mad, modernist master in his portraiture, Altenberg's writings stake his own claim to an anguished identity. Beyond the comedy of smuggling in bottles of Slivovitz and soliciting sexual favours from nurses, Altenberg's feuilleton shows his participation in the modernist strategy to construct genealogies of greatness based on claims to mental illness.

MODERNIST GENEALOGIES

Altenberg's referencing of van Gogh indicates the status this artist had in the city's modern art circles. Van Gogh was first exhibited posthumously in Vienna at the major Impressionism show held at the Secession in 1903, just one year before the German art historian Julius Meier-Graefe – the lead curator – published his seminal *Modern Art*.[21] In keeping with his view that nineteenth-century art was driven by individuals, rather than by social, political or economic forces, Meier-Graefe constructs van Gogh as a sickened and self-destructive genius, made great by his madness. He writes on a van Gogh self-portrait:

> No one who has seen this tremendous head with the square forehead, the staring eyes and despairing jaw can ever forget it. It is so full of terrible grandeur of line, colour and psychology that it takes one's breath away. It is hard to know whether one is repelled by its monstrous exaggeration of beauty, or by the lurking madness in the head that conceived it.[22]

Van Gogh's significance for Vienna's modernists lay in the relationship between madness and genius he embodied, a relationship which was kept at a premium through subsequent exhibitions of his work in the city in 1906 and 1909. In connecting Kokoschka with van Gogh, Altenberg participates in constructing a modernist genealogy where artists are related to each other psycho-biographically and where value is bestowed on those works which reveal the 'lurking madness' behind their inspiration and execution.

Yet Altenberg's review, written back in 1911, is also unusual for its critical approach to the notion of madness and genius. Altenberg's ambivalence towards Kokoschka is revealed in his biting characterisation of the artist as 'in-authentically mad'. This characterisation was an important corrective to the Viennese reviews – albeit not one which was taken up by the city's critics and curators – and it was ahead of its time. In her work on the reception of van Gogh, Griselda Pollock points to how developments in psychiatry in the late nineteenth and early twentieth century worked to re-constitute the myth of mad genius which – as seen in the work of Meier-Graefe – was so central to the narrative of modern art history. She argues: 'The discourse on madness and art [in modernism] operates to sever art and artist from history and to render both unavailable to those without the specialised knowledge of its processes, which art history claims for itself.'[23] Such a mythologising discourse diverts attention from the strategic manoeuvring of artists and patrons, the vested interests which make and break reputations, and the agendas which drive the formation of communities. As Altenberg astutely observed, these dynamics were at play in the conception and reception of the Hagenbund show.

After all, Kokoschka's place in this modernist genealogy was only made possible by Loos's decision to invest in a portfolio of portraiture. Many of the sitters painted by Kokoschka were horrified by the results, but Loos's book of contacts enabled Kokoschka to produce a body of work which was large enough and cohesive enough to conceal these personal politics. Kokoschka's two rooms at the Hagenbund, filled with works largely rejected by the sitter and thus amassed by Loos, presented a unified image of an intimate modernist community both supportive of and connected to the young artist. Their shared identity as 'mad' modernists overlaid the transactional processes that defined the portrait-painting project, and the personality clashes which dogged it. Loos wasn't able to entice Meier-Graefe to Vienna to view the portraits, despite appeals to his contacts, but the project still succeeded in fixing Kokoschka as Vienna's answer to van Gogh.[24]

P.S.

Kokoschka dominates today's scholarship on the history of modern art in Vienna 1900. But he was not the only ambitious portrait-painter connected to the city's modernist communities. One year after he sat for Kokoschka, Altenberg posed for another, equally active artist – the Vienna-born, Academy-trained Max Oppenheimer – in a portrait that was exhibited at Oppenheimer's first one-man-show at Heinrich Thannhauser's Moderne Galerie in Munich (fig.50).[25] The exhibition opened in May 1911 and included portraits on canvas of the leading-lights of Vienna's intellectual circles. Altenberg was joined by Loos and the literary figures Heinrich Mann (fig.51), Franz Blei (fig.52), and Arthur Schnitzler (1862–1931), to give but a few examples. Oppenheimer had beaten Kokoschka by being the first to have his own one-man-show, with a portfolio of portraits that seriously rivalled that shown at the Hagenbund. Moreover, Altenberg's portrait is known only through a black and white reproduction which – significantly – is in the first monograph devoted to Oppenheimer by Wilhelm Michel, published in just 1911.[26] In other words, at the tender age of 26, Oppenheimer was a significant enough artist to warrant his own single-artist publication, more significant, it would seem, than Kokoschka.

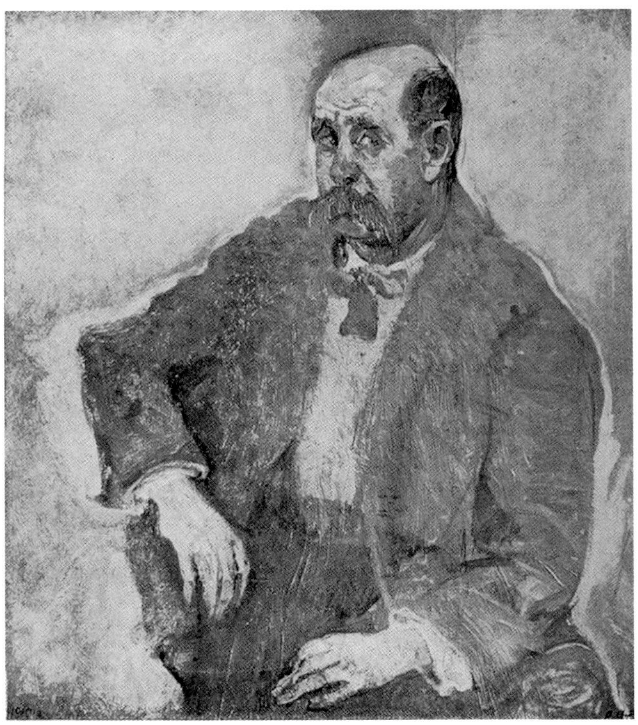

50 Max Oppenheimer, *Portrait of Peter Altenberg*, 1910, present whereabouts unknown. Formerly in the collection of Carl Meinhard, Berlin. Published in Wilhelm Michel, *Max Oppenheimer* (Munich, 1911)

This early reception of Oppenheimer's work makes his near obliteration from subsequent histories of Viennese modernism all the more striking. In the catalogue of the 2002 exhibition of Kokoschka's early portraits at the Neue Galerie, New York[27], works by Oppenheimer were reproduced alongside a number of Kokoschka's, highlighting that there were two participants in the imaging of the city's 'mad' modernists. However, no essay dealt with Oppenheimer's contribution to Vienna's portrait-painting scene or his

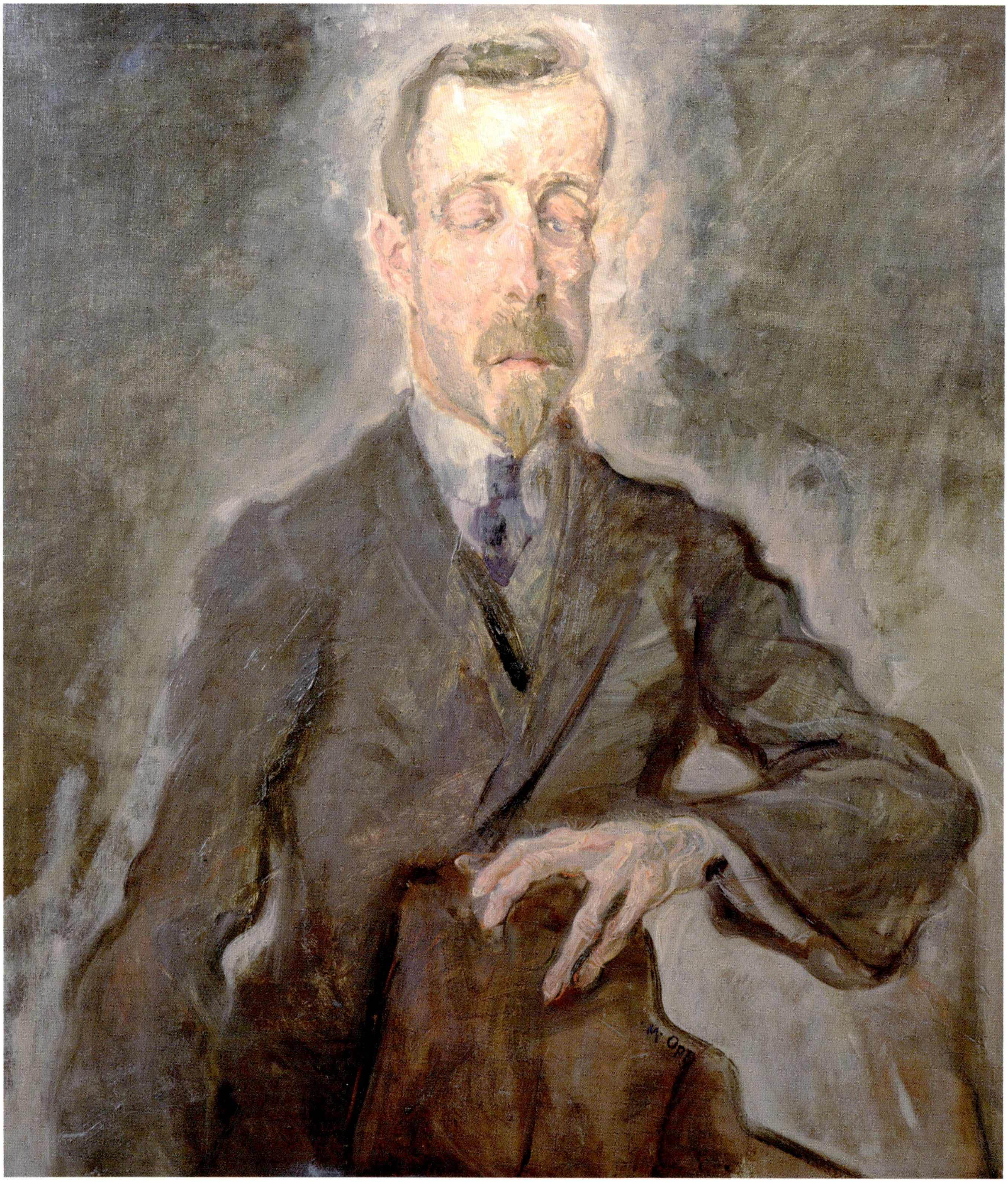

Opposite:
51 Max Oppenheimer,
Portrait of Heinrich Mann,
1910, oil on canvas,
88 × 80 cm (34⅝ × 31½ in).
Wien Museum

52 Max Oppenheimer,
Portrait of Franz Blei,
1911, oil on canvas,
79 × 70 cm (31⅛ × 27½ in).
MUMOK, Vienna

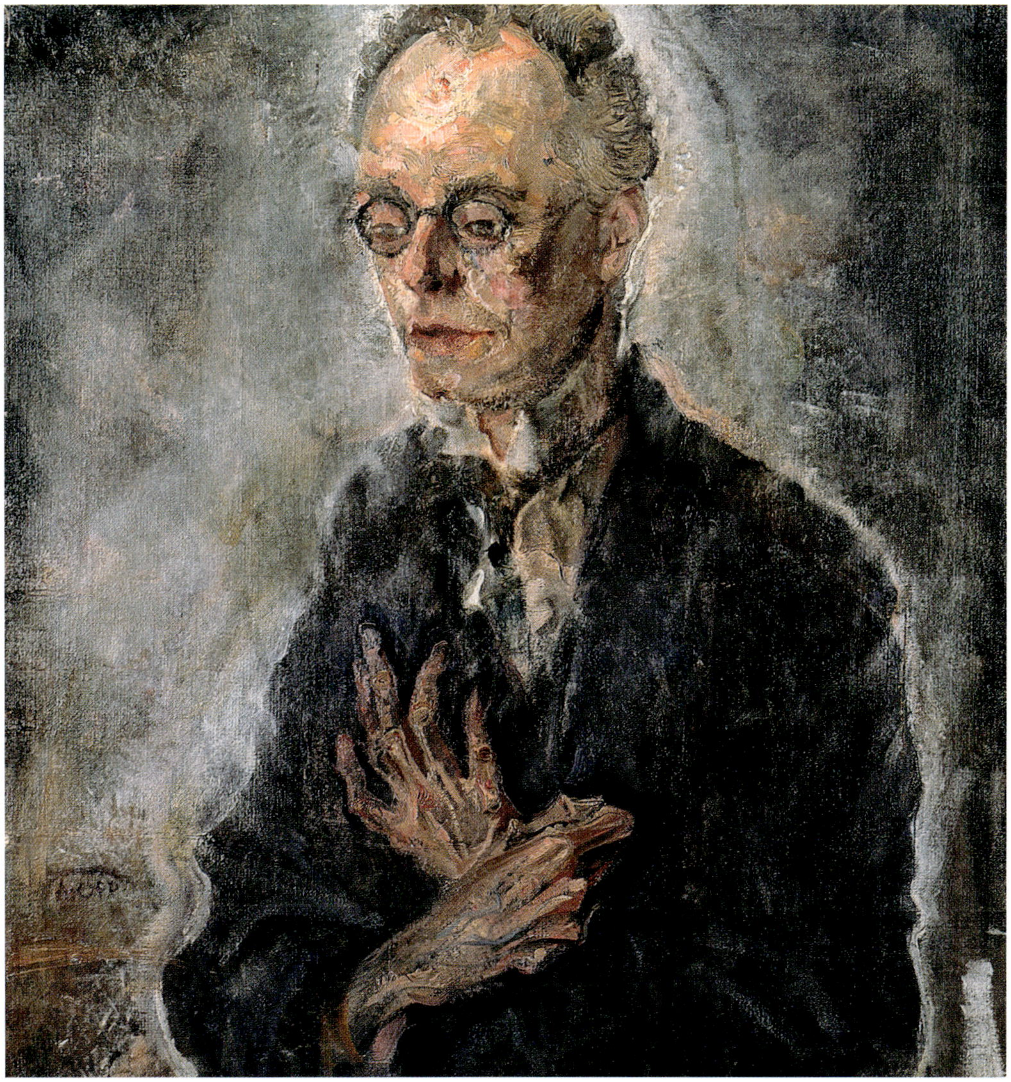

own, exactly contemporaneous development of an aesthetic which *also* emphasised the nervous disposition of the sitter through the representation of their debilitated body and the hallucinatory animation of the pictorial space surrounding them. This reluctance to engage with Oppenheimer's central role in the forging of the city's 'mad' modernist identity stems from a feud that erupted between the artist and Kokoschka. Kokoschka and Oppenheimer, along with the actor Ernst Reinhold, were friends (fig.53), but by 1911 Oppenheimer's success was such that it put the brakes on Kokoschka's own emergent status. The artist, mobilising his friends in Vienna and Berlin, responded with a vicious attack on Oppenheimer, 'the plagiarist', which centred on who could lay claim to the invention of the psychological portrait.

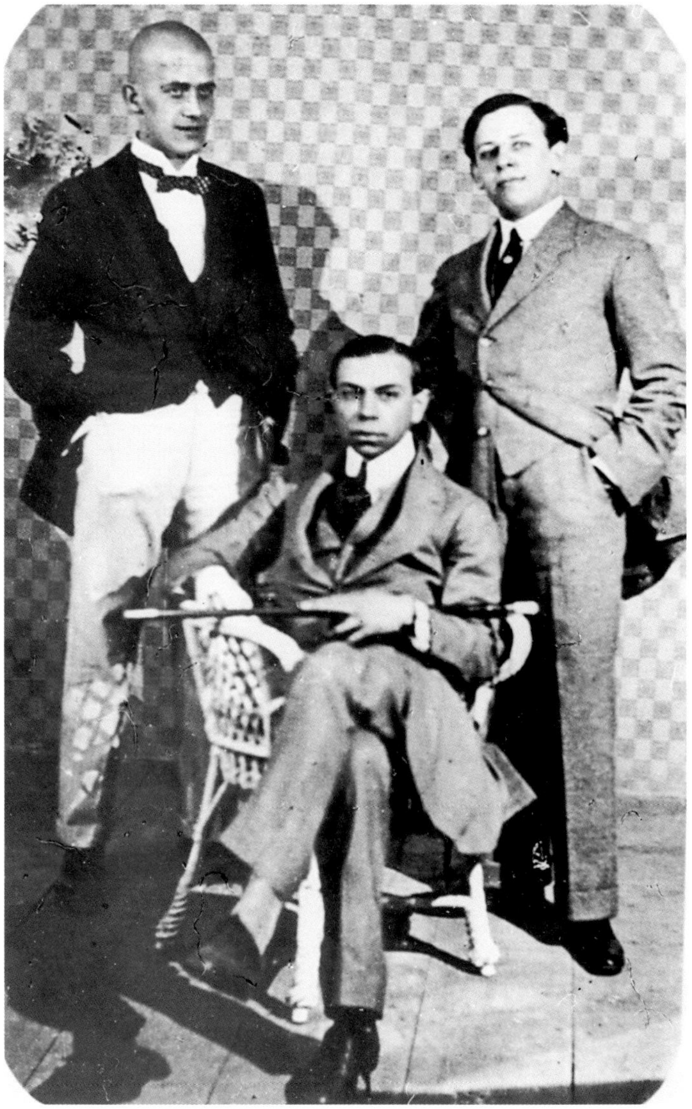

53 Photograph of Oppenheimer, Kokoschka and Ernst Reinhold. Collection Universität für angewandte Kunst Wien, Oskar-Kokoschka-Zentrum, Vienna

In a letter to Lotte Franzos (fig.45) he complained bitterly that: 'My friend Oppenheimer is teaching the Munich-people about my art before I can do it myself.'[28] He also contacted Herwarth Walden, his *Der Sturm* friend, with the news that: 'It's not perhaps known to you that I have a shadow here in Vienna, one by one my pictures are being copied – Oppenheimer.'[29] Loos, who had previously supported Oppenheimer, retaliated by trying to organise Kokoschka's own solo-show, stating in a letter to *Der Blaue Reiter* founder Franz Marc that this was particularly crucial for audiences in Munich where 'the feeble Kokoschka-copyist and swindler Herr Oppenheimer has crept in.'[30] The poet Else Lasker-Schüler also leapt to Kokoschka's defence in a letter addressed to her former friend Oppenheimer, published in the Berlin-based *Der Sturm*. She wrote:

> Dear Max Oppenheimer... Gladly did I go with you to your exhibition in Munich, but it was not your pictures hanging on the walls, only Oskar Kokoschka's... You are, I assume, in love with Kokoschka. Your pictures are works that have been plucked and therefore lack roots. I liked very much the portrait of Heinrich Mann (fig.51). It was like a gleaming copy and I saw in its colours and rhythms, not just the writer but also the painter Oskar Kokoschka, not you...[31]

The impact of this letter was redoubled in Vienna, when it was reprinted in Kraus's *Die Fackel* within an article entitled 'Kokoschka and the Other', in which Kraus reiterated with characteristically caustic wit the difference between talent (Oppenheimer) and genius (Kokoschka).[32] The character defamation campaign thus operated across three cities, Vienna, Berlin and Munich, showing the remarkable ability of the modernist community not only to close ranks but also to turn aggressively against individuals in attacks laced with homophobia (Lasker-Schüler claims the homosexual Oppenheimer is 'in love' with his friend). The repercussions of this assault on Oppenheimer were not perhaps evident at first – he secured two further one-man-shows in 1913 at Thannhauser's Munich gallery and the Kunstsalon Pisko, Vienna. But as the twentieth century moved on, it was Kokoschka's name that became synonymous with Vienna 1900. Oppenheimer – discredited and abandoned by Loos's circle – was effectively written out of art history, relegated – as here – to a postscript.

Where did Altenberg stand in this campaign? Despite his antipathy towards Kokoschka, he did not champion the cause of 'the Other'. 'Authentic' shows Altenberg's grudging acceptance of the new artist on the scene, an artist patronised by the group of friends who he also relied upon to haul him out of difficult waters – whether financial, professional or personal. Altenberg's silence speaks of the high stakes of friendships in the intellectual circles of Vienna 1900 – friendships which were hard won and easily lost. Kokoschka's 'madness' may have been in-authentic, but Altenberg had his own position as the 'genuinely neurasthenic' poet of modern times to protect. And so, it is Kokoschka's portrait of the animated Altenberg (fig.42) – shakily holding forth from his *Stammtisch* in the Löwenbräu restaurant in the Teinfaltstrasse – that graces the cover of the recently published translation of his selected prose.[33] Such a choice reveals the lasting ability of the portrait to conceal the differences that *really* defined Vienna's 'mad' modernist community.

NOTES

1. For further information on the rise of the Hagenbund see Elizabeth Clegg, *Art, Design and Architecture in Central Europe 1890–1920* (New Haven: Yale University Press 2006), pp. 104–5, and Robert Waissenberger, 'Hagenbund 1900-1938', *Mitteilungen der Oesterreichische Galerie*, 16, no. 60 (1972), pp 54–111.
2. Kunstausstellungen, 'Sturm und Drang', *Österreichische Volks-Zeitung*, 13 February 1911, pp 1–2.
3. The other artists included were Robin Andersen, Robert Eckert, Anton Faistauer, Paris von Gütersloh, Hermann Haller, Bernhard Hoetger, Karl Hofer, Sebastian Isepp, Anton Kolig, Erwin Lang, Richard Asir von Rziha and Franz Wiegele.
4. I am indebted to Harold B. Segel's *The Vienna Coffeehouse Wits, 1890–1938* (Vienna: Purdue University Press, 1993) for this term to describe Peter Altenberg. For another account of Altenberg's relationship with Kokoschka see Leo A. Lensing, 'Scribbling Squids and the Giant Octopus: Oskar Koksochka's Unpublished Portrait of Peter Altenberg' in *Turn-of-the-Century Vienna and its Legacy: Essays in Honour of Donald G. Daviau*, ed. by Jeffrey B. Berlin, Jorun B. Johns, Richard H. Lawson (Vienna: Edition Atelier, 1993), pp 193–220.
5. Peter Altenberg, 'Authentisch' in *Simplicissimus*, 16, no. 36 (1911), 621. I would like to thank Edward Neather for the translation of this text.
6. Altenberg, 'Authentisch'.
7. Oskar Kokoschka, letter to Adolf Loos from Berlin, 23 December 1910, in *Oskar Kokoschka : Briefe I 1905–1919* (Düsseldorf: Claassen, 1984), p. 15.
8. Kurt Hiller, 'Oskar Kokoschka' *Der Sturm*, 1, no. 19 (1910), 150. Else Lasker-Schüler, 'Oskar Kokoschka' *Der Sturm*, 1, no. 21 (1910), p. 166.
9. Hiller, p. 150.
10. Josef Strzygowski, 'Junge Künstler im Hagenbund', *Die Zeit*, 9 February 1911. The portrait of Kraus is now lost. A photograph is reproduced in Johann Winkler and Katharina Erling, eds., *Oskar Kokoschka: Die Gemälde 1906–1929* (Salzburg: Galerie Welz, 1995), no. 26.
11. Hans Tietze, 'Ausstellung Jungwiener Künstler im Hagenbund', *Fremdenblatt*, 10 February 1911, pp 21–22.
12. See also Gemma Blackshaw, 'The Pathological Body: Modernist Strategising in Egon Schiele's Self-Portraiture', *Oxford Art Journal*, 30 (2007), pp 377–401.
13. Franz Grüner, *Die Fackel*, 12, no. 317/318 (1911), p. 18.
14. Karl Michael Kuzmany, 'Sonderausstellung von Malerei und Plastik', *Kunst und Kunsthandwerk*, 14 (1911), pp 129–130.
15. Arthur Roessler, 'Hagenbund', *Arbeiter-Zeitung*, 4 February 1911, pp 1–2. I have used Frank Whitford's excellent translation of this difficult review in *Oskar Kokoschka: A Life* (London: Weidenfeld & Nicolson, 1986) pp 73–74.
16. Altenberg, 'Authentisch'. In this exchange, Altenberg references the actual visit of the Archduke to the Hagenbund, after which he apparently expressed his desire to 'break every bone' in Kokoschka's body. See Werner Schweiger, *Der Junge Kokoschka: Leben und Werk 1904–1914* (Vienna: Brandstätter, 1983), p. 195.
17. Strzygowski, *Die Zeit*, 9 February 1911 (as note 10).
18. See for example Richard von Krafft-Ebing's monumental catalogue of the sexual perversions, *Psychopathia Sexualis: With Especial Reference to the Antipathetic Sexual Instinct* (London: Staples Press, 1965). First published in German in 1885.

19. Letter from Altenberg to Engländer written from Steinhof in April, 1913, reproduced in Egon Friedell, ed., *Das Altenbergbuch* (Vienna: Wiener Graphischen Werkstätte, 1921), pp 58–9.
20. Altenberg, 'Sanatorium für Nervenkranke', *Simplicissimus*, 16, no. 41 (1912), p. 724.
21. First published in German as *Entwicklungsgeschichte der modernen Kunst, Vergleichende Betrachtung der bildenden Künste, als Beitrag zu einer neuen Aesthetik*, (Stuttgart: Julius Hoffmann, 1904).
22. Julius Meier-Graefe, *Modern Art: Being a Contribution to a New System of Aesthetics*, English translation, (London: Heinemann, 1908), p. 209.
23. My brackets. Griselda Pollock, 'Artist Mythologies and Media Genius, Madness and Art History', *Screen*, 21, no. 3 (1980), pp 57–96 (p. 65).
24. In a letter to Walden of 4 October 1910, Loos sought his help in contacting Meier-Graefe. Quoted in Georg Brühl, *Herwarth Walden und Der Sturm* (Cologne: DuMont, 1983), p. 33.
25. For a discussion of this see Marie-Agnes von Puttkamer, *Max Oppenheimer – MOPP (1885–1954) Leben und malerisches Werk mit einem Werkverzeichnis der Gemälde* (Vienna: Böhlau, 1999), pp 52–65.
26. Wilhelm Michel, *Max Oppenheimer* (Munich: Georg Müller, 1911). Roessler drafted the first monograph on Oppenheimer. The defamation campaign meant that he never published it, although Kokoschka seemingly read the manuscript and summarised it for Walden: 'He is the Modern of Vienna, he sees ghosts in the most secret sorrows of the soul, he prefers to wallow in wounds, he will end up mad – all this is gathered from my critics.' This appears to be projection on Kokoschka's part, which makes his choice of language, replete with metaphors of disease and madness, all the more interesting. Herwarth Walden, 'Michels Reinfall', *Der Sturm*, 2 (1911–12), p. 667, n. 678.
27. Tobias Natter, ed., *Oskar Kokoschka: Early Portraits from Vienna and Berlin 1909–1914*, exh. cat. (New York: Neue Galerie, New Haven: Yale University Press, 2002).
28. Letter from Kokoschka to Franzos, March, 1911. Quoted in von Puttkamer, p. 59.
29. Letter from Kokoschka to Walden, 1911. Quoted in von Puttkamer, p. 59.
30. Letter from Loos to Franz Marc, November, 1911. Quoted in von Puttkamer, p. 59.
31. Else Lasker-Schüler, 'Briefe nach Norwegen', *Der Sturm*, 2 (1911–12), p. 710.
32. 'Notizen Kokoschka und der andere', *Die Fackel*, vol. 13, no. 339–40 (1911).
33. Peter Altenberg, *Telegrams of the Soul: Selected Prose of Peter Altenberg*, trans. by Peter Wortsman (New York: Archipelago Books, 2005).

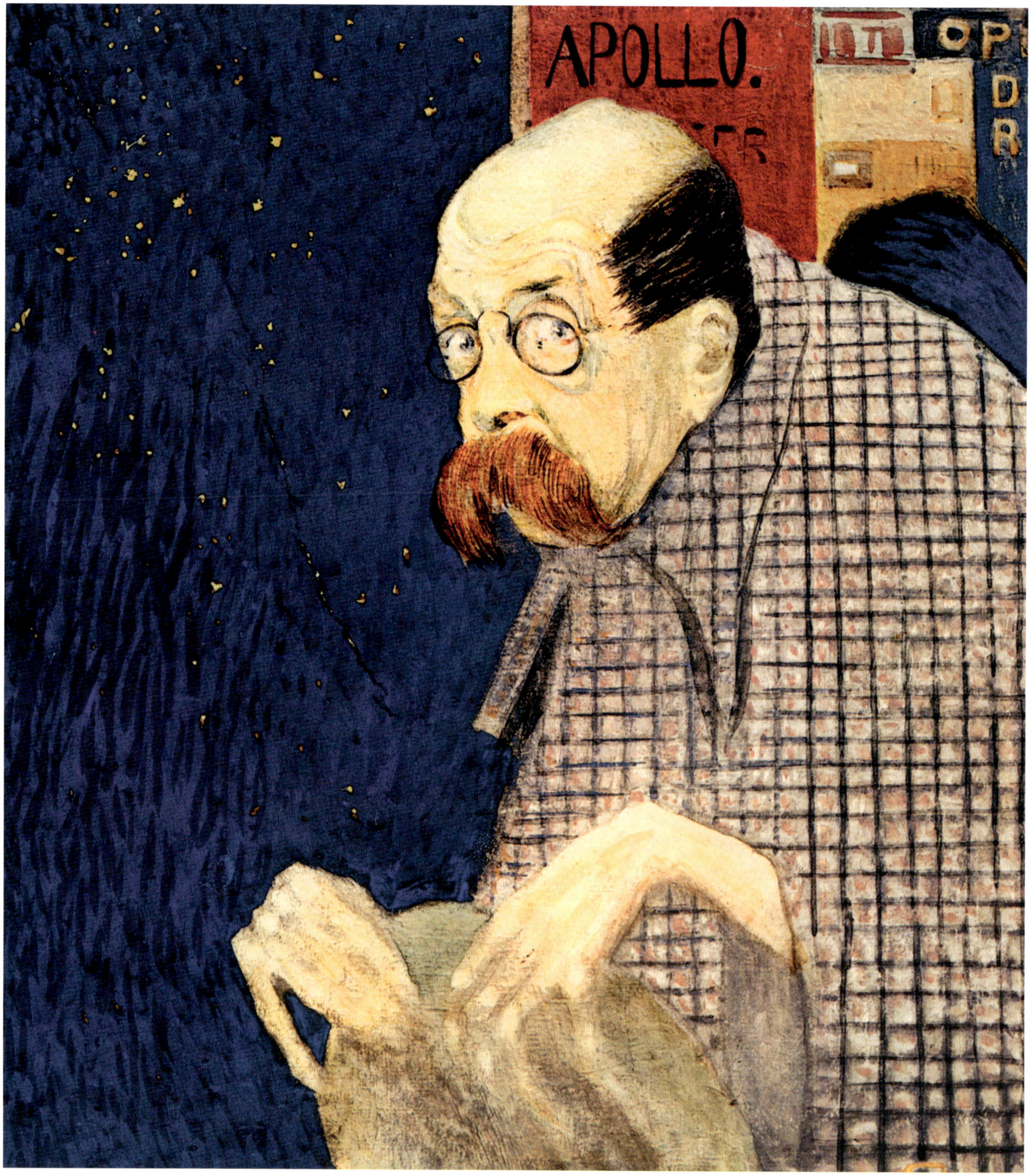
APOLLO.

Chapter 4

Gustav Jagerspacher, *Portrait of Peter Altenberg*, 1909

GEMMA BLACKSHAW

The Munich-based artist and Secession member Gustav Jagerspacher produced a number of caricatures of Peter Altenberg, Vienna's famed night owl, including this pastel drawing of 1909 (fig.54). Jagerspacher remains a shadowy figure in histories of the modernist circles of the two cities, despite being a regular at Altenberg's *Stammtisch*, yet this image of his family friend has achieved recognition through its association with Adolf Loos's American Bar.[1]

Jagerspacher depicts the writer anxiously peering out from behind his Pinz Nez spectacles, wearing the distinctive checked wool coat that denoted his winter attire, with a hat clutched in his long and agitated fingers. This clothing was just as important to the crafting of Altenberg's idiosyncratic persona as the walrus moustache and walking-stick which he was similarly rarely seen without (fig.55). In the spirit of *Selbstdarstellung*, it ensured that the self-styled 'Fool of Vienna' – whose life and work were both inextricably linked and audience-dependent – was always identifiable.[2] Such clothing also operated as the signifier of Altenberg's personal/professional identity as the

54 Gustav Jagerspacher, *Portrait of Peter Altenberg*, 1909, watercolour and pastel applied wet on wove cream paper applied to board, 39.8 × 32.9 cm (15⅝ × 13 in). Neue Galerie, New York

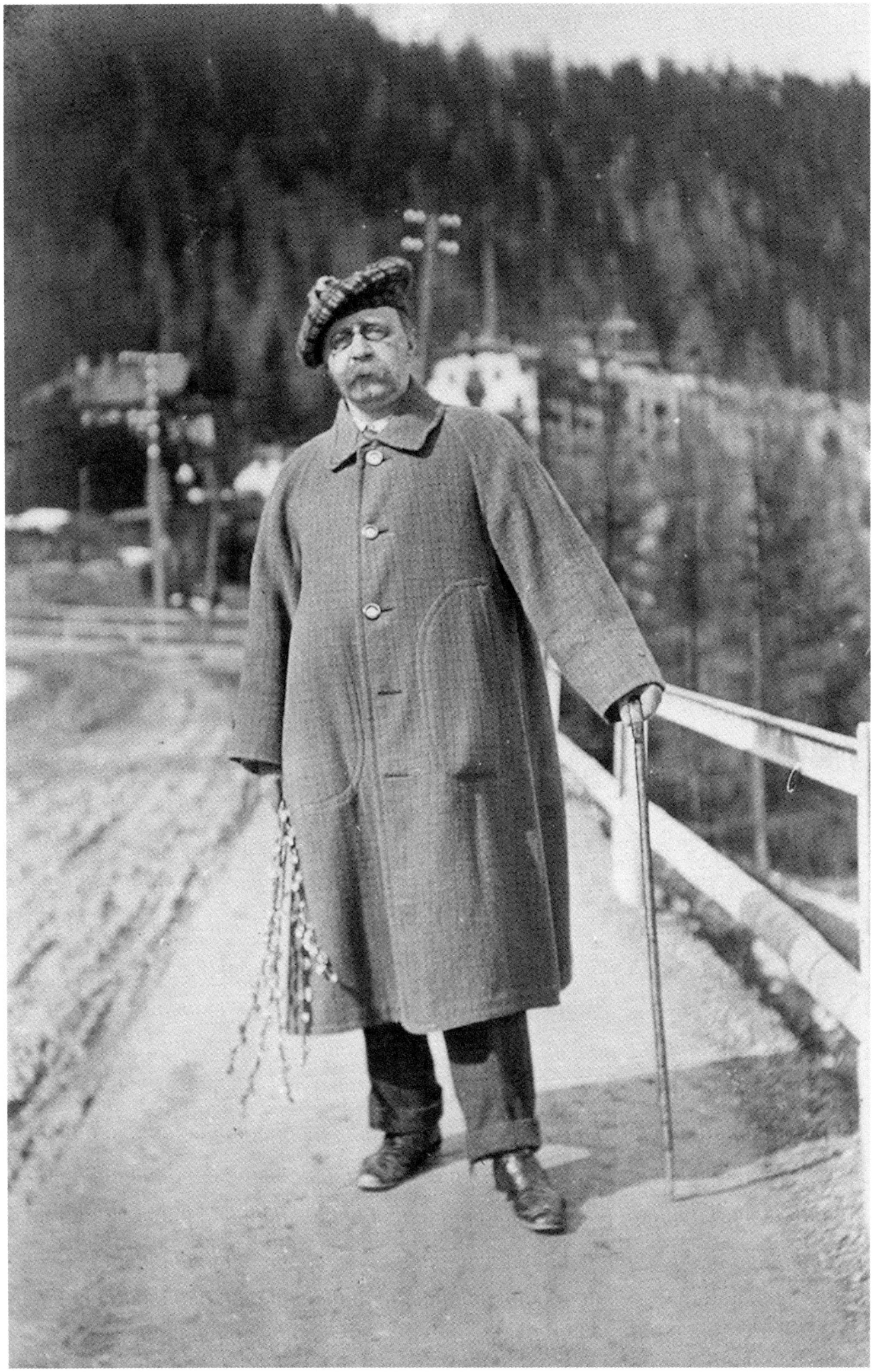

55 Peter Altenberg on the Hochstrasse, Semmering, Easter 1912. Wien Museum

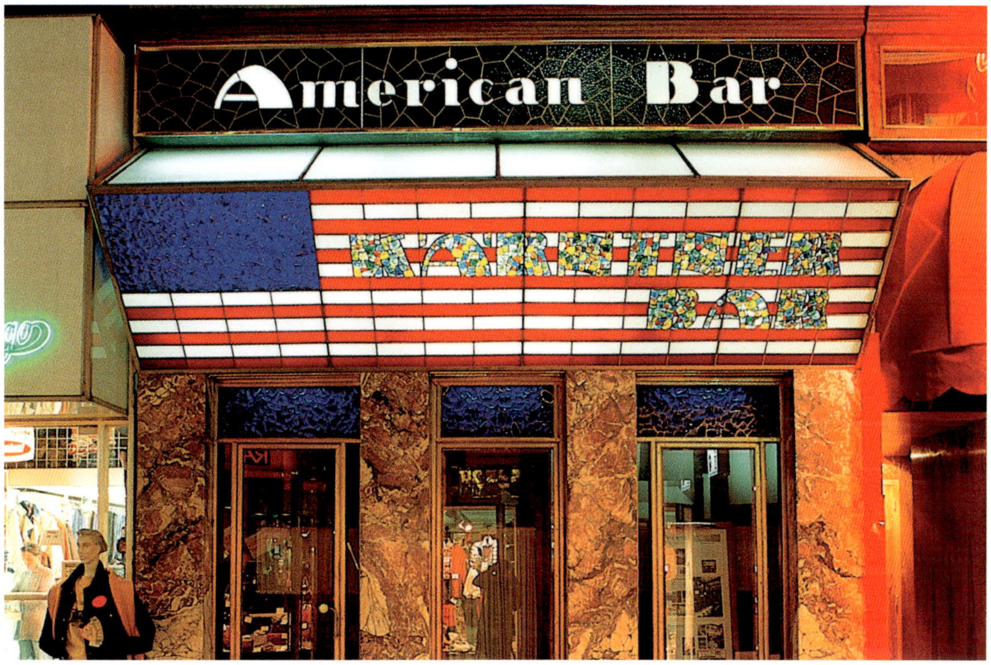

56 View of entrance to Adolf Loos's American Bar, 1908

quintessentially nervous man of modern times – hard-drinking, caffeine-stimulated, mentally anguished. As Loos remarked in 1919: 'Nowadays, the more modern a man's nerves, the more tightly buttoned his coat. As far back as fifteen years ago, Peter Altenberg was wearing a belt with an ordinary jacket. That may well have looked strange, but his nerves demanded it.'[3] Altenberg's participation in this construction of his identity is further evident in the inscription on the drawing in Altenberg's hand, dated February 1909, which reads: 'Are we not all only Karikatures from the truly and ideal wishes, which God and Nature made with our souls and our bodies?!?'[4] The writer and doctor Arthur Schnitzler, who often socialised alongside Altenberg, was certainly sceptical enough to suggest that his condition wasn't quite genuine, being more like the behaviour of 'a professional neurotic'.[5]

Though often retreating to the rural holiday resort of Semmering, at a restorative distance from the city's night-spots, Altenberg's identity was an urban one. Accordingly, Jagerspacher depicts him against the star-studded sky of Vienna's streets in a portrait which was entitled 'Nachts' on its first publication in Egon Friedell's homage to the writer, *Das Altenbergbuch*, published in 1921, two years after Altenberg's death.[6] Caught whilst scurrying to a bar or cafe, Altenberg appears – hunched and startled – against an urban corner, his bald head and wrinkled brow framed with a poster advertising the Apollo, a variety theatre on the Gumpendorferstrasse.[7] Despite the inclusion of this poster, Jagerspacher's drawing was destined for Loos's tiny and exclusive bar off the Kärtnerstrasse, which opened in 1908 (fig.56). Taking as his lead Altenberg's own preference for being photographed in, and identified with, favourite places such as the

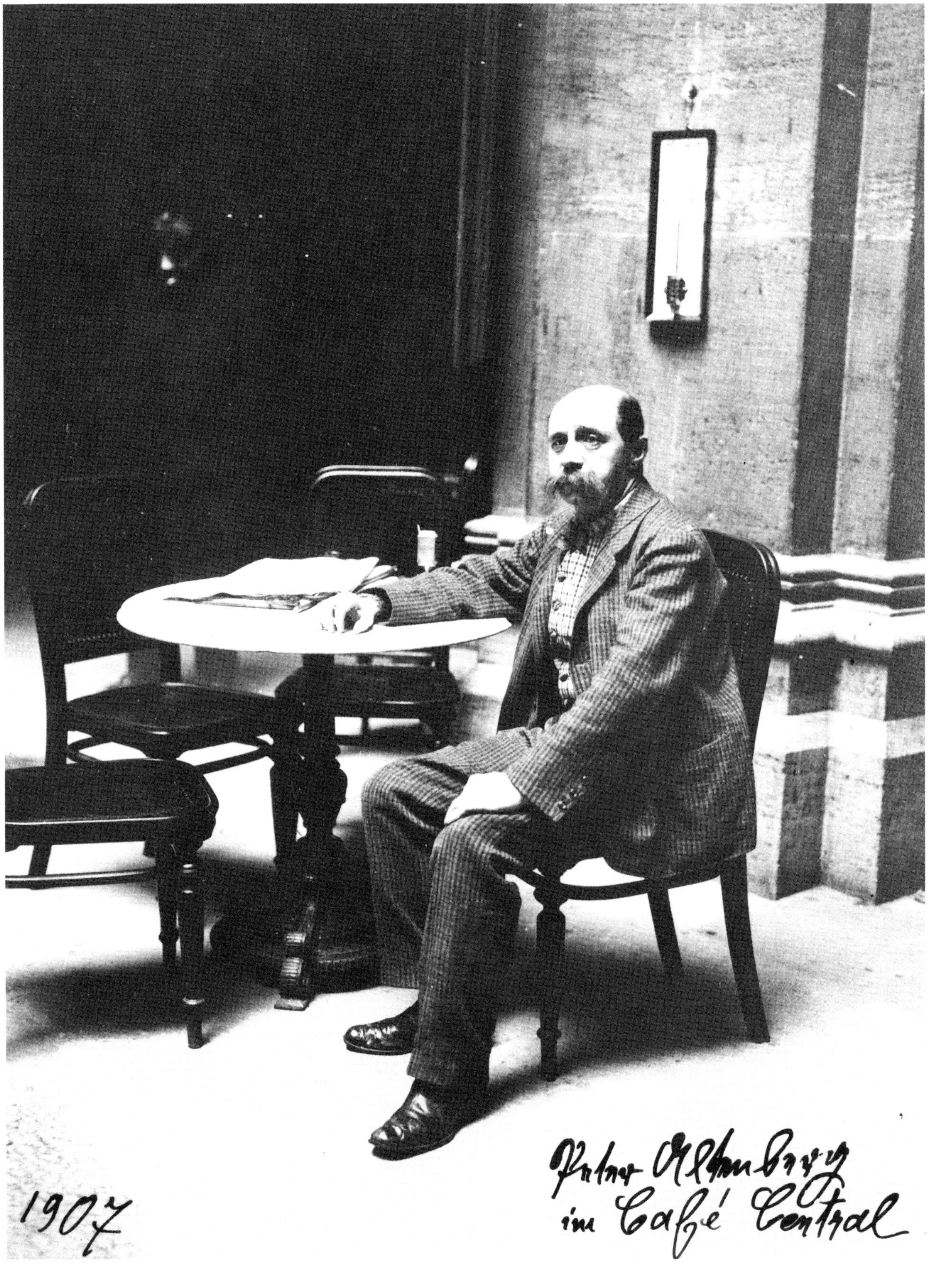

1907
Peter Altenberg
im Café Central

Opposite:
57 Inscribed photograph, 'Peter Altenberg im Café Central', 1907. Wien Museum

Right:
58 Photograph of interior, 1909, of Adolf Loos's American Bar, 1908. Bundesdenkmalamt, Vienna

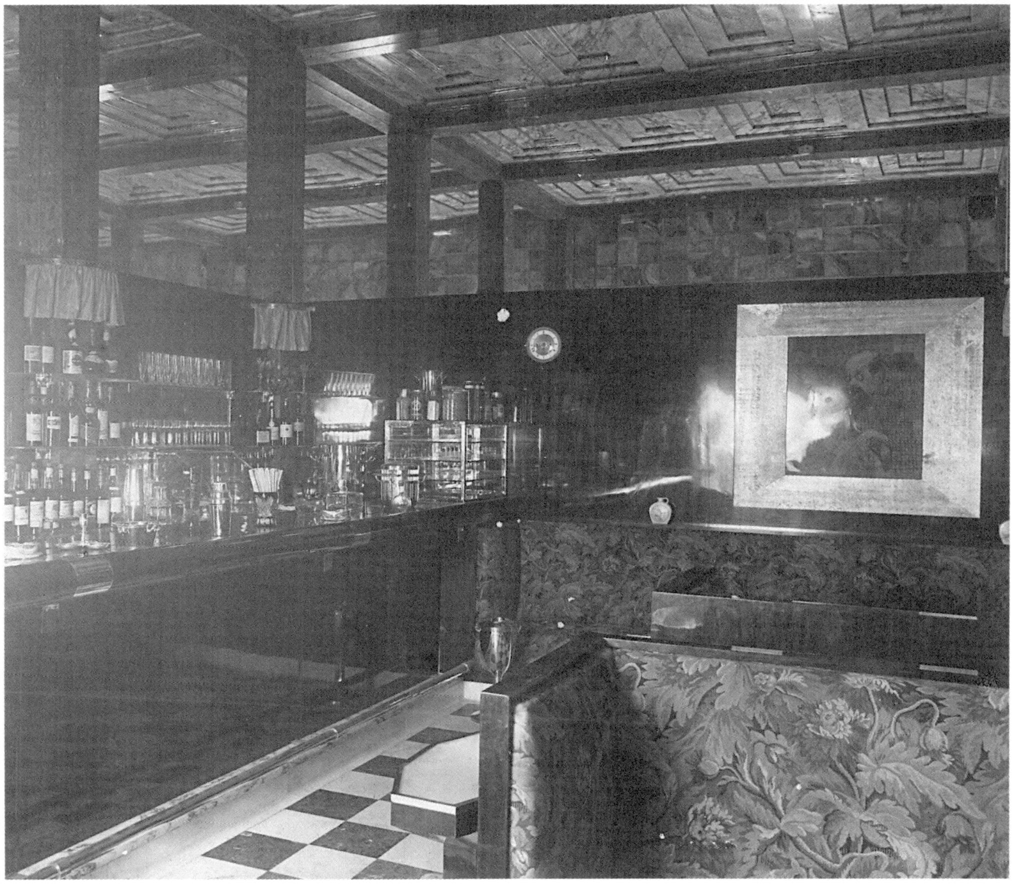

Cafe Central (fig.57), Loos displayed the caricature on the back wall of the bar, as seen in a photograph of 1909 (fig.58). The drawing was later removed, but it represented for Loos an ideal identification of the bar with the writer. Keen to document this, Loos later produced a photo-montage of the interior in which he inserted Jagerspacher's drawing in a canny marketing ploy which is still at play – today's visitor can enjoy a Loos Martini underneath a replica of the drawing.

Jagerspacher's caricature was one of many completed during a particularly fraught period in Altenberg's life. Living a transitory existence in the Hotel London, with the temptations of the First District on his doorstep, letters from Altenberg to his brother signal his decline. In 1909 he wrote: 'The end is not far off. My depression consumes my living body. Even getting up is torture. All that's left is the sort of sleep that is a precursor of death. My misspent life now takes its revenge. This fearful loneliness murders my unhappy nerves'.[8] This state of fear and exhaustion is represented in another of Jagerspacher's caricatures, completed in 1913, just before Altenberg was committed to Steinhof mental hospital (fig.59). Altenberg sits amongst the remnants of a shattered

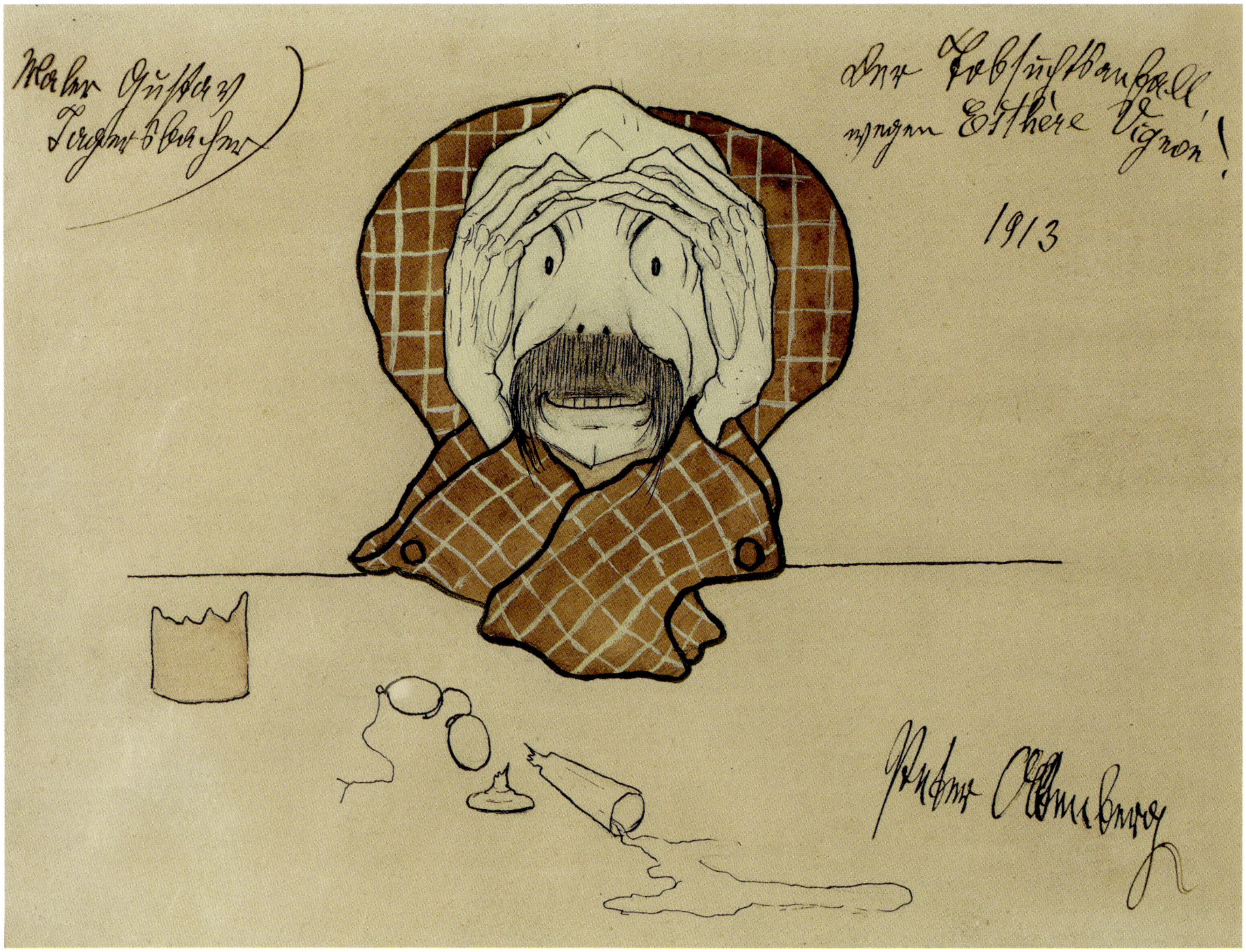

59 Gustav Jagerspacher, caricature of Peter Altenberg, 1913. Wien Museum

Opposite:
60 Gustav Jagerspacher, caricature of Peter Altenberg (Midnight: Lunch-time) Published in 'Der Liebe Augustin', no.13 (1904), 190

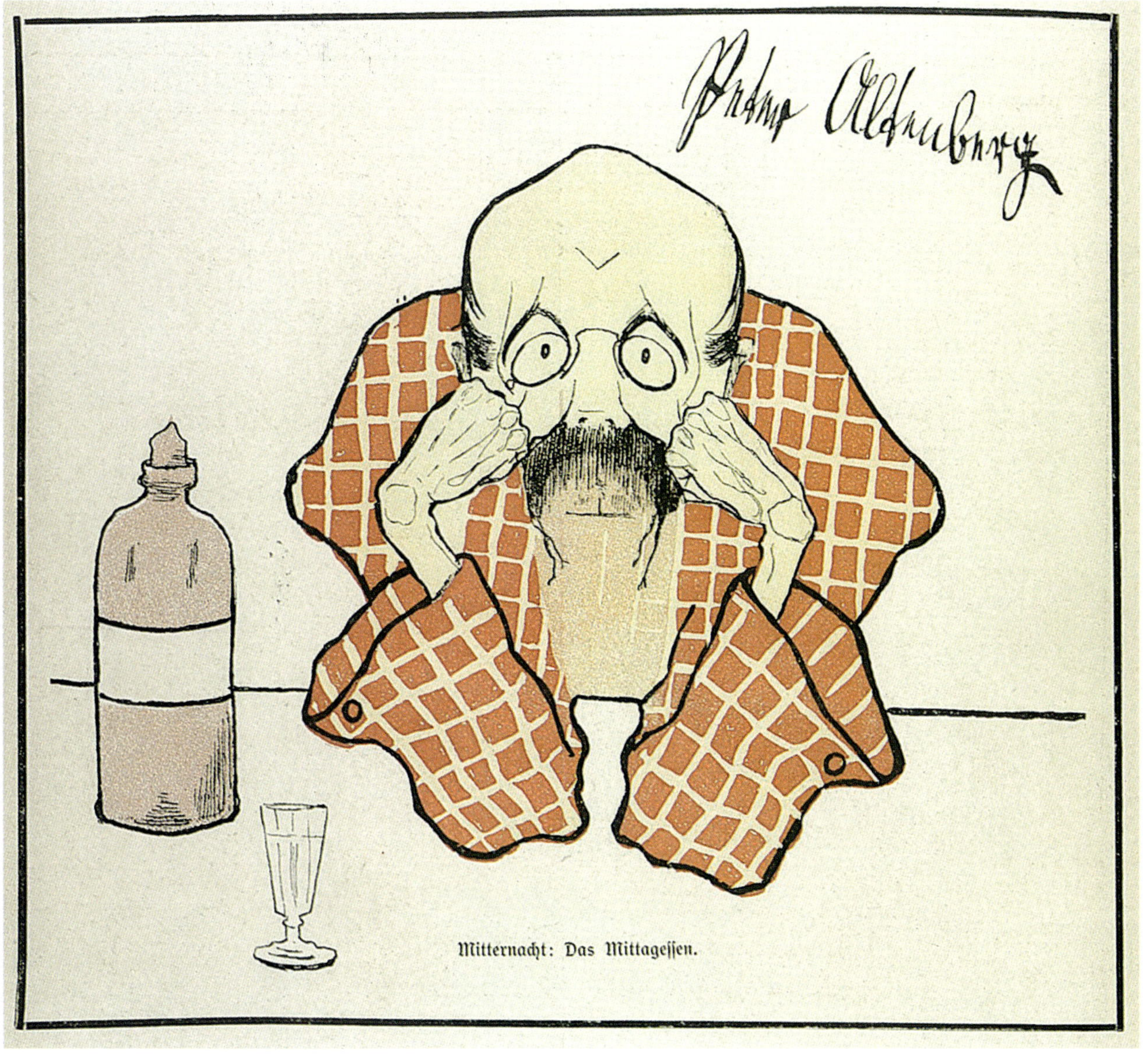

Mitternacht: Das Mittagessen.

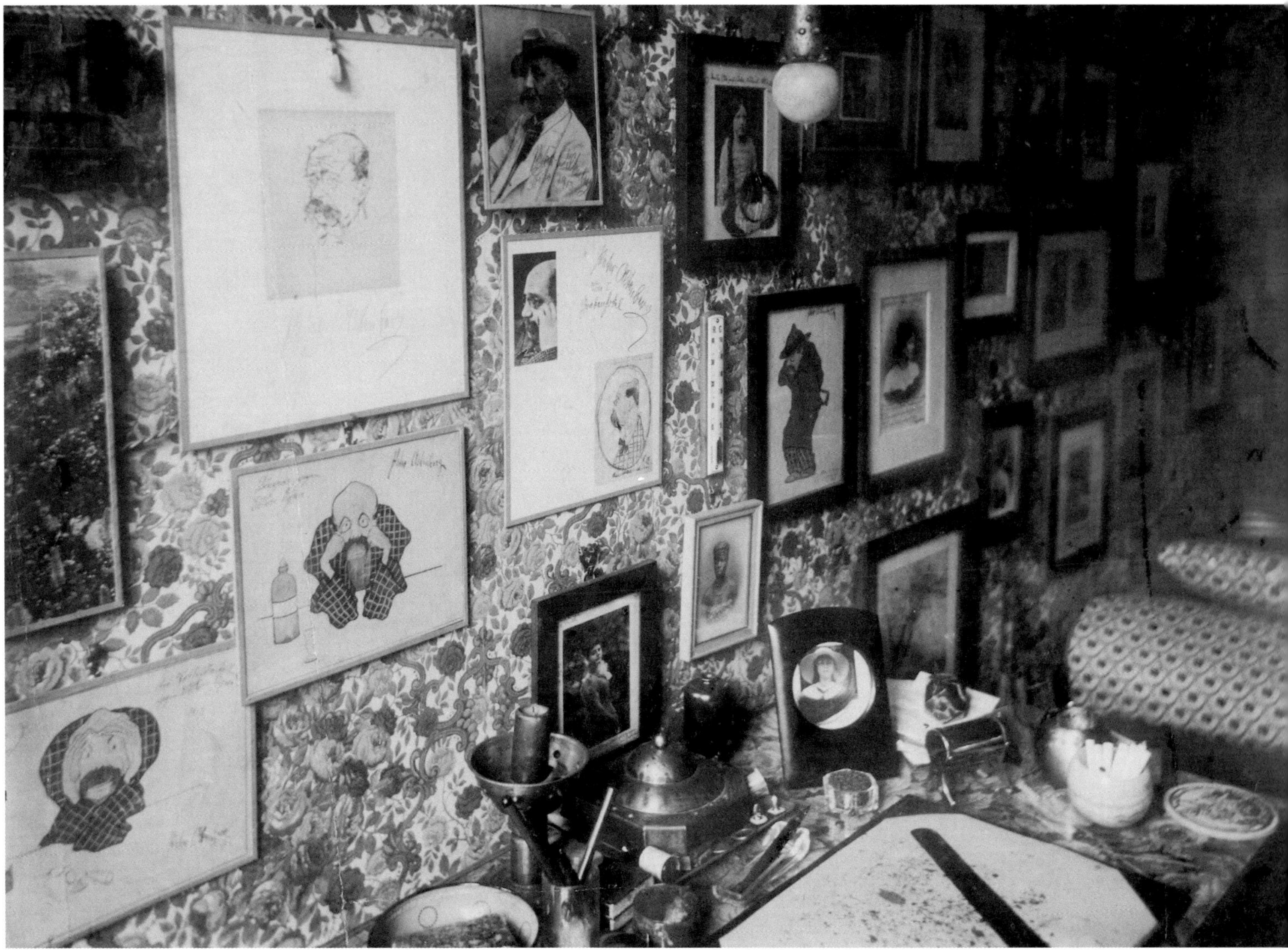

61 Interior of Peter Altenberg's room in Hotel Graben, 1914
Wein Museum

bottle of alcohol and a broken glass, spilling its contents out across the bar table. His Pinz Nez has fallen to the table-top and he clutches his head, his eyes wide open with terror. Such an image deliberately recalls Edvard Munch's *The Scream* of 1893 (fig.60) which was well-known in publication after Munch's production of a lithograph version (Munch's profile in Vienna was such that the Secession devoted an exhibition to his work in 1904). *The Scream* articulated the alienation of the individual in the modern world, a state which Altenberg was to make entirely his own. Altenberg certainly approved of Jagerspacher's image – photographs of his room in the Hotel Graben on the Dorotheergasse taken in 1914 show it in a display of other caricatures hanging above his writing desk (fig.61).

NOTES

1. For a discussion of the American Bar see Burkhard Rukschcio and Roland Schachel, *Adolf Loos: Leben und Werk* (Salzburg: Residenz, 1982). For more information on Jagerspacher see Heinz Lunzer, *Peter Altenberg: Extracte des Lebens* (Vienna: Residenz, 2003), p. 48. This portrait was clearly an important one for Altenberg. Jagerspacher completed another, smaller version of the image in gouache for Altenberg in 1914. Altenberg wrote the same inscription – although this time in German – on the white mount of the image, along with the commemorative words that it had been 'made by the painter Gustav Jagerspacher'. It was framed and displayed in his rooms at the Hotel Graben. This image is now held in the Wien Museum.
2. For a further discussion of *Selbstdarstellung* – the theatrical parade of the 'private' self in public spaces – see Tag Gronberg, *Vienna: City of Modernity* (Bern: Peter Lang, 2007), pp 37–67.
3. Adolf Loos, *Trotzdem*, ed. by Adolf Opel (Vienna: Prachner, 1982), p. 150. Quoted and translated in Janet Stewart, *Fashioning Vienna: Adolf Loos's Cultural Criticism* (London: Routledge, 2000), p. 104.
4. This inscription is written by Altenberg in black ink and – interestingly – in English.
5. Arthur Schnitzler, *My Youth in Vienna* (London: Weidenfeld and Nicolson, 1971), p. 178.
6. Egon Friedell, ed., *Das Altenbergbuch* (Vienna: Wiener Graphischen Werkstätte, 1921).
7. The Apollo-Theater opened in 1904 and was known for its variety-theatre programme and its operettas, particularly during the years 1911–19. For further information see Marion Linhardt, *Residenzstadt und Metropole: Zu einer kulturellen Topographie des Wiener Unterhaltungstheaters (1858–1918)* (Tübingen: Niemeyer, 2006).
8. Friedell, pp 52–3.

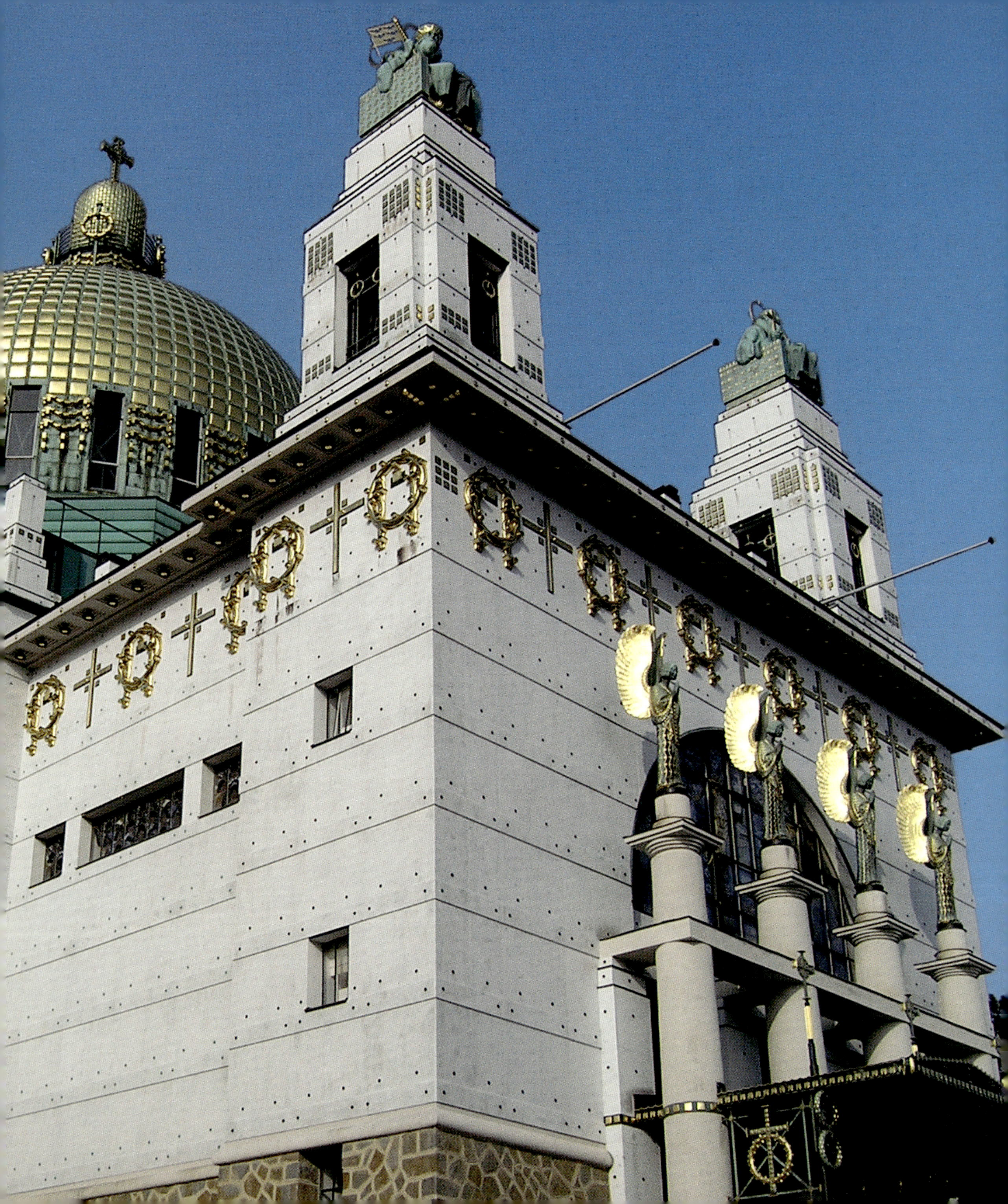

Chapter 5

Modernity follows madness? Viennese architecture for mental illness and nervous disorders

NICOLA IMRIE AND LESLIE TOPP

Around 1910, a person of means suffering from depression and nervous exhaustion could have checked herself into Purkersdorf Sanatorium, a sanatorium for nervous ailments tucked into parkland at the furthest edges of Vienna. The setting for their treatment was a small complex focused on an exquisite white box of a building, designed as a total work of art, characterised by simple lines, the latest building technology and the repeated motif of the square (fig.62). During the same period, a Viennese working class person who began to suffer from paranoid delusions would be delivered to 'Steinhof', the new state psychiatric institution on a prominent slope overlooking Vienna from the west and visible for miles around (fig.63). The setting for his confinement (and treatment) was a city in itself, the highest point of which was a bright white and gold church, also a *Gesamtkunstwerk*, designed with hygiene and unobstructed sightlines in mind. On the terraces below it, flat-roofed pavilions were arranged according to a precise proportional system, on either side of a central axis leading down from the church – men on one side and women on the other.

66 Otto Wagner, St Leopold's Church, Steinhof Psychiatric hospital, 1907

This chapter takes as its starting point the fact that in Vienna, two of the most

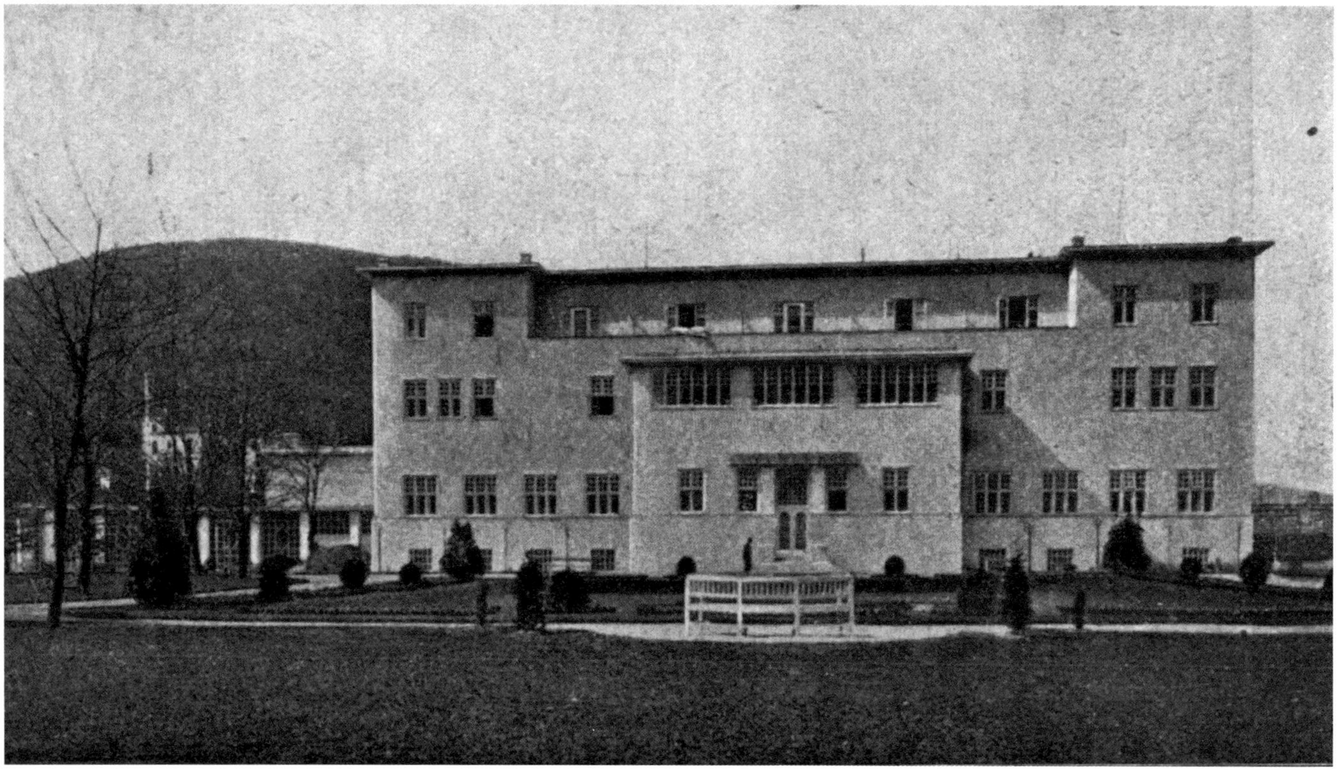

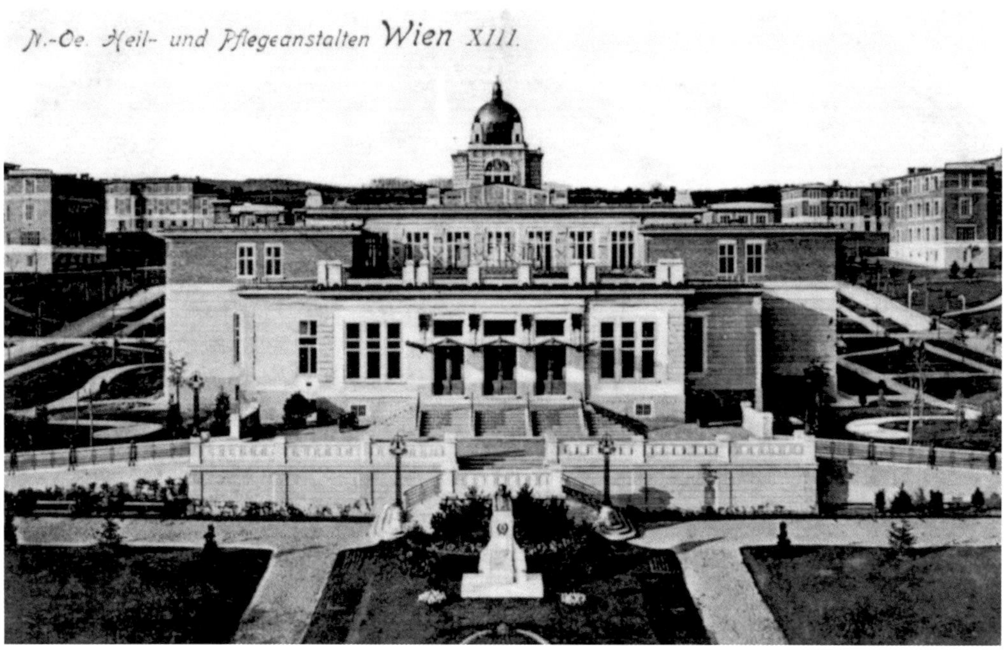

Above:
62 Josef Hoffmann, Purkersdorf Sanatorium, 1904–5, photograph showing east façade, *Offizielles Jahrbuch 1909 des Zentralverbandes der Kur-und Heilanstalts-Besitzer resp. Leiter in Österreich*, 1909

Left:
63 Postcard view, 1919, of Lower Austrian Provincial Institution for the Cure and Care of the Mentally and Nervously Ill 'am Steinhof' (Vienna), opened 1907

important psychiatric establishments also represented key moments in the early development of modern architecture and design. It outlines the development of and the psychiatric thinking behind the two institutions, and explores the important differences between the private sanatorium for nervous ailments and the state asylum, as well as their similarities. It concludes by suggesting some answers to the question: did modernity follow madness?

THE STEINHOF PSYCHIATRIC HOSPITAL AND ITS PREDECESSORS

The Lower Austrian Provincial Institution for the Care and Cure of the Mentally Ill and for Nervous Disorders 'am Steinhof', to use its original official name, was a complex of 60 separate buildings arranged according to a carefully devised site plan (fig.64). In addition to accommodation for 3,000 male and female patients and staff, it included a community centre (with theatre), a church, a farm, a plant nursery, common kitchens and laundries, an infirmary, administrative offices and a mortuary, all set in landscaped parkland

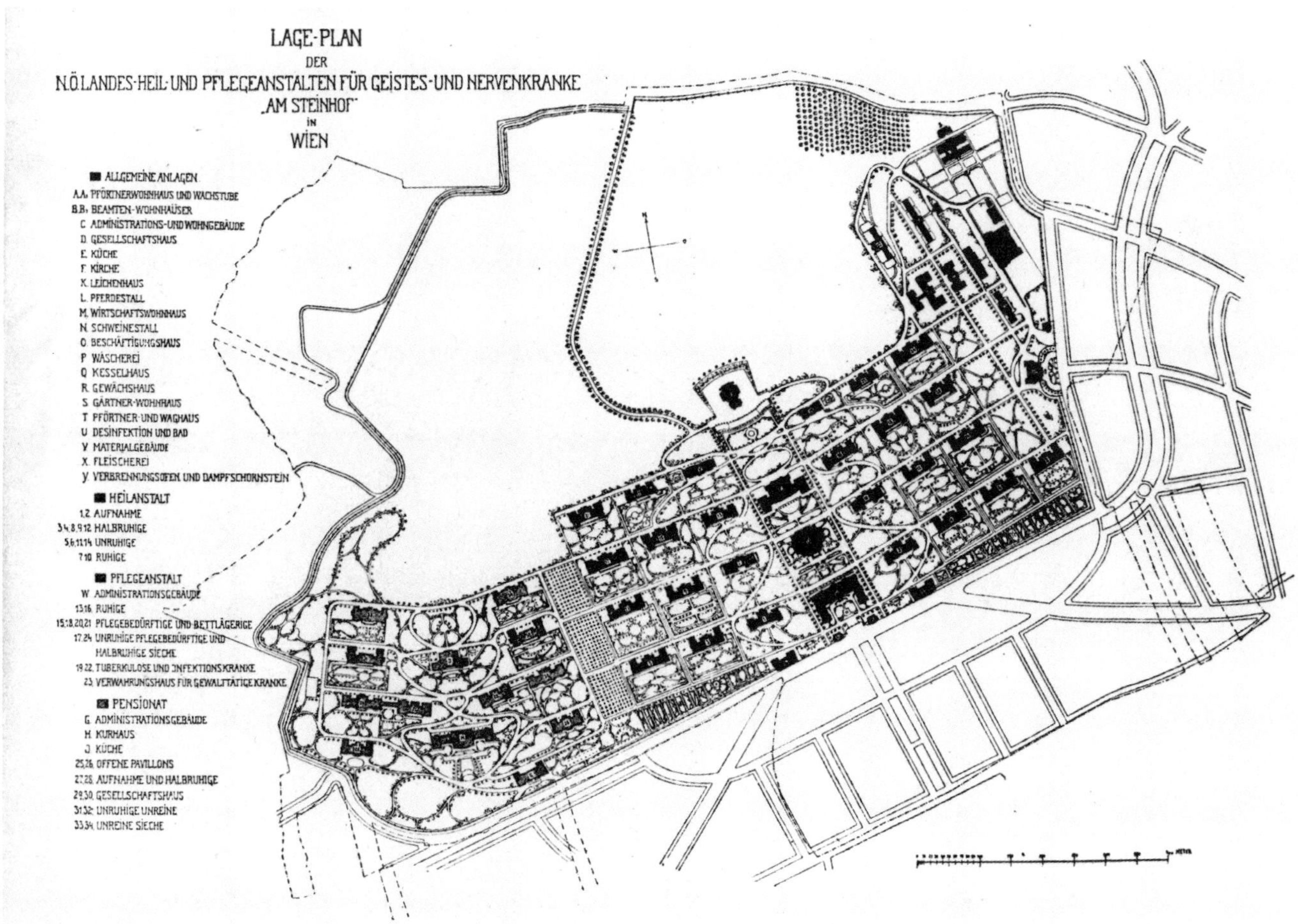

64 Otto Wagner, site plan for the Steinhof psychiatric hospital, opened 1907. *Auszug aus den Verwaltungstätigkeit der christlichsozialen Landtagsmehrheit in den Jahren 1902–1908.* Vienna: Wahlkomitees der christlichsozialen Partei für den I. Bezirk, 1908. n.p.

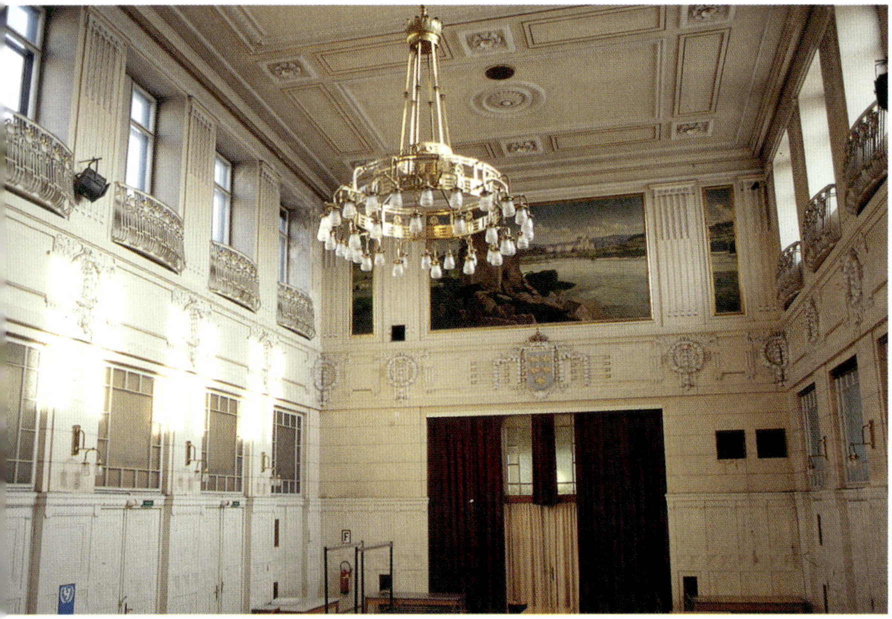

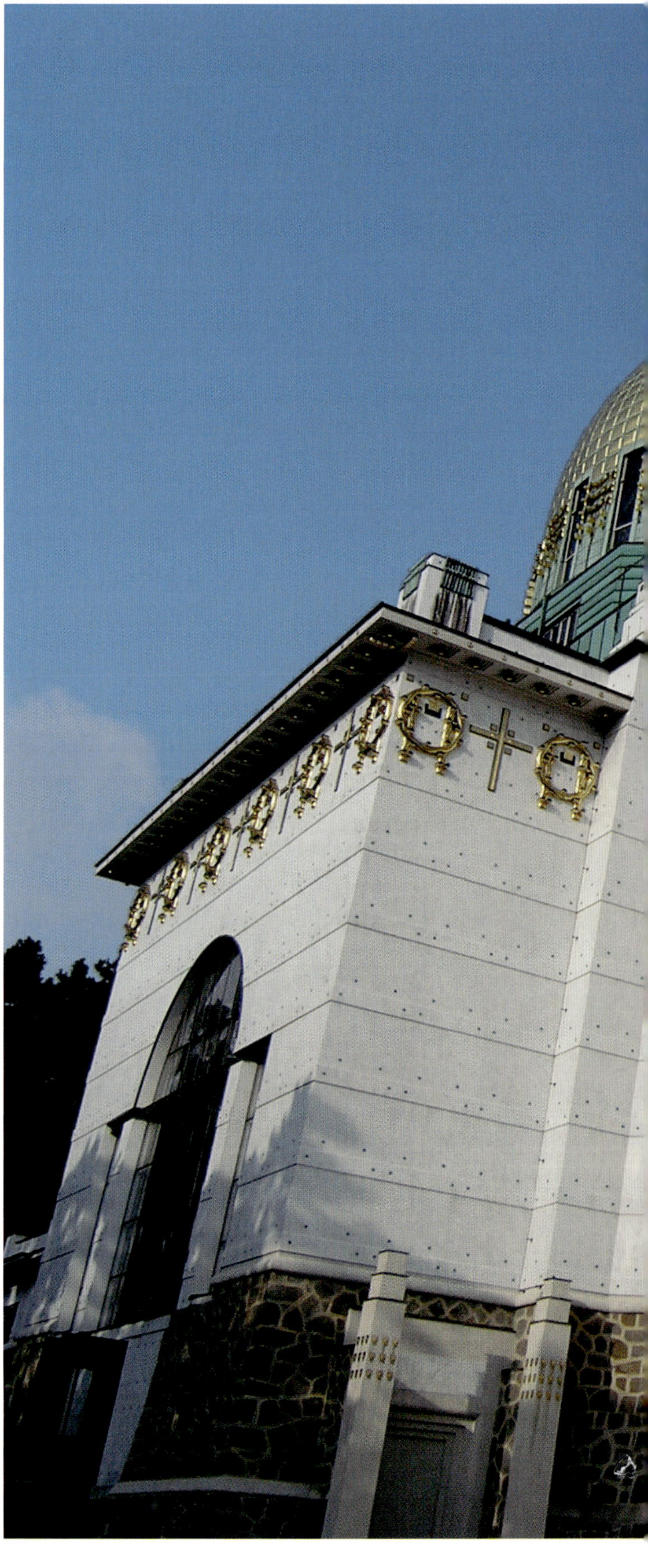

Above:
65 Ballroom, Steinhof
psychiatric hospital, 1907

Right:
66 Otto Wagner,
St Leopold's Church, Steinhof
psychiatric hospital, 1907

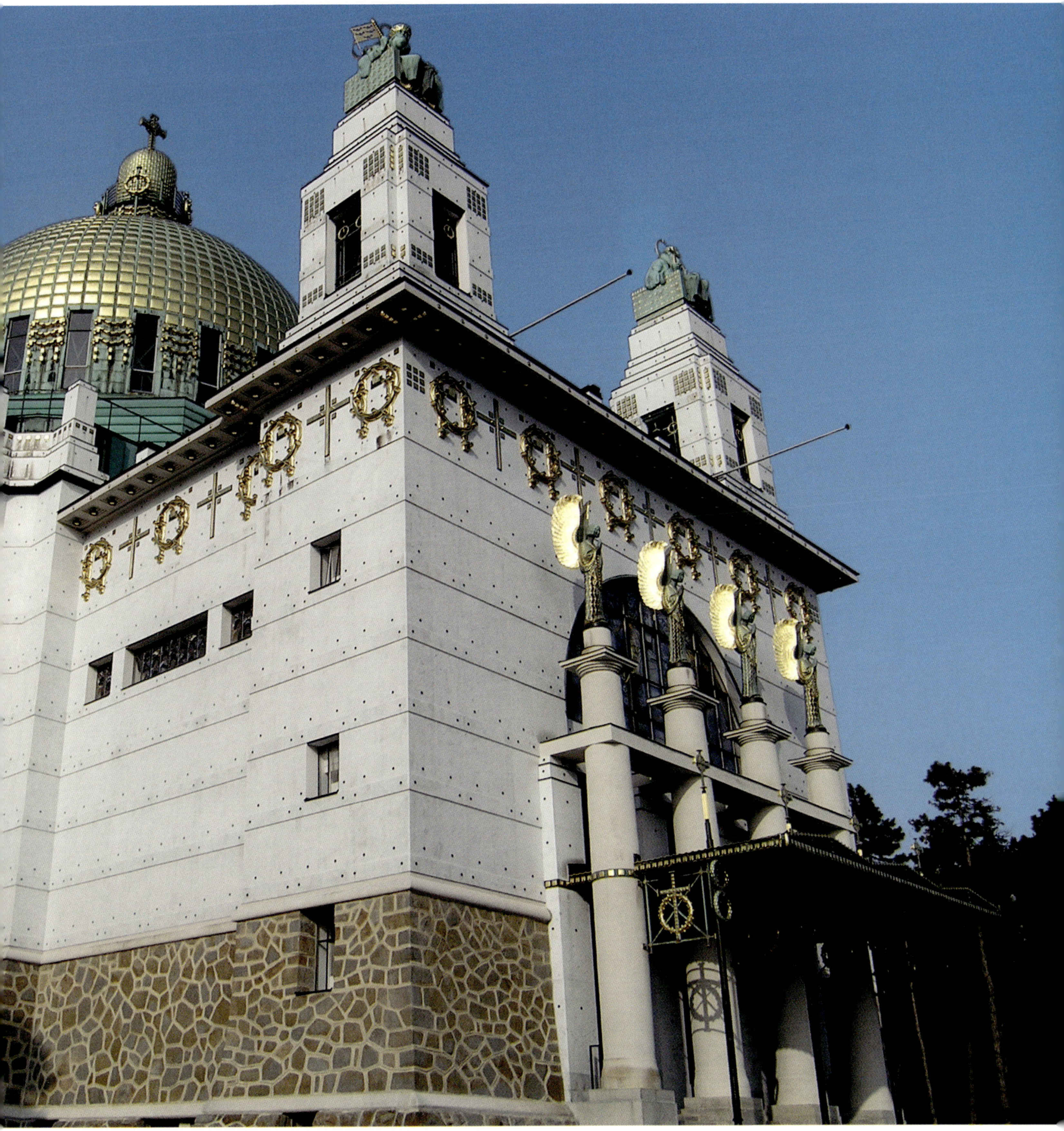

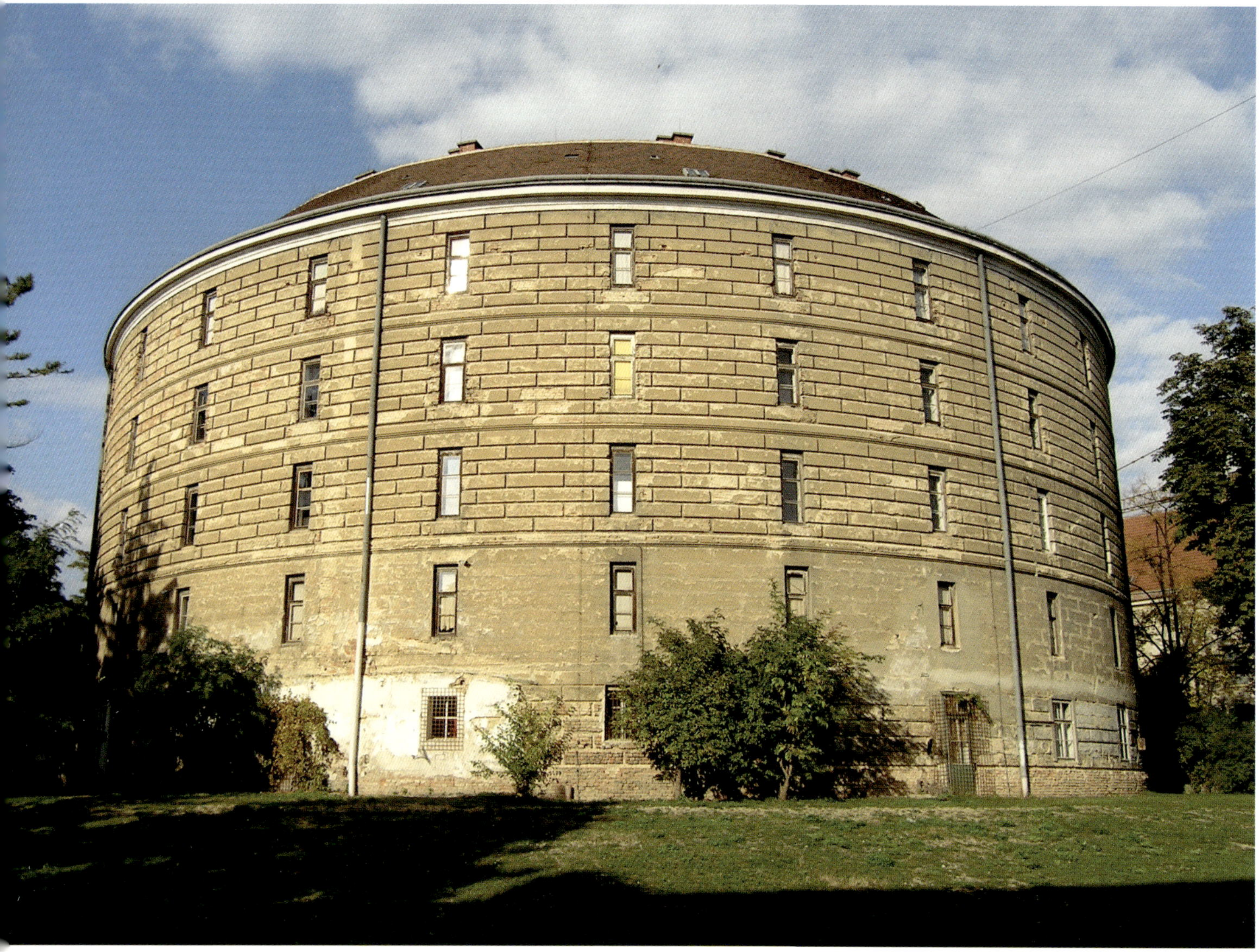

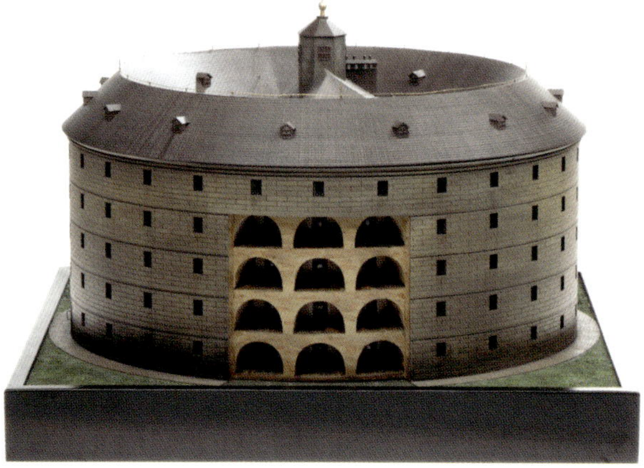

Above:
67 Narrenturm, Vienna, 1784

Left:
68 Narrenturm, Vienna, 1784. Model (undated). Replica of model in Nieder-Österreichisches Landesmuseum Technisches Museum Vienna

(figs 65, 66). The art critic Ludwig Hevesi described it as 'a white city, sparkling in the bright summer sun'.[1]

Institutions for the mentally ill had not always been built in this manner. Two Viennese examples help to illustrate the changes in design for and treatment of mental illness since the late eighteenth century. The 'Narrenturm' (literally 'Fools' Tower') was built in 1784 at the edge of the new General Hospital of Vienna.[2] It still stands today (now housing a pathological-anatomical museum), a cylindrical building of five storeys, each storey consisting of a ring of 28 cells, each with a single barred window and a heavy wooden door opening onto a circular corridor, lit by windows onto central courtyards (figs 67, 68). The Narrenturm confined 140 men and women who were considered dangerously insane. The purpose of the building was purely custodial; many inmates were chained to the walls and provided only with straw mats for sleeping and the most rudimentary nourishment. There was no provision for outdoor activities. What is interesting about the design of the Narrenturm is its careful regularity and use of simple, rational, repeated volumes within the strikingly clear overall volume of the cylinder.[3] When psychiatrists around 1900 looked back at the Narrenturm, it was with a sense largely of superiority but also of admiration for the care and rationality with which it was designed in this early period.[4]

The Narrenturm was replaced in 1853 as the main institution for the mad in Vienna by the new Vienna Lunatic Asylum (*Irrenanstalt*) at Brünnlfeld (fig.69).[5] This institution embodied important developments that had taken place in asylum architecture since the 1790s. On the one hand, it had become much more common to confine people seen to suffer from mental disorders in dedicated institutions (as opposed to putting them in prisons, or workhouses, or caring for them at home). On the other, the idea developed that confinement itself could be curative, as long as the spaces within which it took place, and the daily regime, were effectively designed. The Vienna asylum was set in extensive landscaped grounds and modelled on a country estate with a multi-winged house at the centre, divided along a central axis into sections for male and female patients. The domestic allusions in the architecture were meant to suit a regime in which patients were permitted a greater degree of freedom, using the grounds and dayrooms in a semblance of normal life, with cells only for use in cases of violent derangement. Chains and locks were for the most part replaced by a system of 'moral management', in which a highly regimented daily programme and strict hierarchies of doctors, staff and patients, maintained order.[6]

By the end of the nineteenth century, the tenets of moral management of the insane had not changed, but a new architectural framework was developed for them. German psychiatrists advocated the 'villa system' of asylum planning. In place of a single rambling building surrounded by parkland, multiple smaller pavilions or 'villas' were arranged across most of the institution's site. The villa system was primarily inspired by the desire further to increase the freedom possible for patients within the confines of the institution. Multiple separate pavilions allowed for the careful categorisation of patients according to

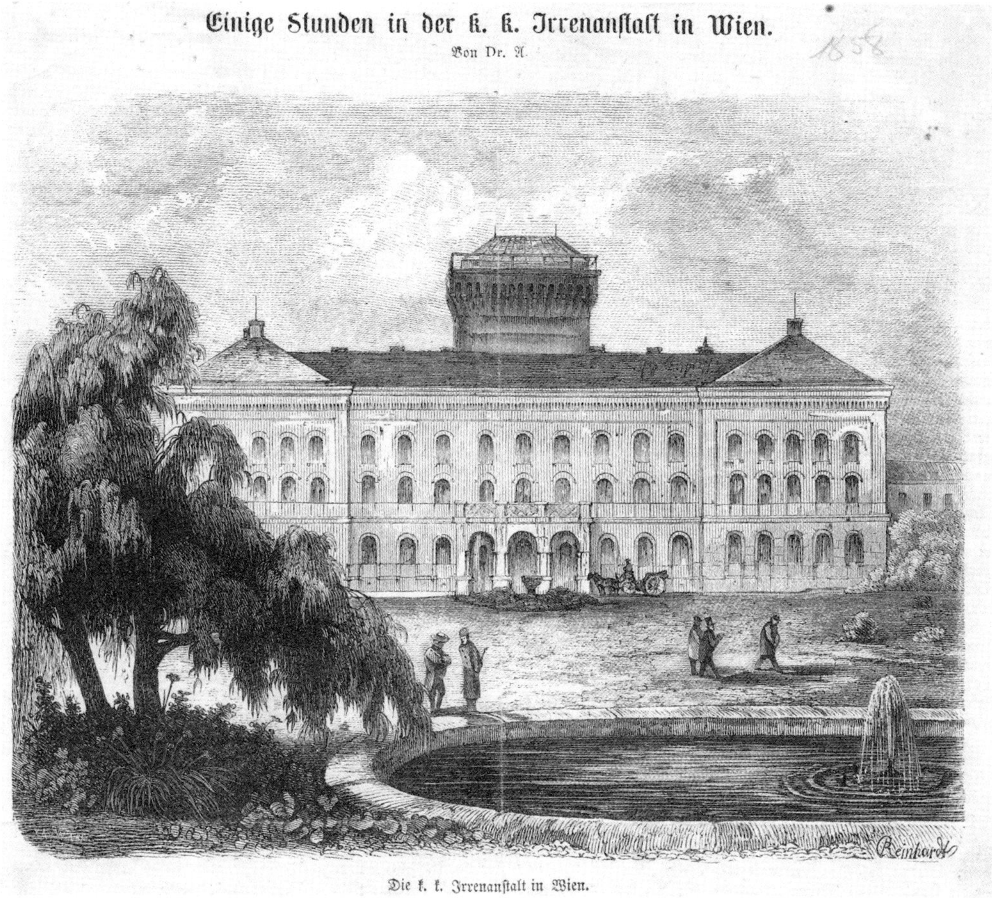

69 Vienna Asylum at Brünnlfeld with grounds, drawing, 1858 by H. Reinhardt

their behaviour and a tailoring of the design of each pavilion to the relative security needs of that group.[7] At Steinhof, the pavilions closest to the central axis housed the 'quiet' patients, with 'semi-agitated' and 'agitated' patients at a graduated remove from the centre. The 'quiet' pavilions contained only dormitory accommodation and common day rooms and offered direct access to the institutions' grounds (fig.70). The pavilions for semi-agitated patients gave onto large gardens surrounded by openwork fences, while those for agitated patients had walled gardens and verandas enclosed by wire mesh (fig.71).[8]

Other perceived benefits of the villa system were better ventilation of the wards and the sense patients had, both through views from inside and through easy access to the outdoors, of proximity to nature. Elevated sites were favoured for this reason – patients, having been removed from the unhealthy city, should be relocated to a healthful setting with restful views. (Steinhof's site on a south-east facing slope at the edge of the Vienna Woods fulfilled this requirement better than most.) Advocates also pointed to the sense of normality fostered by the imitation of a village or settlement, enlivened by the busy activities of its occupants as they moved around the grounds in the open air.[9]

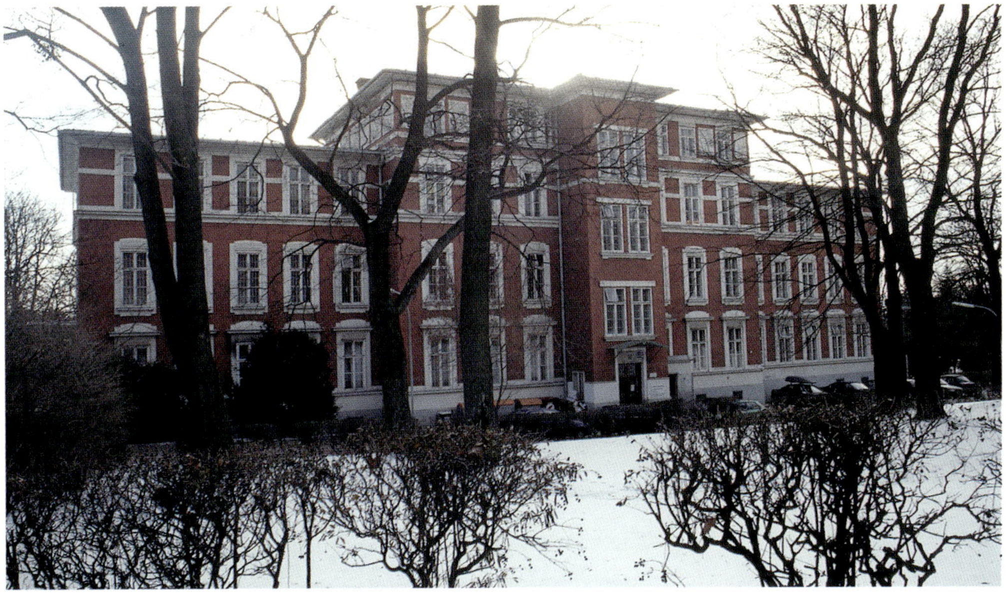

70 Pavilion for quiet patients, Steinhof

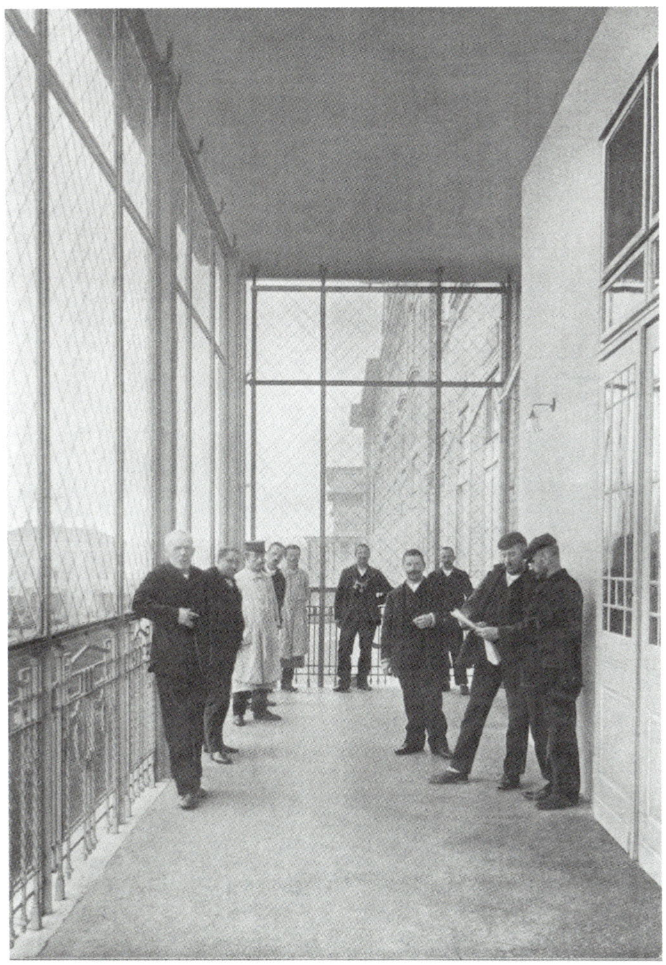

71 Male patients on the veranda of a pavilion, Steinhof, from *Die niederösterreichischen Landesirrenanstalten und die Fürsorge des Landes Niederösterreich für schwachsinnige Kinder, Jahresbericht über die Zeit vom 1908–9* (Vienna, 1909), n.p.

THE PURKERSDORF SANATORIUM

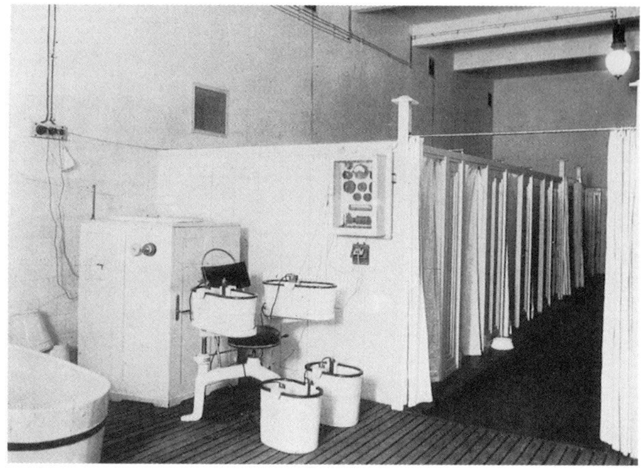

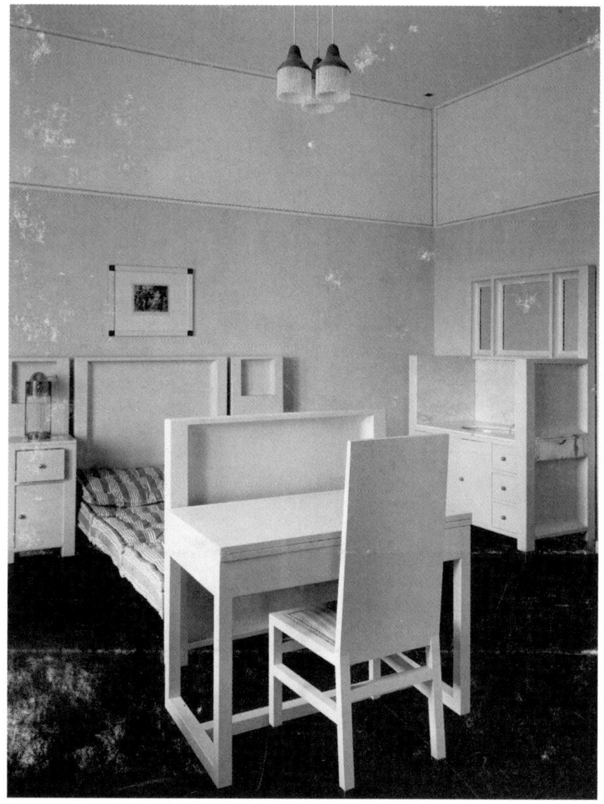

The Purkersdorf Sanatorium belonged to a newer medical building type, the sanatorium for nervous ailments, which shared some of the features of the villa system asylum while also differing in important ways. The location of Purkersdorf Sanatorium, in fact of any sanatorium for nervous ailments, was of the utmost importance. In the 1911 annual report, physician in chief, Ludwig Stein, underlined the therapeutic benefits of light, air and the surroundings of the Vienna Woods. He also advocated the removal of patients to a sanatorium far from their usual domestic, social and professional environment.[10] These were two fundamental elements of the holistic approach to the treatment of nervous ailments around 1900, which was promoted by leading psychiatrists such as Richard von Krafft-Ebing in Vienna and Paul Julius Möbius in Leipzig. Influenced by American doctor George Beard, they believed that the physical and social environment of modern cities was responsible for causing the physical symptoms of nervous exhaustion. They prescribed a range of physical therapies to combat these symptoms which included a strict daily regime of light and fresh-air cures, hydrotherapy, electrotherapy, active and passive exercise (mechanotherapy), special diets, carefully regulated sleep and suggestive psychotherapy known as psychological influencing.[11]

The design of Purkersdorf Sanatorium corresponds closely to the holistic approach to treatment. The materials and technology utilised and the flat surfaces and crisp edges of Hoffmann's design (see fig.113) created an environment which could be easily cleaned, so that high levels of hygiene – important to the sanatorium's health-giving image – could be maintained. Large windows brought light into each room of the sanatorium while specially invented ventilation systems within each window supplied the sanatorium with fresh air.[12] Such design features demonstrate an awareness of the design of tuberculosis sanatoria, where the architecture and mountain landscapes were utilised to treat one of the most prevalent diseases around 1900. In new tuberculosis sanatoria, patient bedrooms were orientated to allow for the greatest amount of light and had exterior balconies for outdoor air cures.[13] In the same way, the internal arrangement of space at Purkersdorf Sanatorium, as well as external details such as the flat roof, also met the needs of therapy. Balconies provided spaces for light and air cures while indoor spaces for therapy, e.g. bathing facilities, were located on the ground

Top:
72 Josef Hoffmann, hyrdrotherapy room, Purkersdorf Sanatorium. *Innen-Dekoration* 17 (1906), 319

Above:
73 Josef Hoffmann, patient room, Purkersdorf Sanatorium. MAK – Austrian Museum of Applied Arts / Contemporary Art, Vienna

floor, the public social and dining spaces on the first floor and finally patients' private rooms on the second floor (figs 72, 73). Services, kitchens, laundry and workshops were contained in the basement. This arrangement and division by function of space facilitated the sanatorium's daily routine.

The division of functional spaces points to the influence of another building type on design of Purkersdorf Sanatorium: the grand hotel. Typically, the ground and perhaps the first floor of a hotel would be given over to public spaces for dining and entertainment while the upper floors would be reserved for the guests' private rooms or suites. Kitchens, laundry and other services would be contained in the basement.[14] Given the bourgeois and even aristocratic clientele at the profit-making, fee-paying Purkersdorf Sanatorium, this link to hotel architecture is not surprising.[15]

While the affluent sought treatment for their nervous ailments in the new world of Purkersdorf Sanatorium, the same section of society found relief in a very different approach to treatment in a contrasting setting: psychoanalysis in Sigmund Freud's consulting room. Purkersdorf Sanatorium provided treatment in a totally designed, hygienic environment which orientated patients in their new and isolated physical world and daily routine. In contrast, Freud's comfortable, upper middle-class doctor's office, packed full of archaeological artefacts, works of art and the famous couch covered with an oriental carpet, was a place to dig, as it were, into the archaeology of a patient's mind (fig.74).

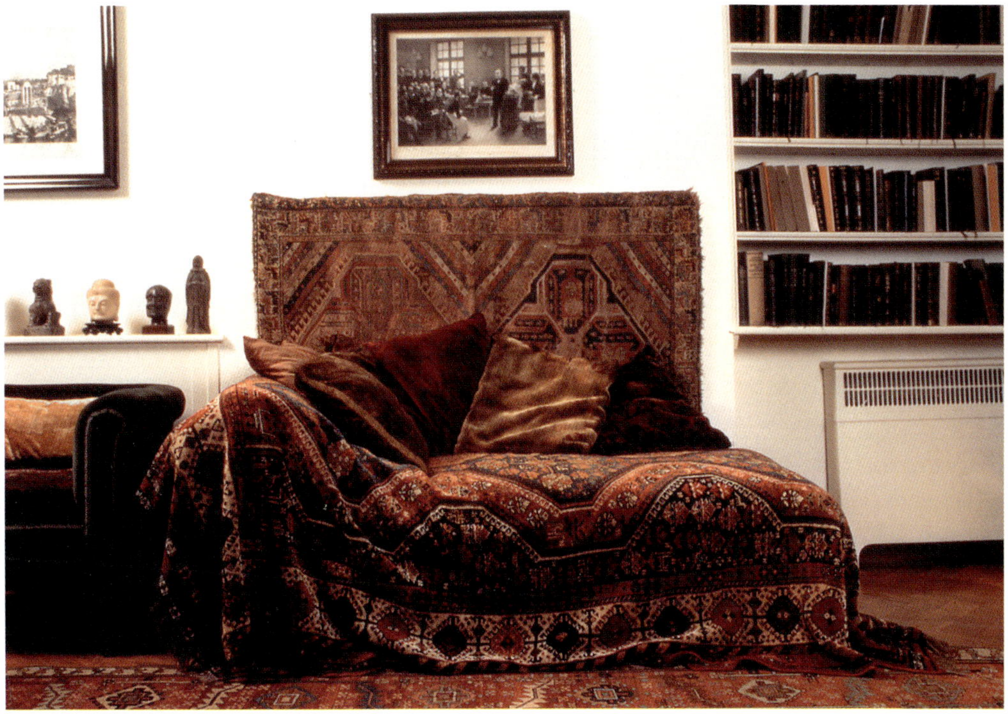

74 Sigmund Freud's consulting room with couch at 20 Maresfield Gardens. Freud Museum, London

ASYLUM VERSUS SANATORIUM

When making distinctions between the architecture and organisation of asylums and sanatoria for nervous ailments, it is important to keep in mind both perceptions about different degrees of mental disorder and, just as importantly, issues of social class. Matters including the financing of the construction and upkeep of an asylum or sanatorium, its design and interior decoration and the separation of patients were all as much connected to social hierarchies as they were to illness.

It was often difficult to establish exactly where a nervous ailment ended and mental illness began. However, this distinction was essential as it determined where an unwell person would end up. Admission to an asylum occurred only with official certification from a doctor, which was legally binding and meant that the patient was confined in the asylum until the psychiatrists deemed the patient well enough to be discharged to their family or to a sanatorium or spa to convalesce. This was the case at both state-run asylums caring for working class and poor patients and at private, fee-paying asylums caring for affluent patients in more comfortable surroundings. Admission to sanatoria for nervous ailments however was entirely voluntary. Prospective patients (generally) participated in the decision to seek treatment. Moreover, patients at these sanatoria were, according to the advertisements at least, most definitely not mentally ill.[16] It was of the utmost importance to voluntary middle and upper class patients and their families that no associations were made with the dread and shame of mental illness. The location of many sanatoria for nervous ailments in coastal, mountain or rural spa resorts helped to address this concern.

The sanatoriums were owned by either a non-medical businessman or by the physician in chief who was responsible for financing the construction of the sanatorium building, its upkeep and marketing. The sanatorium business produced its owner's livelihood in addition to paying the salaries of medical and other staff. Thus, excluding mentally ill patients was one strategy adopted by sanatorium owners to maintain their reputation and income. Another strategy was to make use of architecture and interior decoration to attract a specific type of patron,[17] while a further tactic was to advertise the most advanced technology and therapeutic facilities available. State-financed and -run asylums had a quite different agenda to fulfil. Their patient population was an involuntary one which meant that designers' attention could be focused more exclusively on what was deemed by psychiatric experts to be necessary for the treatment and management of the asylum population, without being overly concerned about patients' individual needs or predilections. That said, designers were answerable to the tax-paying public and its representatives, and planners expressed the desire to overcome the negative public image of the asylum through a friendly and transparent built environment.[18]

Strict categorisation of patients was instituted at state asylums, including the rigid separation of the sexes into two distinct sections. There was no such spatial categorisation of patients in the much smaller sanatoria for nervous ailments. In fact male and female patients' rooms could be directly adjacent to one another, as in a hotel. This suggests that social class was often a determining factor in interactions between the sexes, although Purkersdorf Sanatorium maintained separate spaces for male and female social activities. However, this was the norm in the outside world: for example, the café was a predominantly male space while the salon was predominantly female. Another discrepancy based on class rather than illness can be seen in the patient bedroom. On the one hand, at Steinhof and other asylums, patients often slept in dormitories with single rooms (in some cases called 'cells') reserved for patients in a disturbed state. On the other hand, at sanatoria for nervous ailments, the privacy of an individual room was seen as a requirement of affluent patients (see fig.73). The physical environment of asylums and sanatoria was thus influenced strongly by both illness and social class. However, there are examples of sanatoria that blur these distinctions; two examples in Vienna show planners and designers blending the two institutional types and grappling with the issues described above.

BETWEEN THE SANATORIUM AND THE ASYLUM

The Steinhof 'Sanatorium'

One of the most unusual aspects of the new institution at Steinhof was the inclusion of a large 'Sanatorium' section (see fig.64, where it is labeled 'Pensionat').[19] While most of the institution (as was standard for state asylums across Europe) was intended for local people who did not have the means to support themselves while in care, a distinct group of ten patient pavilions (with service buildings) to the south west of the main complex was designated for fee-paying patients from across the Empire and beyond. The title 'Sanatorium' was meant to signify the higher class status of this part of the institution, by conjuring up associations with private, exclusive facilities such as the Purkersdorf Sanatorium. It also signalled another novel aspect of the Steinhof mission, which was that the institution accepted not only people with mental illness, but also people suffering from nervous disorders. The association of nervous disorders with affluence corresponded to widely held medical and social beliefs, as we have seen.

The admission of patients with nervous illness and the inclusion of a high-profile 'sanatorium' were also part of a concerted publicity campaign surrounding the new institution (fig.75). Advocates of Steinhof insisted that it represented a departure from the old, forbidding and remote 'closed' institutions, objects of fear among the general populace. While private sanatoria were eager to maintain a sharp distinction between what they offered and the 'madhouse', Steinhof co-opted the name 'sanatorium' in order to soften the image of the state asylum.[20] The 'Kurhaus' in the centre of the sanatorium complex was equipped with the latest physical therapy equipment and included a swimming pool and verandas for the 'Luftkur' (fig.76). The residential pavilions were

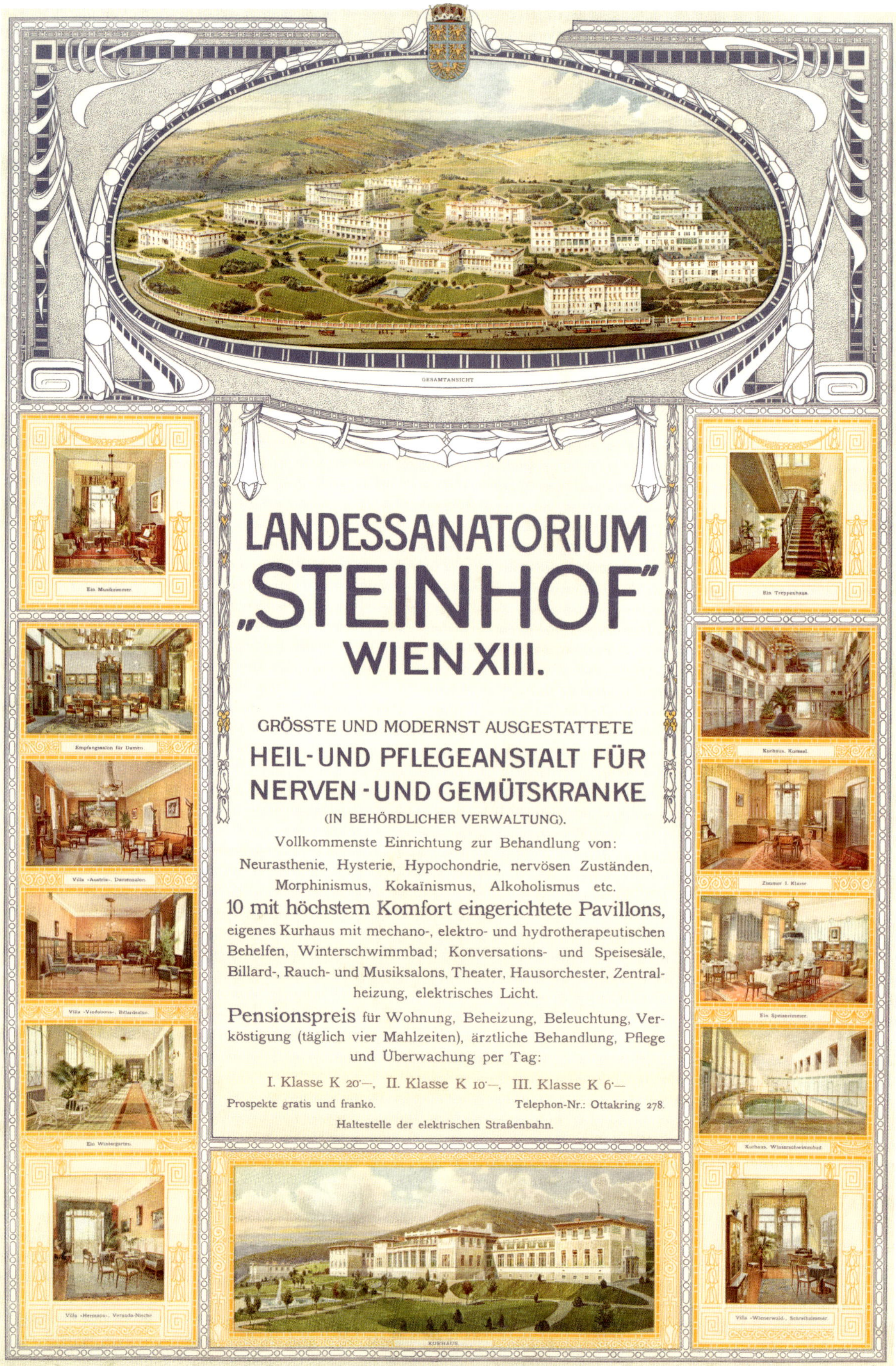
GESAMTANSICHT
LANDESSANATORIUM
„STEINHOF"
WIEN XIII.
GRÖSSTE UND MODERNST AUSGESTATTETE
HEIL- UND PFLEGEANSTALT FÜR
NERVEN - UND GEMÜTSKRANKE
(IN BEHÖRDLICHER VERWALTUNG).
Vollkommenste Einrichtung zur Behandlung von:
Neurasthenie, Hysterie, Hypochondrie, nervösen Zuständen,
Morphinismus, Kokaïnismus, Alkoholismus etc.
10 mit höchstem Komfort eingerichtete Pavillons,
eigenes Kurhaus mit mechano-, elektro- und hydrotherapeutischen
Behelfen, Winterschwimmbad; Konversations- und Speisesäle,
Billard-, Rauch- und Musiksalons, Theater, Hausorchester, Zentral-
heizung, elektrisches Licht.
Pensionspreis für Wohnung, Beheizung, Beleuchtung, Ver-
köstigung (täglich vier Mahlzeiten), ärztliche Behandlung, Pflege
und Überwachung per Tag:
I. Klasse K 20·—, II. Klasse K 10·—, III. Klasse K 6·—
Prospekte gratis und franko.
Telephon-Nr.: Ottakring 278.
Haltestelle der elektrischen Straßenbahn.
Ein Musikzimmer.
Empfangssalon für Damen.
Villa »Austria«. Damensalon.
Villa »Vindobona«. Billardsalon.
Ein Wintergarten.
Villa »Hermann«. Veranda-Nische
Ein Treppenhaus.
Kurhaus. Kursaal.
Zimmer I. Klasse
Ein Speisezimmer.
Kurhaus. Winterschwimmbad
Villa »Wienerwald«. Schreibzimmer
KURHAUS

Opposite:
75 Erwin Pendl, poster advertising the Provincial Sanatorium 'Steinhof', *c.*1907. Otto-Wagner-Spital, Vienna

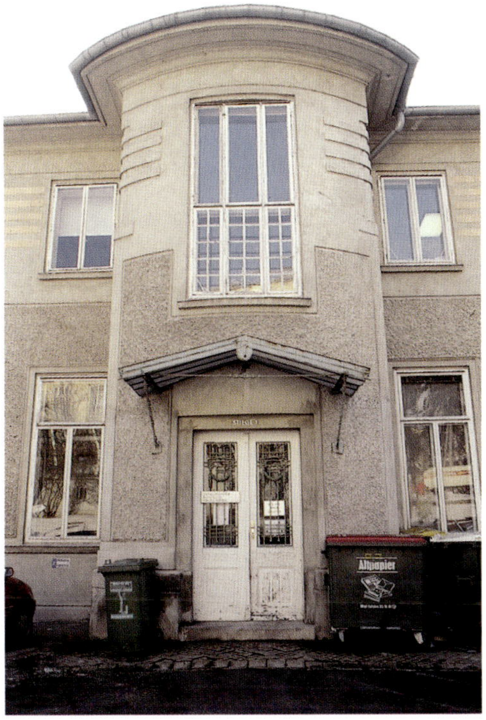

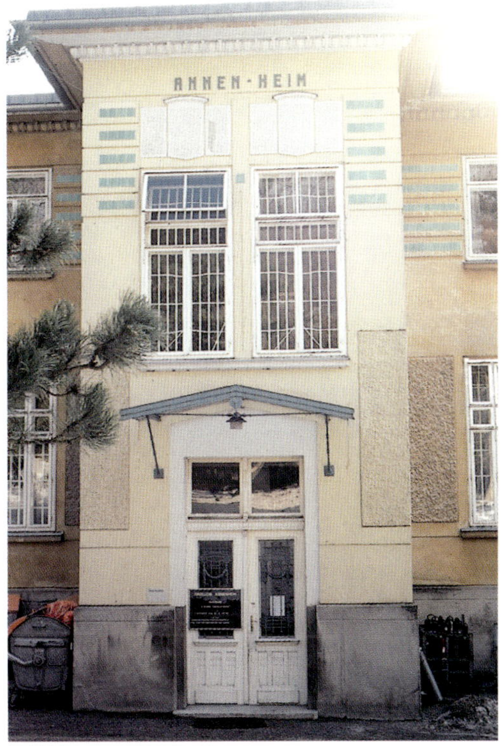

Right:
76 Kurhaus, Steinhof Sanatorium, (detail)

Far right:
77 Villa for patients, Steinhof Sanatorium, (detail)

designed in a similar Jugendstil mode to those in the main institution, but were on a grander scale, and eschewed bare brick in favour of white stucco (fig.77).[21]

The Nervenheilanstalt Rosenhügel

The *Nathaniel Freiherr von Rothschild Stiftung für Nervenkranke*, a sanatorium for nervous ailments built between 1910 and 1912 at Rosenhügel, Vienna also blurred the boundaries between the asylum and sanatorium building types. Facilities included on the one hand, a *Kurmittelhaus* or therapy building, typical of middle and upper class sanatoria and spas. On the other, there were farm buildings and workshops for work therapy which were not features of these more privileged environments. But the main, visible difference to the conventional, hotel-like sanatorium was that Nervenheilanstalt Rosenhügel was built according to the villa system (fig.78). This unusual combination of facilities signalled the fact that this was another hybrid institution: a sanatorium for nervous ailments, funded through charity and intended for the working classes.

During the 1890s it was recognised that the working classes were also at risk of developing nervous ailments and thus required their own sanatoria. Krafft-Ebing, Möbius and Austrian public health official Fédor Gerényi made repeated calls from 1891 onwards for the establishment of *Volksnervenheilanstalten* (sanatoria for nervous ailments for the working classes and poor). The first was established by Dr Heinrich Laehr near Berlin in 1898 on a philanthropic basis and was clearly based on ideas set out by Möbius in 1896.[22] The benefactor and designers of the Rosenhügel sanatorium modelled it closely on this precedent.

The use of the villa system (rather than the grand hotel type) indicated an openness to the techniques of asylum planning; establishing a distance from the asylum for the sake of squeamish upper-class customers was not a strong concern here. The pavilions, with their emphasis on space, simplicity, hygiene and ventilation, also stood in concerted contrast (as they did in state asylums) with the assumed poor hygiene and over-crowding in the domestic environments of working class patients at Rosenhügel. The separation of patients and activities into distinct pavilions also helped to address the well-known sensitivity to noise and other environmental irritations suffered by nervous patients.[23]

The complex at Rosenhügel consisted of an administration pavilion, the *Kurmittelhaus*,

78 Postcard showing aerial view of Clinic for Nervous Disorders, Rosenhügel, *c.*1931

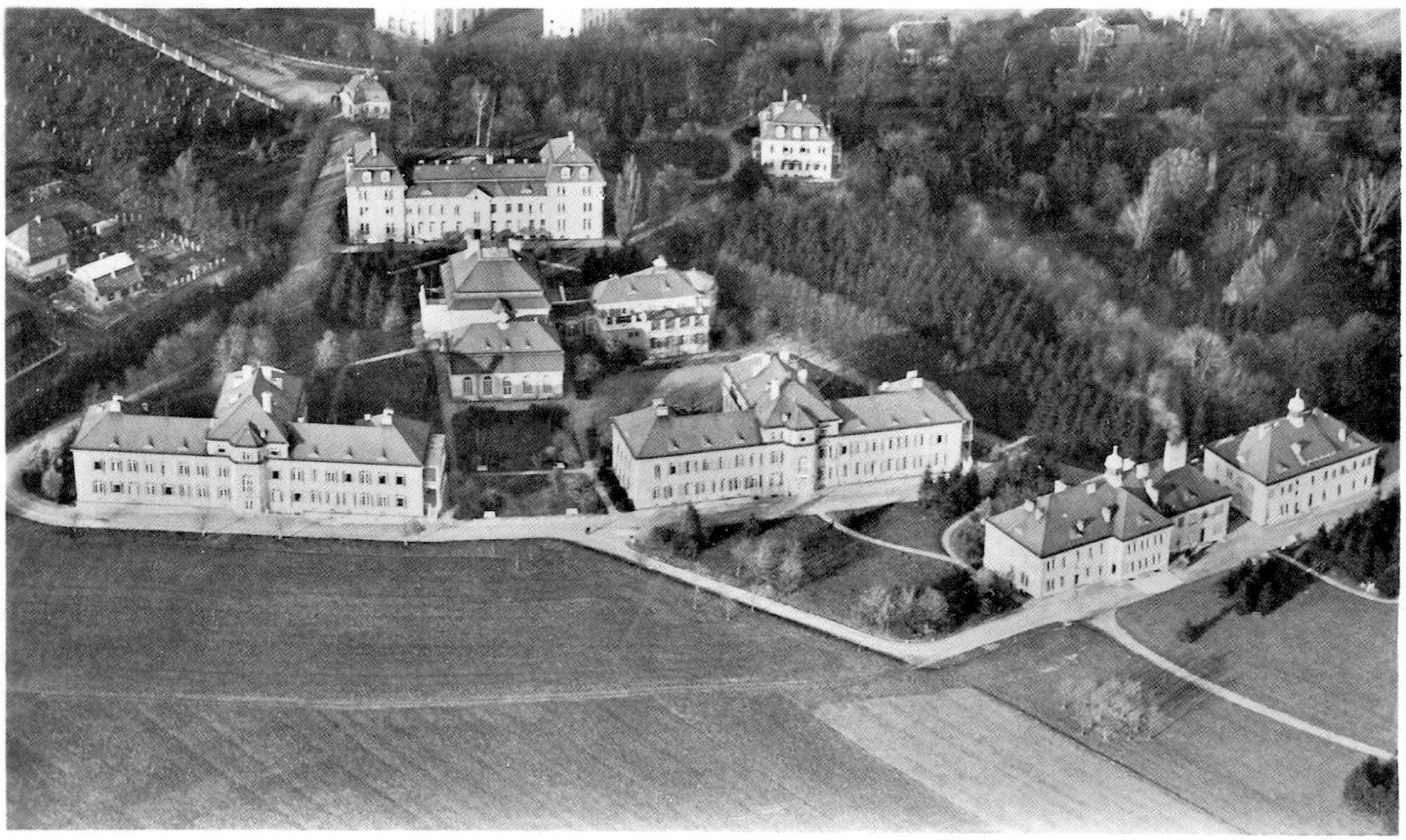
Fliegeraufnahme: Nervenheilanstalt Rosenhügel

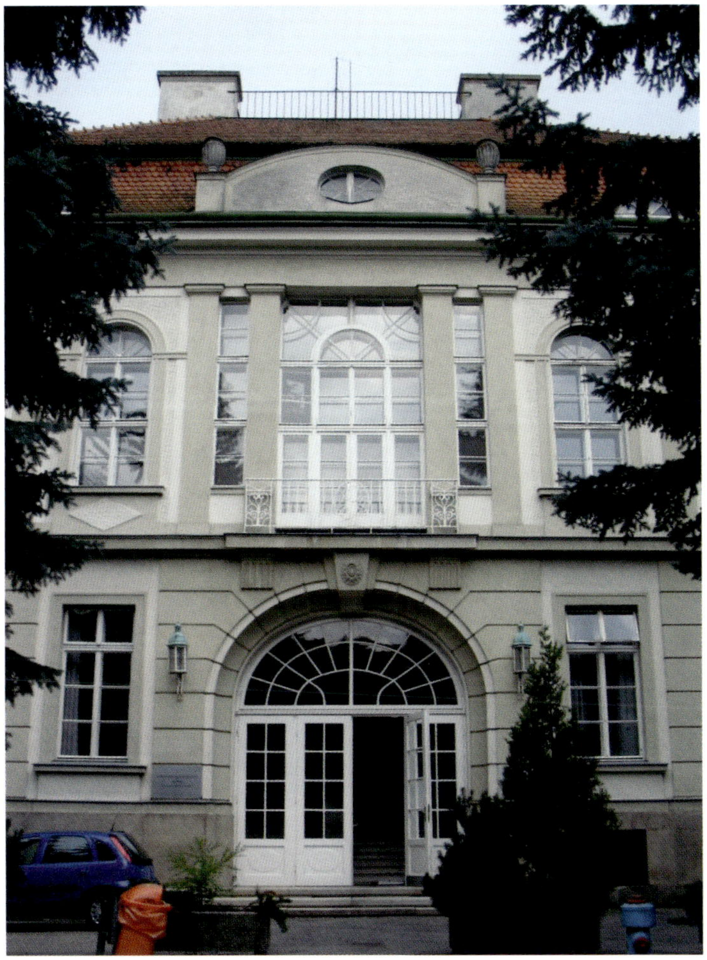

79 Pavilion at Clinic for Nervous Disorders, Rosenhügel, Vienna

two residential pavilions (separating male and female patients), a services pavilion (kitchens, laundry, etc), a farm, a medical director's house and porter's lodge. Functions were thus divided into separate pavilions as well as among designated zones within each pavilion. Patients were given the novel experience of an individual room or at most a room shared by two or three patients with the requisite space, light and fresh air to assist their recovery. In the absence of severely disturbed patients, working class patients could be given the privacy of the single or small shared room without the risk that it would be confused with an isolation cell.

At Rosenhügel, the blurring of boundaries between the design of this sanatorium for nervous ailments and of asylums built around 1900 was very much associated with the social class of its patients. The villa style design met the benefactor's, psychiatrists' and architects' assumptions about the negative aspects of patients' everyday living conditions, while the spa facilities provided the necessary range of treatment to cure nervous ailments. Rosenhügel pioneered the idea of the *Volksnervenheilanstalt* in the Austro-Hungarian Empire and stood for the belief that nervous ailments could affect any human being, regardless of social class. The pioneering mission at Rosenhügel was however not reflected entirely by an equally pioneering architectural style. Externally the pavilions were designed in a conventional, neo-baroque style (fig.79); internally however the modern construction materials remained visible as part of a simple, hygienic aesthetic reminiscent of Purkersdorf Sanatorium.

MODERN ARCHITECTURE AND THE IMAGE OF THE INSTITUTION

The account above shows that the design of both asylums and sanatoria was closely bound up with psychiatric thinking, and that psychiatrists took the lead in determining the site, layout and placement of buildings. This did not however mean that the visual impression given by the building or complex of buildings was seen as unimportant. With the development of the illustrated press and emphatically visual advertising material, the image projected by the building was an important factor to be considered, especially

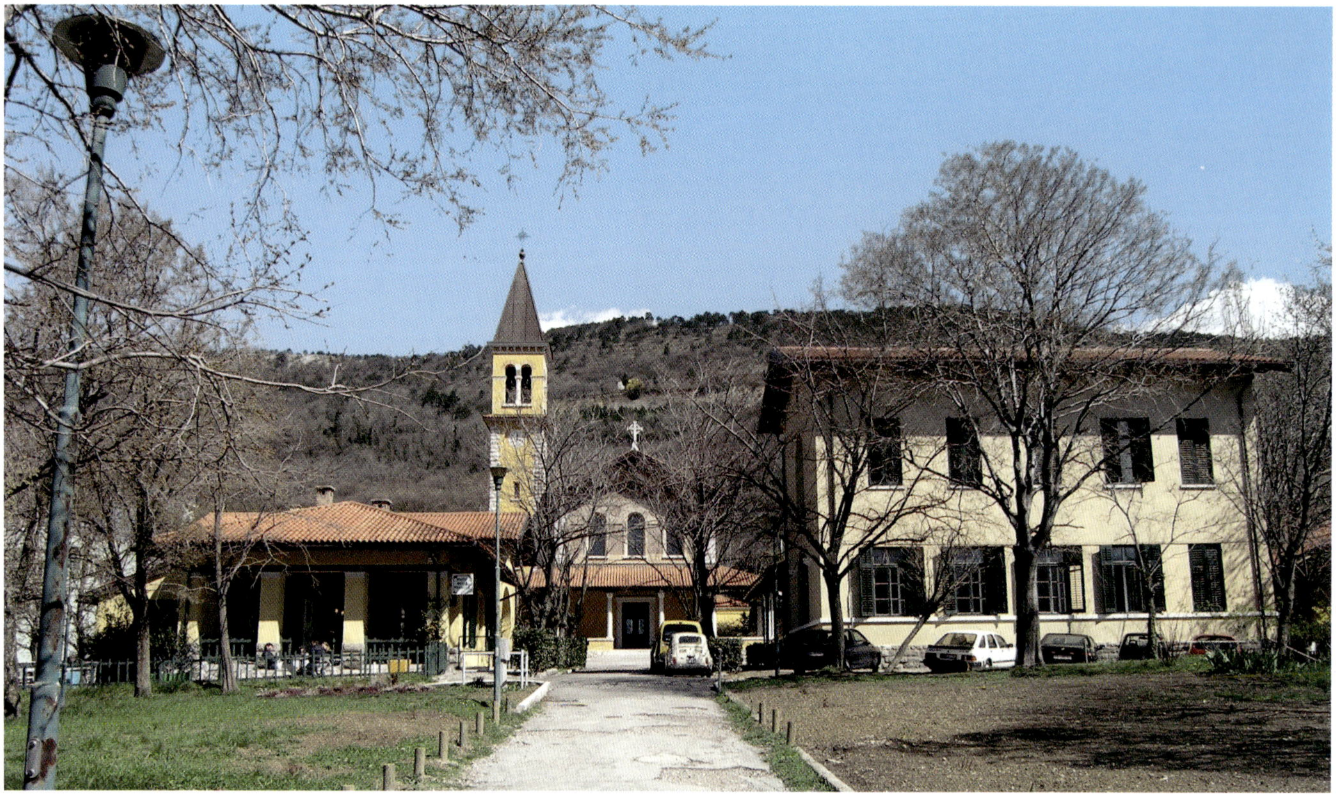

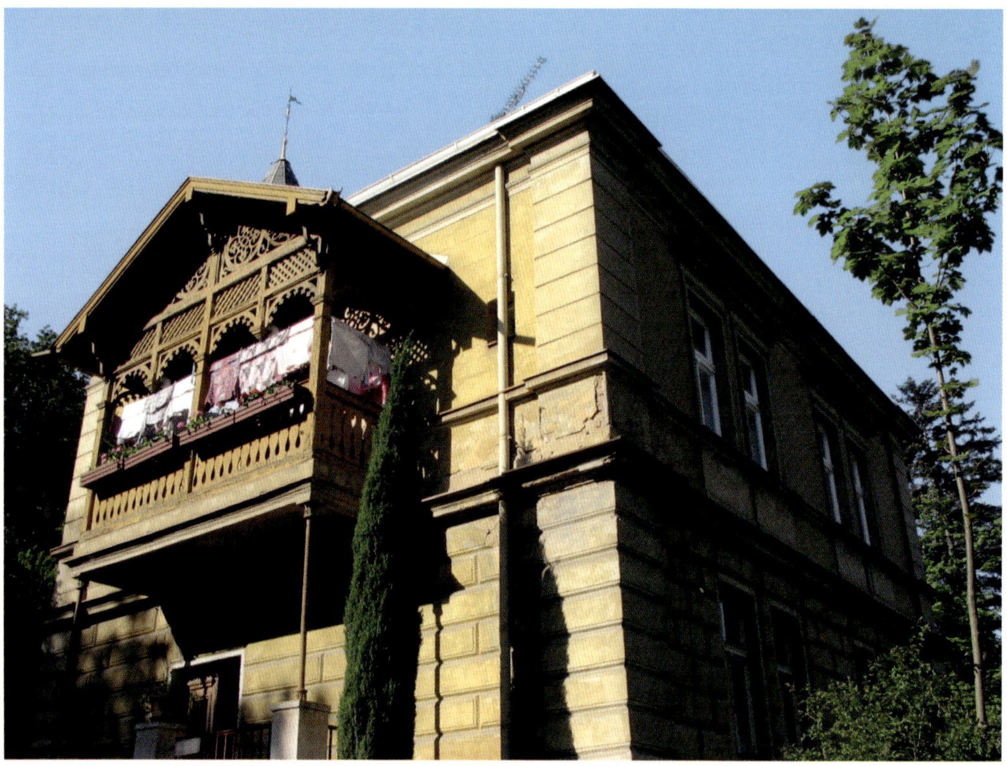

Above:
80 View of church and workshop buildings, Trieste asylum

Left:
81 Pavilion from first stage of development, Sanatorium Dr Šimsa, Prague

by commercial enterprises such as private sanatoria but also by public psychiatric institutions, with their history of public suspicion. The visual impression made by the institution on the patient was also seen as important, and in the case of both asylums and sanatoria, the emphasis was placed on visual landscapes that would distract the patient from the fact of his or her illness and confinement rather than reinforcing it.[24]

So did modernity follow madness? The fact is that, in the first decade of the twentieth century, when modernism in architecture was still in its infancy, most psychiatric buildings (and most buildings of all types) were built in a late historicist mode. The public asylum at Bohnice in Prague, built 1904–1914, was designed by Václav Roštlapil and Václav Heller using a pared down neo-baroque architectural language. For the Trieste asylum (1904–1908), the architect, Lodovico Braidotti, experimented with a range of revivalist 'Italian' styles (fig.80).[25] Sanatorium design in the Habsburg Empire was similarly diverse. Sanatorium Dr Šimsa near Prague encompassed a variety of the styles used. The first phase of the sanatorium complex (completed in 1901) was built in the half-timbered style widely used for rural recreational purposes (fig.81). For the later buildings (1909–1910), designer Bohumil Cerny (who may also have built the first phase) chose a unique, flamboyant neo-baroque and Jugendstil-influenced style (fig.82).[26]

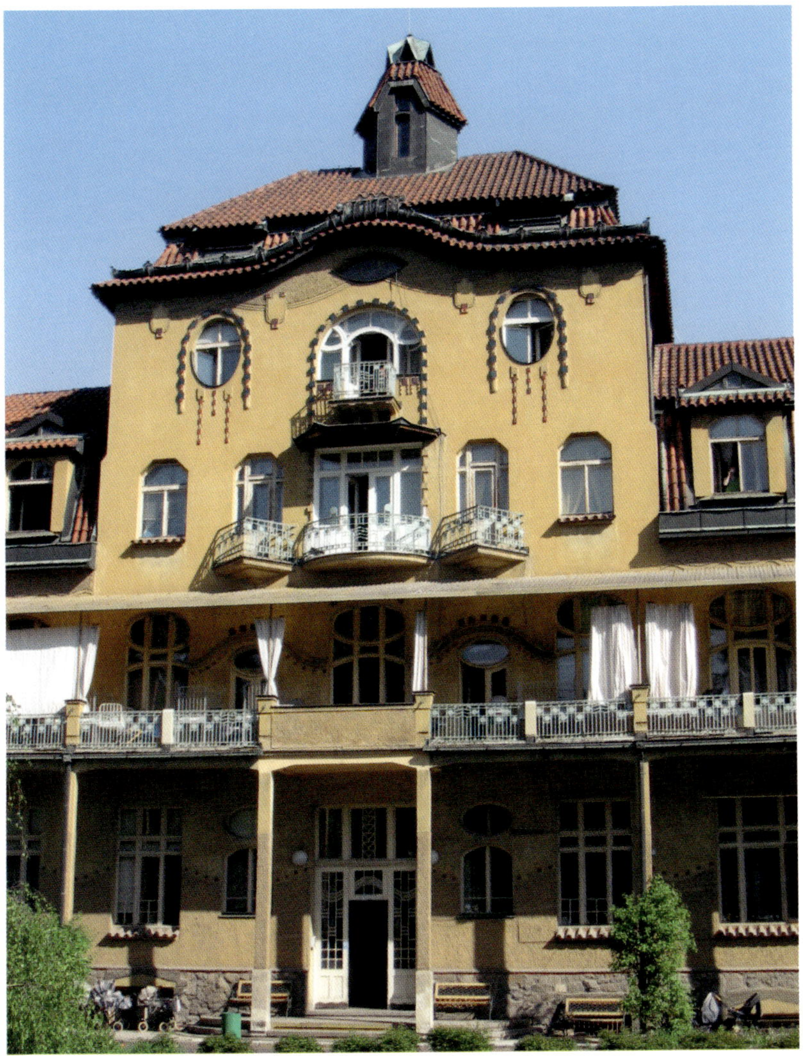

82 Pavilion from second stage of development, Sanatorium Dr Šimsa, Prague

Therefore, there was nothing inherent in the commission for a psychiatric hospital or a sanatorium for nervous ailments before 1914 that demanded a modern architectural vocabulary that eschewed historical references and complex volumes in favour of white walls and formal simplicity. Purkersdorf Sanatorium and the Steinhof psychiatric hospital could only have ended up appearing as they did under the influence of an approach to architecture peculiar to Vienna. It was there that a group of architects deliberately and self-consciously developed a 'modern' architecture around 1900. They opened themselves up to the influence of a scientific world view generally, and more specifically to the inspiration

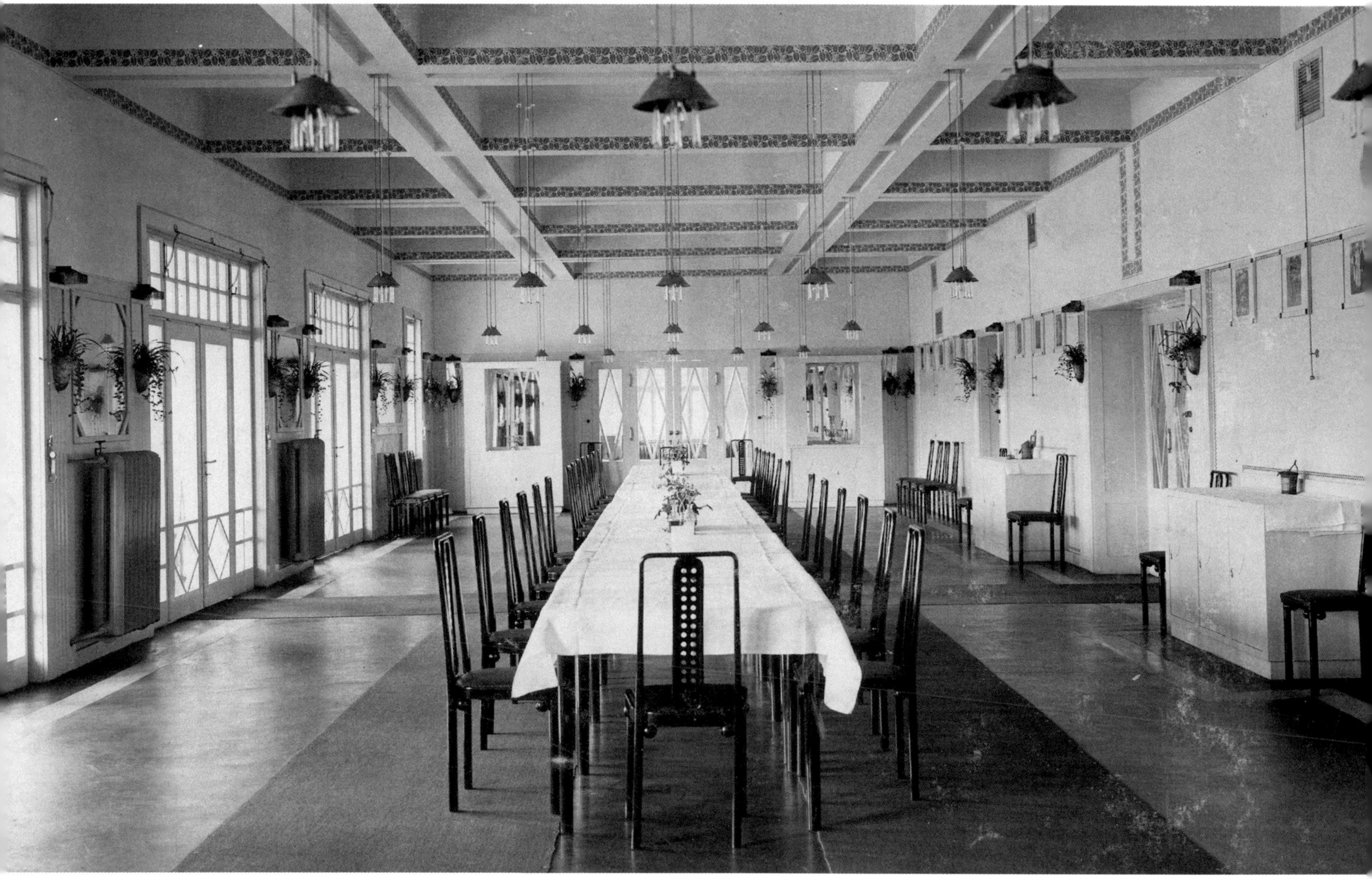

83 Josef Hoffmann, dining room, Purkersdorf Sanatorium, 1904–5. MAK – Austrian Museum of Applied Arts / Contemporary Art, Vienna

provided by those aspects of such psychiatric commissions that corresponded to their own view of society and architecture's potentially transformative role within it.

Steinhof and Purkersdorf were designed by, respectively, the leader and one of the most important pupils of the Wagner School: Otto Wagner and Josef Hoffmann. Wagner, as Professor at the Vienna Academy of Fine Arts, led a highly influential master class in architecture. Students were challenged to distance themselves from the prevailing past-oriented academic approach to design and seek inspiration in the achievements of the present. This meant an orientation towards commissions that were seen to emerge from modern life. Wagner deliberately pursued large public commissions and had a strong interest in urban planning, which he put to use in his design of the site plan for Steinhof. Hoffmann was more active as a designer of residences for the culturally progressive Viennese intelligentsia; his connections with a family of art critics and medics, the Zuckerkandls, gained him the sanatorium commission. The approach to design advocated by Wagner and embraced by Hoffmann was a particular version of the 'truth to purpose'

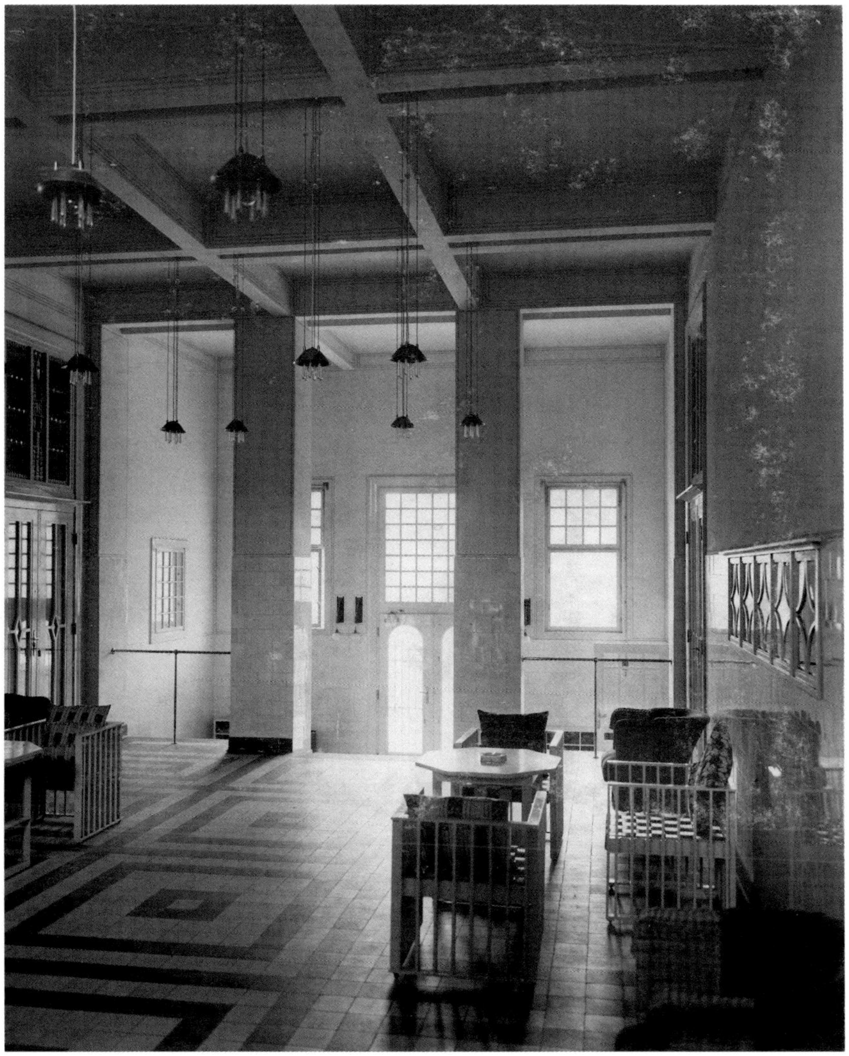

impulse shared by early modernists from Louis Sullivan to Hendrik Berlage. The architect should take the requirements of the commission, both practical and symbolic, as his starting point, answer them directly and simply, and at the same time seek the 'inner truth' of the project, expressing it through the monumental coherence of simple forms and surfaces.[27]

We see this process at play in both projects discussed in this chapter. Hoffmann seems to have analysed the requirements of the sanatorium and at the same time been inspired by the simple, rationalised way of life prescribed to patients, and by the enthusiasm for new machine technologies seen in, for example, the 'mechanotherapy' room (see fig.25). His entrance hall and dining room, for example, are uncluttered and clearly proportioned spaces, easy to clean and to move through, fitting settings for the repeated routines of sanatorium life (figs 83, 84). The ceilings have been built using reinforced concrete, a new building technology, the grid of beams undisguised by the usual covering. Hoffmann's approach to design created a physical environment like no other. It communicated to patients the sense of a new world and a specific purpose: curing their nervous ailments.[28] Wagner's challenge at Steinhof was to provide an aesthetic interpretation of a building brief that already contained detailed prescriptions as to how the spaces should be laid out and the various aspects of the complex organised. Remaining true to these requirements, Wagner also sought to embody their spirit, by drawing on ideas of the utopian settlement developed within his master class.[29] A tightly organised masterplan of simple volumes, set amid a lush green landscape, is focused on a modern monument (at Steinhof, the church) at the apex of a central axis. Wagner picked up on the ambitious transformative social goals of the psychiatrists and government officials who planned Steinhof and expressed them in terms of the language of monumental modernity.

84 Josef Hoffmann, entrance hall, Purkersdorf Sanatorium, 1904–5. MAK – Austrian Museum of Applied Arts / Contemporary Art, Vienna

The Purkersdorf Sanatorium and the Steinhof asylum may not have been typical of psychiatric architecture then or since, but they are highly significant cultural documents. In them, two important visions – psychiatric and architectural – of the transformation of the individual through the built environment combined to produce central monuments of Vienna 1900.

NOTES

1. Ludwig Hevesi, *Altkunst-Neukunst, Wien 1894–1908* (Vienna: Konegen, 1909), pp 249–54. For a detailed account of Steinhof's architecture and planning, see Leslie Topp, 'Otto Wagner's Steinhof Psychiatric Hospital: Architecture as Misunderstanding', *Art Bulletin*, 87 (2005), pp 130–56.
2. Alfred Stohl, *Der Narrenturm oder die dunkle Seite der Wissenschaft* (Vienna: Böhlau, 2000), pp 41–4. For an account of patients and their lives in the Narrenturm, see Andrea Brenner, 'Der Wiener "Narrenturm" und seine PatientInnen – ein erster Arbeitsbericht', in *Vor Freud. Therapeutik der Seele vom 18. bis zum 20. Jahrhundert*, (ed.) Carlos Watzka and Marcel Chahrour (Vienna: Verlag der Ärzte, 2008), pp 45–63.
3. Stohl argues that the precise form of the Narrenturm is deeply implicated in alchemical and numerological calculations.
4. Alexander Pilcz, *Die Irrenbehandlung Einst und Jetzt* (Vienna: Nieder-Österreichische Landesausschusse, 1898); Edmund Holub, 'N.Oe.Landes-Heil – und Pflegeanstalten für Geistes – und Nervenkranke "Am Steinhof" in Wien, XIII' in *Die Irrenpflege in Österreich in Wort und Bild*, (ed.) Heinrich Schlöss (Halle: Carl Marhold, 1912), p. 178.
5. Josef Berze, 'Bauliche Beschreibung und Geschichte der alten Anstalt', *Psychiatrisch-Neurologische Wochenschrift*, 9 (1907), pp 221–6. The Narrenturm continued to operate as an insane asylum until 1870.
6. Berze, pp. 224–5. For moral management see Andrew Scull, *The Most Solitary of Afflictions: Madness and Society in Britain, 1700–1900* (New Haven: Yale University Press, 1993) and Michel Foucault, *History of Madness*. trans. Jonathan Murphy and Jean Khalfa (London: Routledge, 2006).
7. For an account of the villa system, see Leslie Topp, 'The Modern Mental Hospital in Late Nineteenth-Century Germany and Austria: Psychiatric Space and Images of Freedom and Control', in *Madness, Architecture and the Built Environment: Psychiatric Spaces in Historical Context*, (ed.) Topp, James Moran and Jonathan Andrews (New York: Routledge, 2007), pp 241–61.
8. Holub, p. 182.
9. Topp, 'The Modern Mental Hospital', pp 246–51.
10. Ludwig Stein, *Jahresbericht des Sanatoriums Purkersdorf bei Wien für das Jahr 1911 nebst literarischem Anhang* (Vienna: Franz Doll, 1912), pp 15, 32–3.
11. Richard von Krafft-Ebing, *Über gesunde und kranke Nerven*, 5th edn (Tübingen: Verlag der H. Laupp'schen Buchhandlung, 1903), pp 133–73; Paul Julius Möbius, *Über die Behandlung von Nervenkranken und die Errichtung von Nervenheilstätten* (Berlin: S. Karger Verlag, 1896), pp 20–23.
12. Leslie Topp, *Architecture and Truth in Fin-de-Siècle Vienna* (Cambridge: Cambridge University Press, 2004), p. 76.
13. Nils Aschenbeck, *Die Moderne, die aus den Sanatorien kam: Reformarchitektur und Reformkultur um 1900* (Delmenhorst: Aschenbeck & Holstein, 1998), pp 31–2.
14. Herbert Lachmayer, Christian Gargerle and Géza Hajós, 'The Grand Hotel', *AA Files*, 22 (1991), p. 37.
15. For an account of a hotel style sanatorium for nervous ailments, see Nicola Imrie, 'The Architecture and Culture of Sanatoria for Nervous Ailments in the Austro-Hungarian Empire, 1890–1914' (unpublished doctoral thesis, University of London, Birkbeck College, 2008), pp 68–121.
16. Edward Shorter, 'Private clinics in central Europe, 1850-1933', *Social History of Medicine*, 3 (1990), 185; Franz Schalk, 'Sanatorium Dr Schalk' in *Feschrift zum 60. Geburtstag des Prof. J Glax*, ed. by J. Cohn, G. Fodor et al. (Abbazia, 1906), p. 179.
17. For a discussion of the patrons of Purkersdorf Sanatorium, see Sabine Wieber, 'Nervous Bodies and Femmes Fragile: Sculpting the Sanatorium in Vienna 1900', forthcoming.

18. See for example [Edmund] Holub, 'Wir und die Öffentlichkeit!' *Psychiatrisch-Neurologische Wochenschrift*, 9 (1907), pp 357–61.
19. Holub, 'N.Oe.Landes-Heil – und Pflegeanstalten', p. 7.
20. Topp, 'Otto Wagner's Steinhof Psychiatric Hospital', p. 139.
21. An illustrated prospectus for the Steinhof sanatorium shows architecture and interiors being used to sell the institution to an international public. *The Provincial Sanatorium of 'Steinhof' in Vienna (Austria) XIII. Prospectus*, (Vienna: Province of Lower Austria, 1907).
22. Möbius' ideal *Volksnervenheilanstalt* included a pavilion system design, a rural setting where patients could participate in agricultural and horticultural work therapy and foundation upon the financial basis of public subscription with share certificates. See Möbius, pp 25–7.
23. Möbius, p. 26; Ruth Koblizek and Gernot Schnaberth, *Neurologie Rosenhügel Rothschild-Stiftung* (Vienna: Eigenverlag Verein MEMO, 2002), p. 51.This book contains transcripts of original documents and drawings, including the architects' descriptions of the design of the pavilions where the patients' environment is addressed and Möbius' influence can be found.
24. Topp, 'The Modern Mental Hospital', 248–51; Imrie, pp 49–56, 132–4.
25. Heinrich Schlöss, (ed.), *Die Irrenpflege in Österreich in Wort und Bild* (Halle: Carl Marhold, 1912), pp 9–32, 132–9.
26. Imrie, pp 122–72; Schlöss, pp 56–9; Marie Vitochová, Jindřich Kejř and Jiří V?etečka, *Prag und der Jugendstil*, trans. by Ruth and Jiří Kuča, (Prague: V Ráji, 1993), pp 167–8.
27. Topp, *Architecture and Truth*, pp 1–27.
28. Topp, *Architecture and Truth*, pp 63–95; Imrie, pp 29–67.
29. Otto Wagner, *Modern Architecture: A Guidebook to His Students to This Field of Art*. trans. by Harry Francis Mallgrave (Santa Monica: Getty Center for History of Art and the Humanities, 1988).

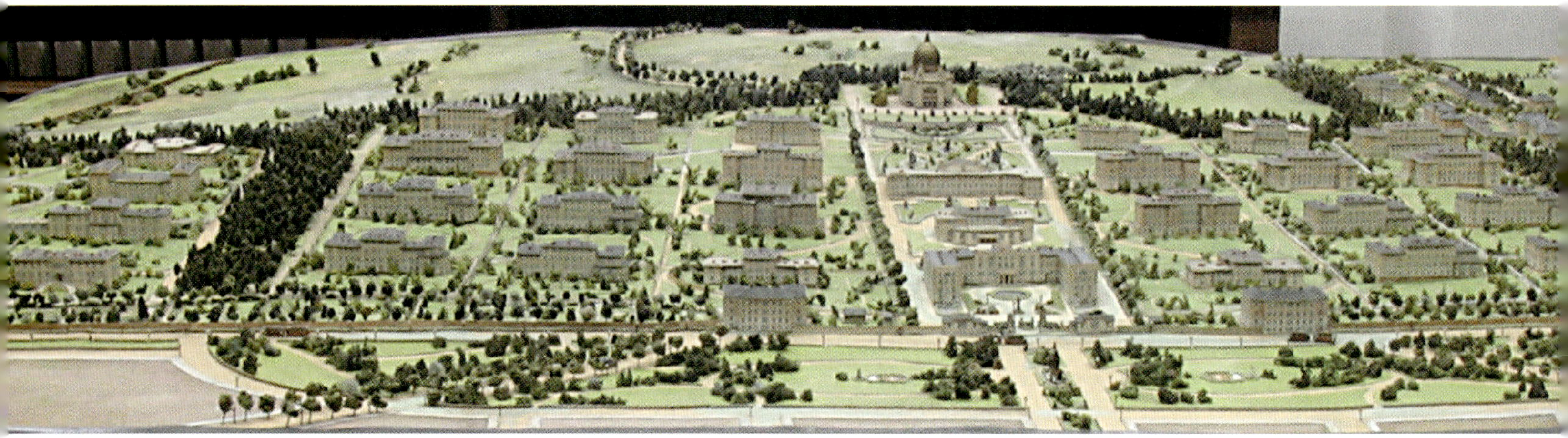

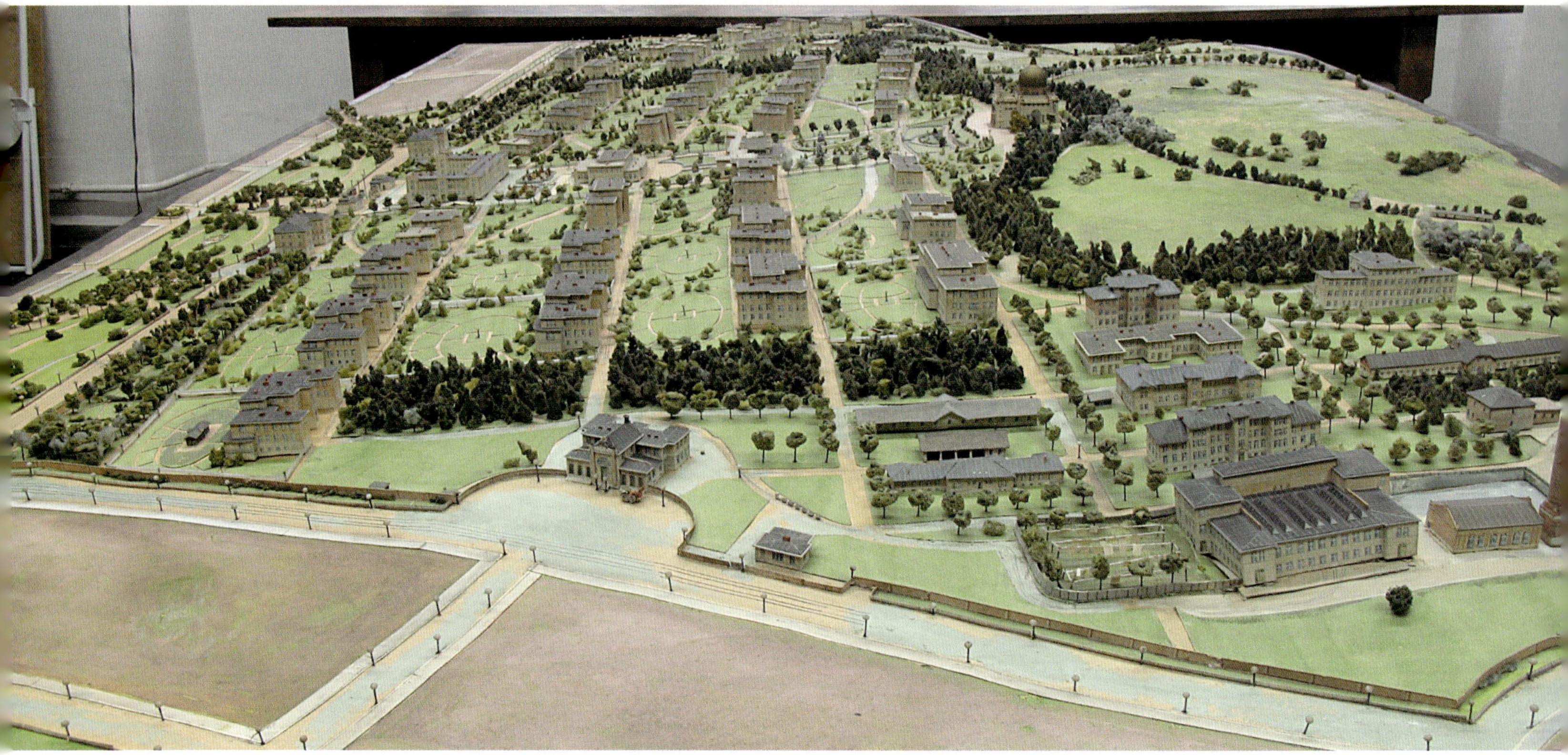

Chapter 6

Erwin Pendl (studio), Model of Lower Austrian Provincial Institution for the Cure and Care of the Mentally and Nervously Ill 'am Steinhof', c.1907

LESLIE TOPP

85, 86 Erwin Pendl (studio), Model of Lower Austrian Provincial Institution for the Cure and Care of the Mentally and Nervously Ill 'am Steinhof', scale 1:640, c.1907, 247 × 154 × 138 cm (97¼ × 60⅝ × 54⅜ in). Technisches Museum, Vienna. Photograph made during the restoration of the model, January 2009

The Lower Austrian Provincial Institution for the Cure and Care of the Mentally and Nervously Ill 'am Steinhof' was opened to great fanfare in October 1907. It occupied 143 hectares on a south-facing slope overlooking Vienna from the west and contained facilities for 2,000 patients, male and female, chronic and curable, affluent and destitute – an enormous number by the standards of any other psychiatric institution previously or since. The three sections of the institution are visible in the model, which was made not by the architect but by a professional model maker commissioned by the Lower Austrian government (figs 85, 86). In the centre, the main institution for acute and chronic patients consists of rows of patient pavilions – women on the left and men on the right – built on five terraces climbing the slope and divided by a central axis of service buildings. To the east, are the mortuary, farm buildings and the pavilion for dangerous patients. To the west, the so-called 'Sanatorium' complex, for fee-paying patients, is oriented away from the rest and built on more generous lines, but shares a common architectural vocabulary of flat roofs and simple, future-oriented volumes.

The asylum's spatial organisation – employing the 'villa system', where the institution was broken down into a complex of individual buildings arranged across extensive grounds – was presented as the epitome and perfection of the science of asylum planning (a sub-discipline of psychiatry in the late nineteenth and early twentieth century that worked towards the perfection of the ideal of the curative and well-managed asylum).[1] Psychiatric tenets were expressed in the language of self-consciously 'modern' architecture and planning, as advocated by leading modern architect of the day Otto Wagner, who himself was responsible for the asylum church and for the aesthetic handling of the institution's urban plan.[2] The rest of the buildings were designed in the same spirit by government-employed architects Carlo von Boog and Franz Berger. Each of the 60 individual buildings is carefully depicted in the model, knitted together by a network of paths and plantings and a range of security enclosures.

The model was part of an elaborate publicity campaign around the opening of Steinhof that focused on the attractive presentation of its modern buildings, frequently executed by Erwin Pendl as models or paintings. Pendl produced accurate depictions of contemporary and historical aspects of the Viennese built environment, often commissioned for publicity and/or educational purposes.[3] The precise impetus for commissioning the model is unknown; we know that before 1914, it was part of a collection of models of health and welfare institutions in Lower Austria that was located at Steinhof and, in 1915, was donated

87 Erwin Pendl, panoramic view of Steinhof Psychiatric Hospital, from N.-Ö. *Landes-Heil- und Pflegeanstalten für Geistes- und Nervenkranken 'Am Steinhof' in Wien*, (1907?) n.p.

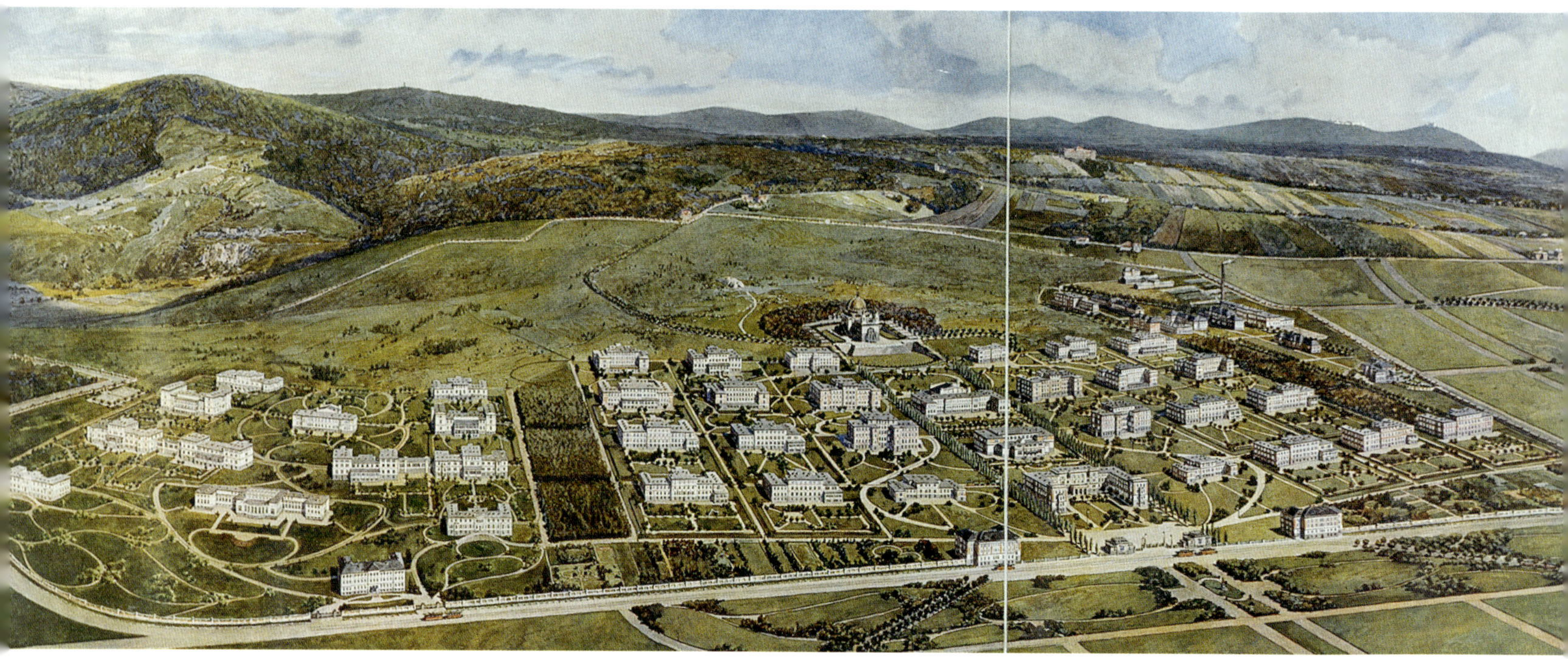

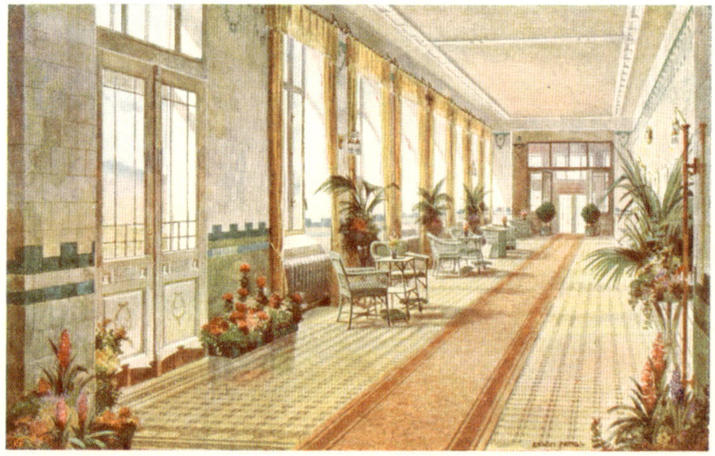

The Cure-house. Promenade.

37

88 Erwin Pendl, interior view of Steinhof Sanatorium Kurhaus, from *The Provincial Sanatorium of 'Steinhof' in Vienna (Austria) XIII. Prospectus* (Vienna: Province of Lower Austria, [1907?]), p. 37

to the Technical Museum in Vienna to form part of a display on the development of hospital architecture.[4] In addition to the model, Pendl produced a panoramic bird's eye view of the complex, in watercolour, for reproduction in a range of celebratory publications marking the opening (fig.87).[5] Pendl also painted a series of watercolour interior views used in advertisements for the Sanatorium complex, the part of the institution equipped with the latest therapeutic equipment and luxurious accommodation and facilities, images of which were meant to attract paying patients from across the Empire and around the world (fig.88).[6] In addition, he was responsible for three murals which can still be seen decorating the interior of Steinhof's theatre building.

The aspect of the complex that received the most attention in the non-medical press was Wagner's church, which formed the central aesthetic node of the complex and which is depicted in Pendl's model with more care and finish than any other building. Wagner used the opportunity presented by the commission to produce a design that both gestured towards traditional religious architecture (as a centrally planned domed structure) and overturned convention through the creation of a bright white interior, equipped with the latest hygienic fittings and furnishings, and offering a completely unobstructed view of the altar from all angles (fig.89). The church, which was used by patients and staff for Roman Catholic worship, was heavily publicised in the architectural press, and in Wagner's own publications, via a series of exquisite presentation drawings and graphically powerful plans (figs 90, 91, 92).[7]

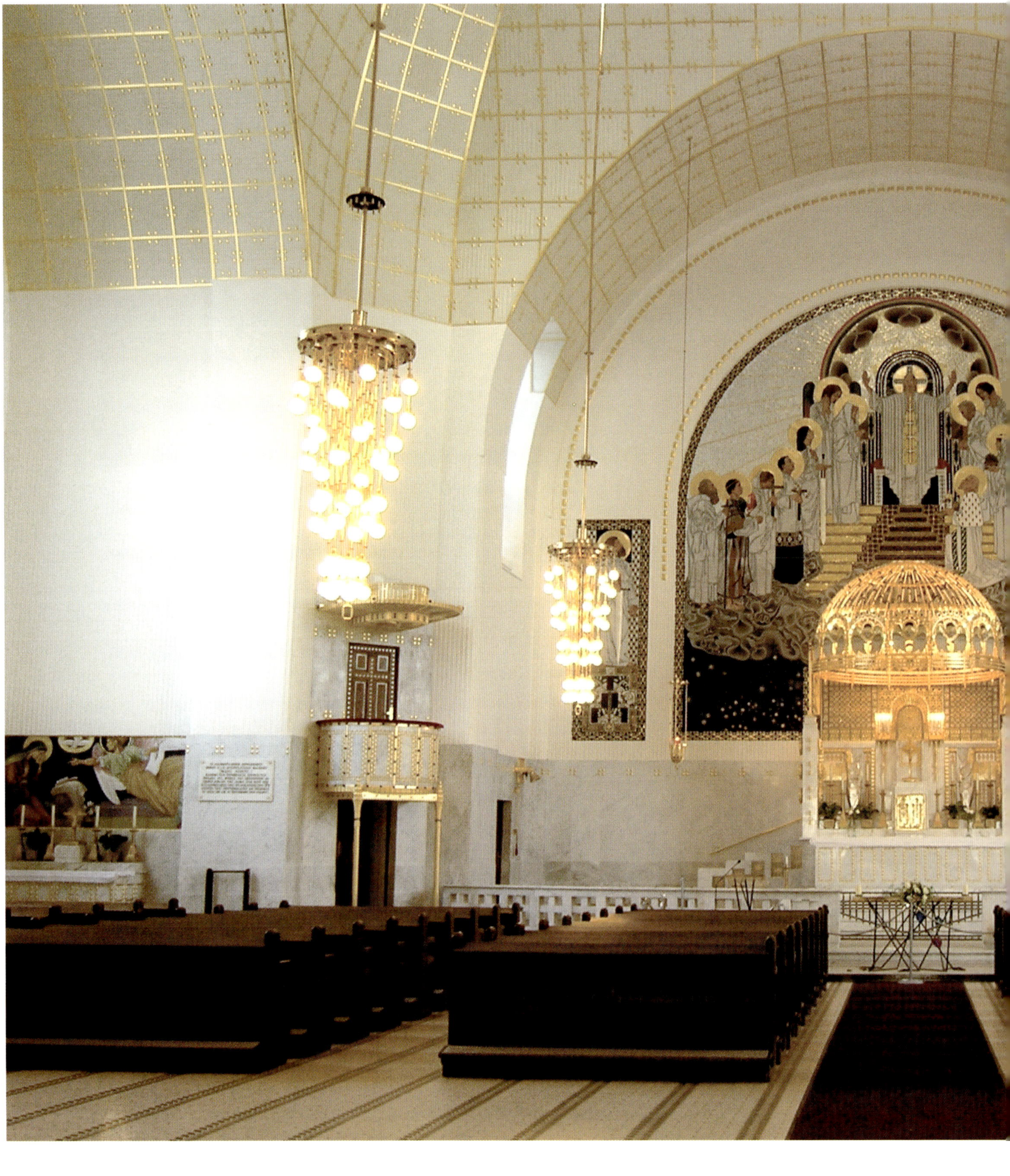

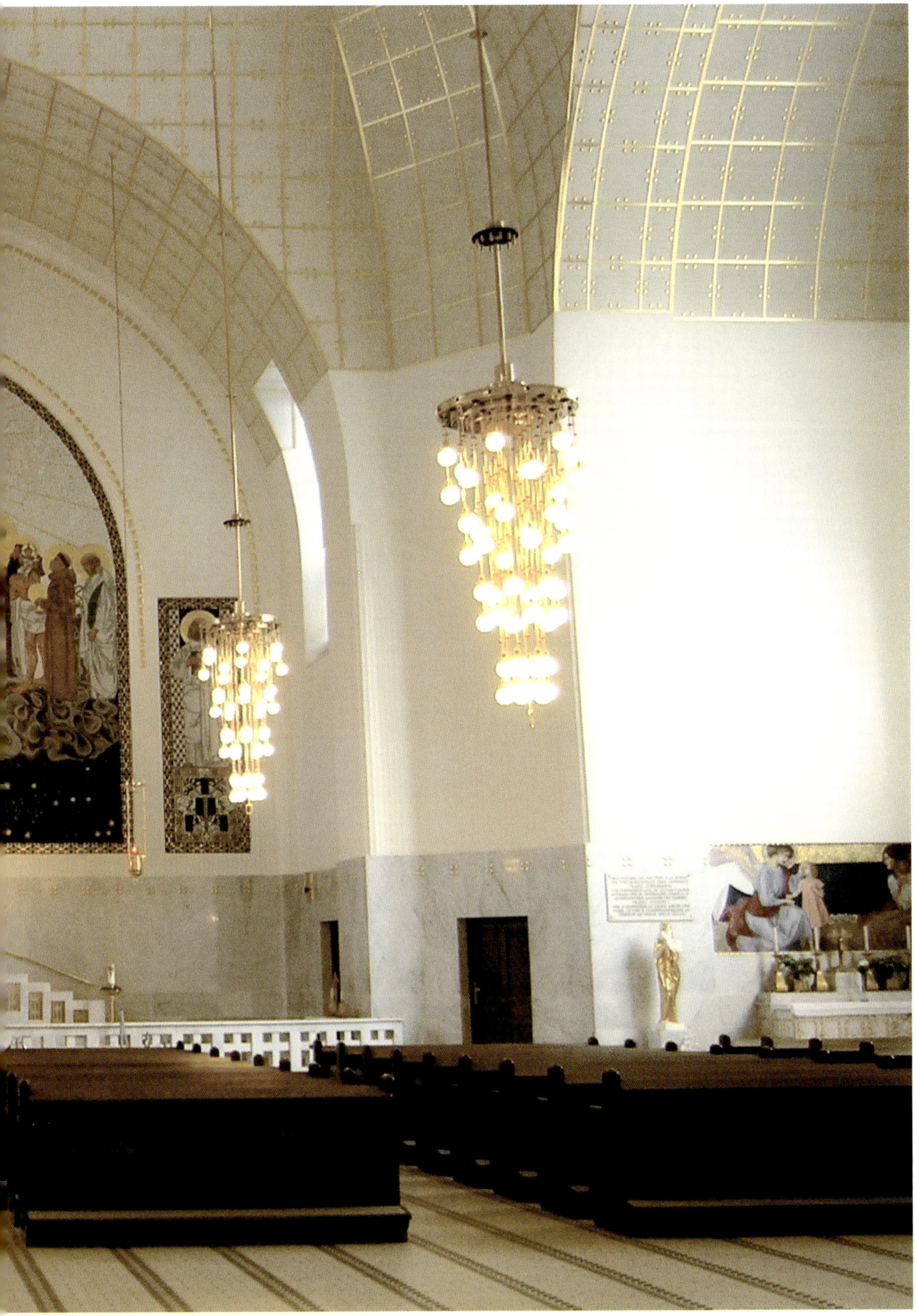

89 Otto Wagner, view of interior, St Leopold's Church, Steinhof Psychiatric Hospital, 1907

Overleaf:
90 Otto Wagner, St Leopold's Church, first design, colour section from N to S in front of altar, coloured pencil, ink, drawing paper on canvas, 55.7 × 48.3 cm (22 × 19 in). Wien Museum

91 Otto Wagner, St Leopold's Church, final design, side façade, pencil, ink, watercolour, drawing paper on card, 68 × 49.9 cm (26¾ × 19⅝ in). Wien Museum

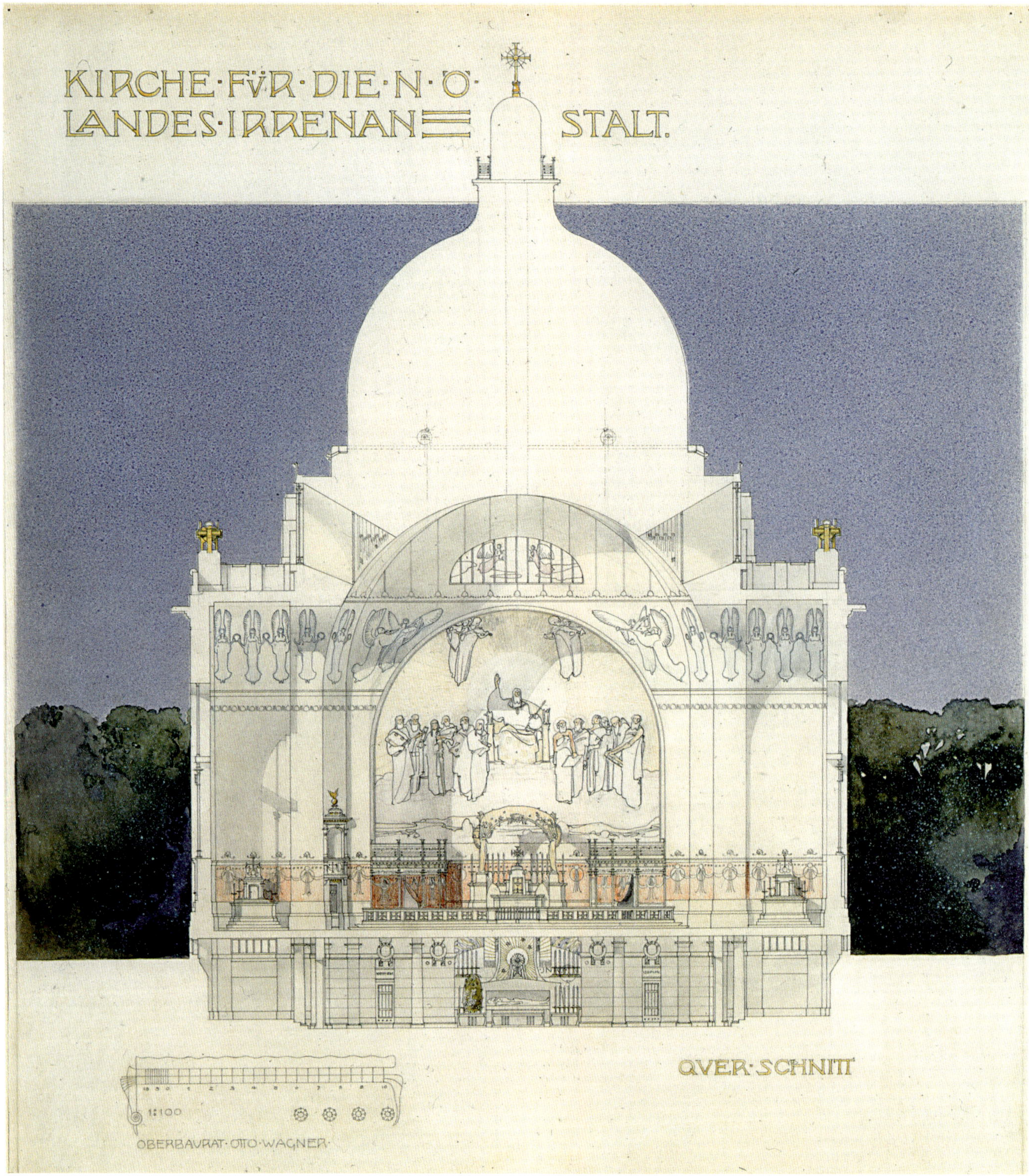
KIRCHE·FÜR·DIE·N·Ö·
LANDES·IRRENAN=STALT.
QVER·SCHNITT
1:100
OBERBAURAT·OTTO·WAGNER·

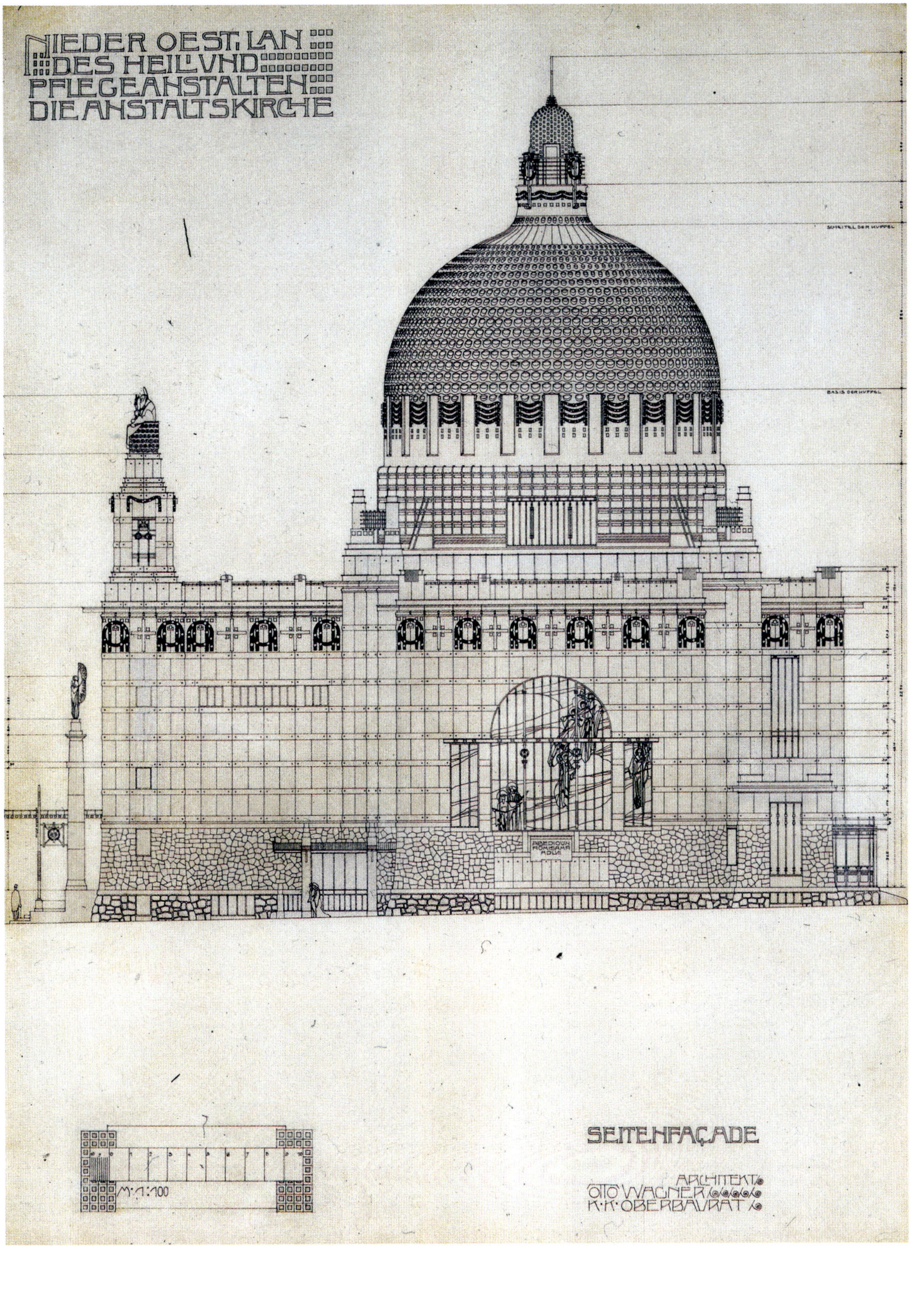
NIEDER OEST. LAN
DES HEIL- UND
PFLEGEANSTALTEN
DIE ANSTALTSKIRCHE
M: 1:100
SEITENFAÇADE
ARCHITEKT
OTTO WAGNER
K.K. OBERBAURAT

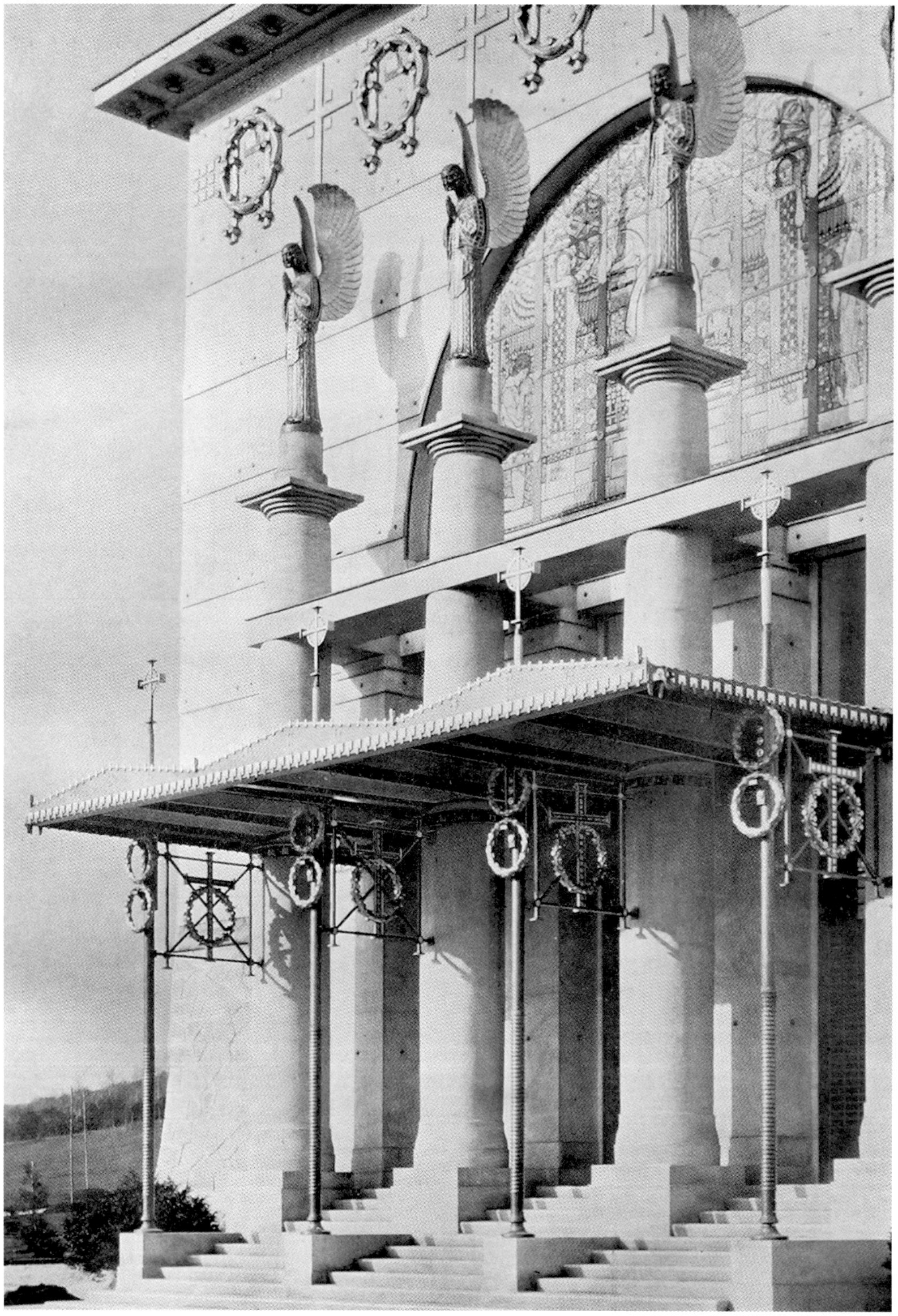

92 Otto Wagner, St Leopold's Church, view of main entrance portal published in *Der Architekt*, 14 (1908), p. 3

NOTES

1. See for example Johannes Bresler, 'Zur Eröffnung der Niederösterreichischen Landes – Heil – und Pflege-Anstalten für Geistes – und Nervenkranke "Am Steinhof" in Wien XIII', *Psychiatrisch-Neurologische Wochenschrift*, 9 (1907), pp 213–15.
2. See Leslie Topp, 'Otto Wagner and the Steinhof Psychiatric Hospital: Architecture as Misunderstanding', *Art Bulletin*, 87 (2005), pp 130–56.
3. Pendl (1875–1945) was well known as a painter of architecture and urban landscapes executing, for example, a bird's eye view of Vienna with Hugo Darnaut. 'Erwin August Pendl', in *Historisches Lexikon Wien*, (ed.) Felix Czeike (Vienna: Kremayr & Scheriau, 1995), iv, p. 514.
4. Technisches Museum Wien, archive, Folder XIV/55 BPA-014471.
5. For example, it formed the first plate of a massive commemorative volume consisting of floor plans and elevations for every building in the institution *N.-Ö.* Landes-Heil-und Pflegeanstalten für Geistes- und Nervenkranken 'Am Steinhof' in Wien, (1907?). There is no bibliographic information given on this volume other than the title. Copies exist in the Niederösterreichisches Landesarchiv and the Niederösterreichisches Landesbibliothek. Reproductions also appeared in 'Festnummer aus Anlass der Eröffnung der Niederösterreichischen Landes-Heil-u. Pflege-Anstalten für Geistes-und Nervenkranke "Am Steinhof" in Wien Am 8. Oktober 1907, *Psychiatrisch-Neurologische Wochenschrift*, 9 (1907), n.p. and printed on the invitation to the opening ceremonies on 8 October 1907 (National Archive of the Czech Republic, Prague, Zemsk? v?bor Praha –1874–1928, Karton 3196, Folder 2).
6. *The Provincial Sanatorium of "Steinhof" in Vienna (Austria) XIII. Prospectus*, (Vienna: Province of Lower Austria, [1907?]).
7. See Otto Wagner, *Sketches, Projects and Executed Buildings* (New York: Rizzoli, 1987), pp 172–80. Sets of presentation drawings and plans for two phases of the church design are in the Wien Museum in Vienna. For a full listing see Otto Antonia Graf, *Otto Wagner*, 7 vols., vol. 1, Das Werk des Architekten, 1860–1902, *Schriften des Instituts für Kunstgeschichte, Akademie der Bildenden Künste, Wien* (Vienna: Böhlau, 1985), i., pp 400–20.

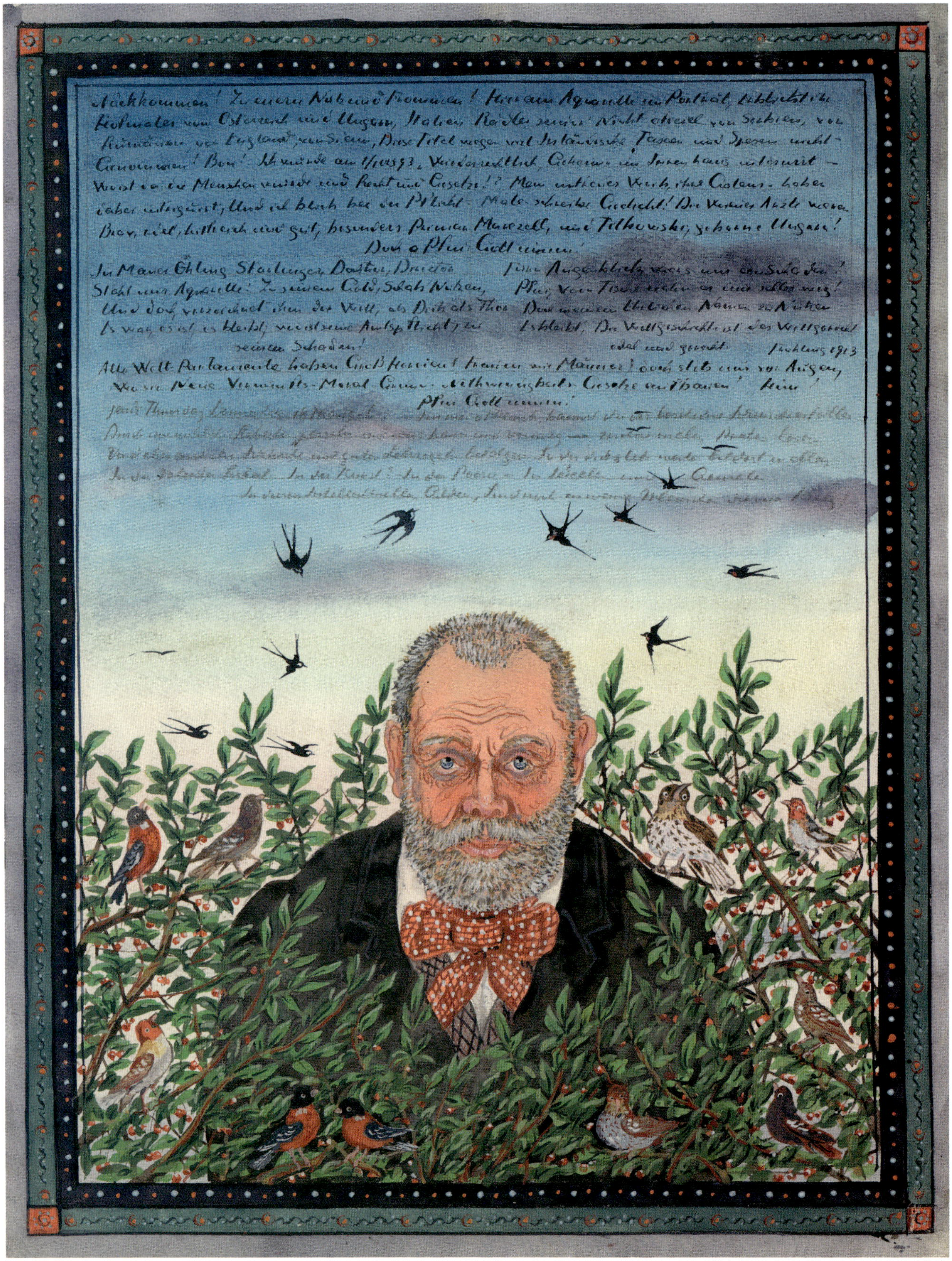

Chapter 7

Josef Karl Rädler, *Untitled* (Self-Portrait), 1913

LUKE HEIGHTON

93 Josef Karl Rädler, *Untitled* (Self-portrait), 1913, watercolour and gouache, with inscriptions, 39.5 × 29.8 cm (15½ × 11¾ in). Christian M. Nebehay Antiquariat & Kunsthandlung

Josef Karl Rädler's creative output – a vast collection of paintings, drawings and texts – was described as 'mannered', 'laboured', 'wooden', 'spiritless' and 'unctious' by doctors at the psychiatric hospital Mauer-Öhling and seen as 'further evidence of the patient's delusional megalomania'.[1] Rädler's work was first made available to the Austrian public in 1994, having been 'discovered' roughly 40 years previously, when more than 400 of his paintings, drawings and writings were found by a nurse in a heap of rubbish at what was then known as the Psychiatrische Krankenhaus Mauer.[2]

Rädler was born in Falkenau, Bohemia in 1844. A master porcelain painter, he came to Vienna when he was 23, where he married and had four children. On 1 October 1893, at the age of 40, he was hospitalised at the behest of his family, who could no longer cope with his severe mood swings. He spent three months in a private institution for the mentally ill at Lainz, before being transferred to the public Vienna psychiatric hospital at Pilgerhain.[3] Diagnosed as suffering from 'circular psychosis with manic tendencies', epilepsy and 'secondary dementia'[4] – akin to what is today known as schizophrenia –

he lived at the psychiatric hospital Mauer-Öhling from 11 August 1905 until his death, at the age of 74, on 13 November 1917.[5]

Rädler began to paint whilst he was a patient at Pilgerhain. There his subject matter comprised mainly pictures of other patients (fig.94), of the institution, of birds, and of views through the trees across the roof-tops of the town, into the corners of which he occasionally incorporated small self-portraits. He worked on paper, using a mixture of quills, pencils, brushes and watercolours. His smallest works were roughly the size of a postcard, his largest 30 × 40 cm. At Mauer-Öhling a far greater range of images found their way into his work. In addition to portrait studies, group scenes, social gatherings and events, he captured images from the daily workings of the hospital; the workshop, the bath-house, the dayroom and the dormitory (fig.95). Although he did not give them titles, Rädler signed and dated almost all of his work, either as 'J. K. Rädler' or as 'The Laughing Philosopher'. In the latter, Rädler alludes sardonically to the profound lack of status he was afforded as a psychiatric patient, permanently removed from society. In his self-portrait of 1913, Rädler depicts himself in a polka dot bow-tie, framed by a tangle of plant life dense with birds (fig.93). The work incorporates all of those basic elements which characterise Rädler's oeuvre as a whole: portraiture, flora and fauna, textual explication and decoration. Taken together, these elements not only serve to give the painting added depth, but also provide us with clues as to Rädler's reflexive attitude towards his own art-making practice.

Throughout his confinement Rädler was permitted, perhaps even encouraged to paint. This was primarily because it kept him out of trouble. Doctors' reports described him as prone to being 'difficult', manic, with a habit of haranguing other patients, or loudly delivering philosophical lectures (some of which may be documented in the works themselves), unless given other means by which to occupy himself. He was equally given to periods of profound depression, feelings of isolation and of despair. At the same time, Rädler may have seen his art as a means to reach out to and interact with others through the prism of his own experience. Other patients are, after all, one of his principal subjects (fig.96). If he does exhibit a tendency towards self-aggrandisement, this is countered by the picture of himself he presents: a tired, deeply unhappy, sympathetic-looking old man (fig.93). But as the Laughing Philosopher, Rädler mocks this image, too, undermining not only his own pretensions but those of his contemporaries, the medical

94 Rädler,
Untitled (Portrait of a man),
1902, watercolour and gouache,
35.4 × 25.3 cm (14 × 10 in).
Christian M. Nebehay
Antiquariat & Kunsthandlung

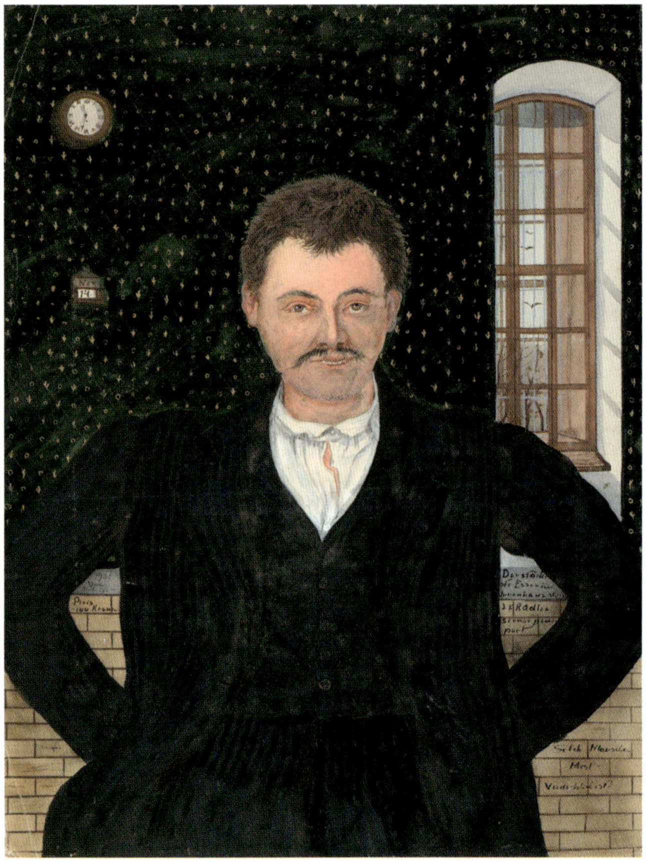

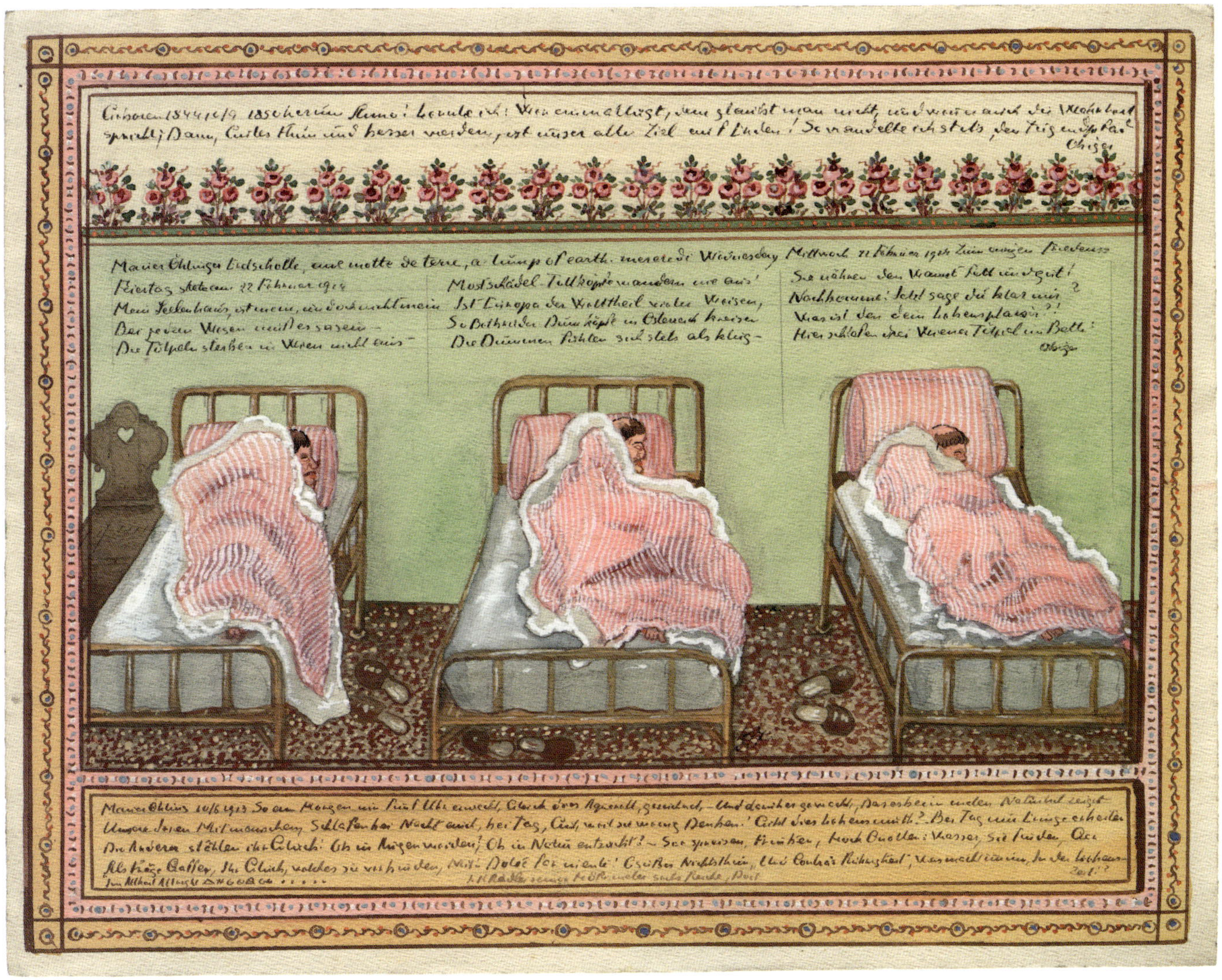

95 Rädler, *Untitled* (In the dormitory), 1913, watercolour and gouache, with inscriptions, 25.7 × 31.8 cm (10⅛ × 12½ in). Christian M. Nebehay Antiquariat & Kunsthandlung

profession, and of the world beyond the asylum's walls. Showing the artist gazing out enigmatically at the viewer from beneath a halo of swallows – traditionally a symbol of hope and resurrection – Rädler's self-portrait is a testament to his recognition of reality, and the reality of his circumstances. In attempting to describe and to understand the limits to which he was subject through art, however, he discovered a means by which those limits might also, momentarily, be overcome.

Highly colourful, often featuring some kind of floral motif, it seems likely that Rädler's visual compositional style was heavily influenced by his previous career as a porcelain painter. He plays with the geometry of the painted surface itself, integrating abstract geometric and perspectival elements into his graphic work, allowing the viewer either to comprehend more than one scene simultaneously, or breaking a scene up into its

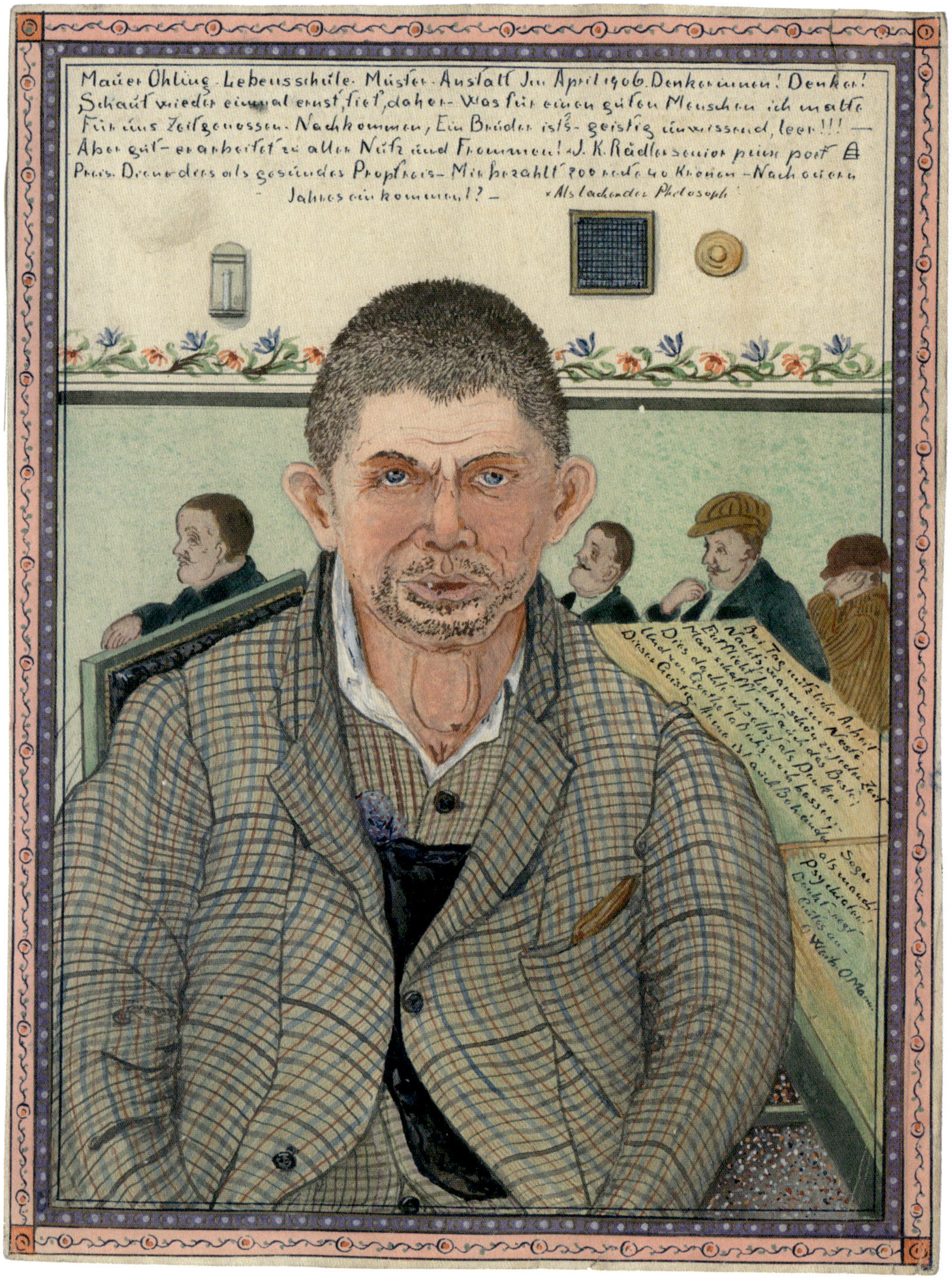

96 Rädler,
Untitled (Portrait of a man),
1906, watercolour and
gouache, with inscriptions,
31.2 × 23.4 cm
(12⅜ × 9¼ in).
Christian M. Nebehay
Antiquariat & Kunsthandlung

Opposite:
97 Rädler,
Untitled (Group portrait),
1905, watercolour and
gouache, with inscriptions,
31.3 × 23.6 cm
(12⅜ × 9¼ in).
Christian M. Nebehay
Antiquariat & Kunsthandlung

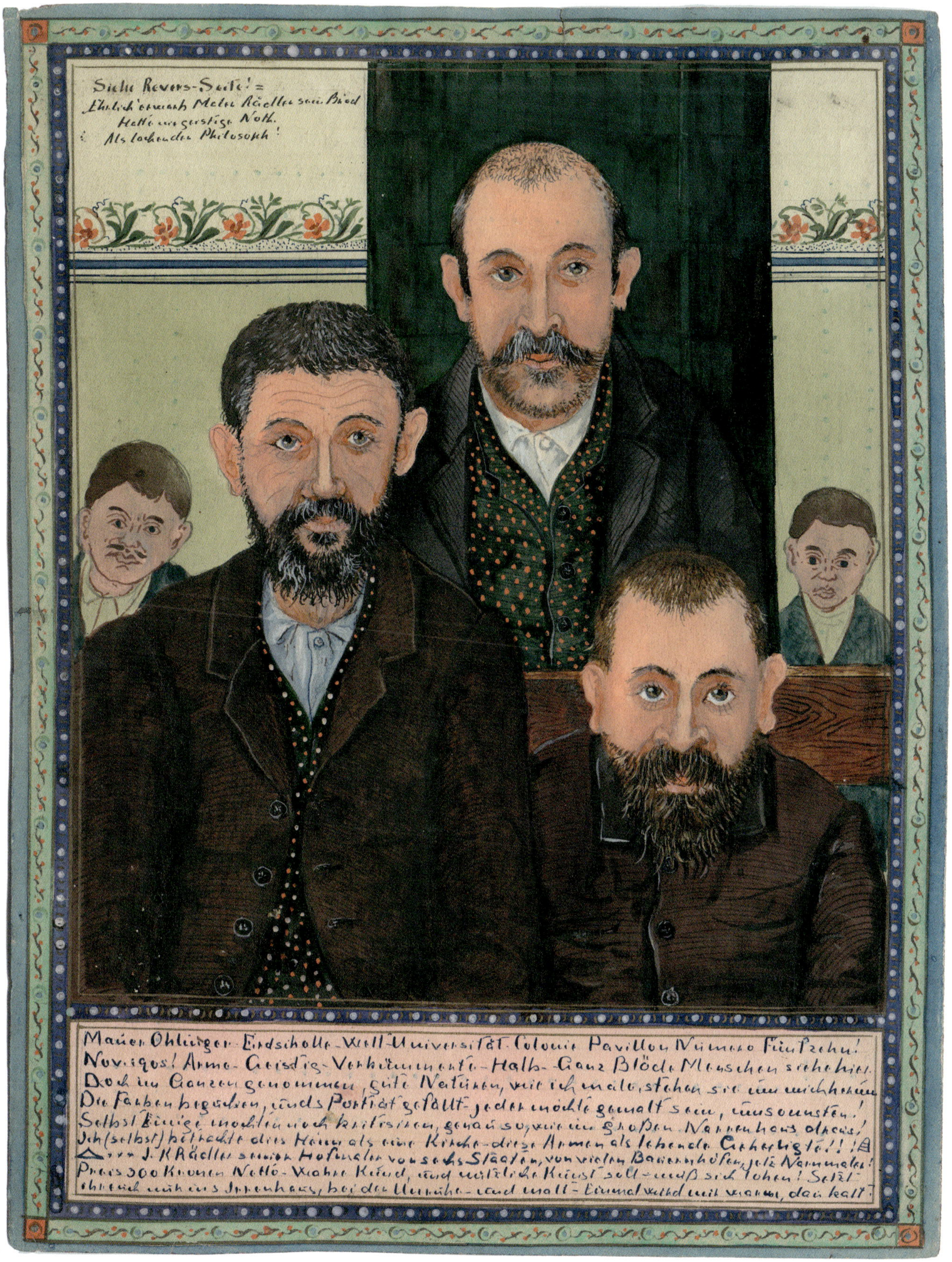
Siehe Revers-Seite! =
Ehrlich erwarb Maler Rädler sein Brod
Hatte nie geistige Noth.
Als lachender Philosoph!
Mauer Öhlinger Erdscholle-Welt-Universität-Colonie Pavillon Nummero Fünfzehn!
Novigos! Arme-Geistig-Verkümmerte-Halb-Ganz Blöde Menschen sieh hier.
Doch im Ganzen genommen, gute Naturen, wie ich male, stehen sie um mich herum
Die Farben begeistern, und's Portrait gefällt-jeder möchte gemalt sein, umsonsten!
Selbst Einige möchten noch kritisieren, genau so, wie im großen Narrenhaus draus!
Ich (selbst) betrachte dies Heim als eine Kirche-diese Armen als lebende Geheiligte!!
J. K. Rädler Hofmaler von sechs Staaten, von vielen Bauernhöfen, jetz Narrenmaler!
Preis 300 Kronen Netto-Wahre Kunst, und natürliche Kunst soll-muß sich lohnen!

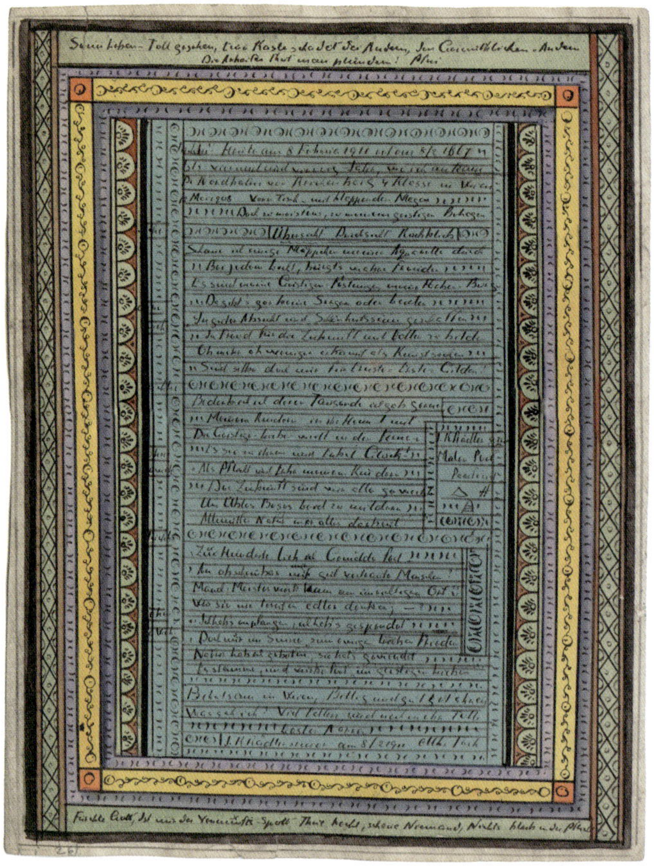

98 Rädler, *Untitled* (Verso of fig. 96), dated 1908, 1911, watercolour and gouache, with inscriptions, 31.2 × 23.4 cm ($12\frac{3}{8} \times 9\frac{1}{4}$ in). Christian M. Nebehay Antiquariat & Kunsthandlung

constituent parts (fig.97). His use of text, intricate networks of symbols and decoration is most pronounced in what are usually (not necessarily correctly) referred to as the works on the 'reverse' side of the paper (fig.98). These are sometimes legible, sometimes not. Often they take the form of a description, poem, essay, stream of consciousness, or extended wordplay. Snippets of personal biography appear alongside a range of recurring themes, notably Rädler's pacifist convictions, his identification with the figures of Schiller and Goethe, and his imaginary travels across the globe.

Contrary to the romantic image of the mad painter, Rädler's style and choice of subject matter might appear somewhat restricted, not to say disappointingly conservative or kitsch. Yet this says more about our own expectations of the art of the mentally ill, than it does about the art of Rädler. Far from exhibiting a 'pathological' or 'naive' fixation with a limited range of themes and images, Rädler employs them as the basis for his experiments with the medium of painting. We see this most clearly in the portraits he completed at Mauer-Öhling, where he regularly employs the device of a painted frame within the frame of the paper, singling out his subject, separating him or her from the work at the same time as he or she becomes the work; a comment, perhaps, on the artificiality, the subjectivism, the *irrationality* of the creative act.

NOTES

1. As quoted in Leo Navratil, *Josef Karl Rädler* (1844–1917), (Vienna: Niederösterreichisches Landesmuseum, 1994), p. 16, my translation. Navratil's book is the standard work on Rädler. See also Luke Heighton, 'Exhibiting Madness, Art and the Asylum: The Creation and Exhibition of Images by Psychiatric Hospital Patients in Vienna, 1890–1914' (unpublished doctoral thesis, University of London, Birkbeck College, 2008).
2. Navratil, pp 13–25.
3. Navratil, p. 13.
4. Navratil, p. 13.
5. Navratil, p. 13.

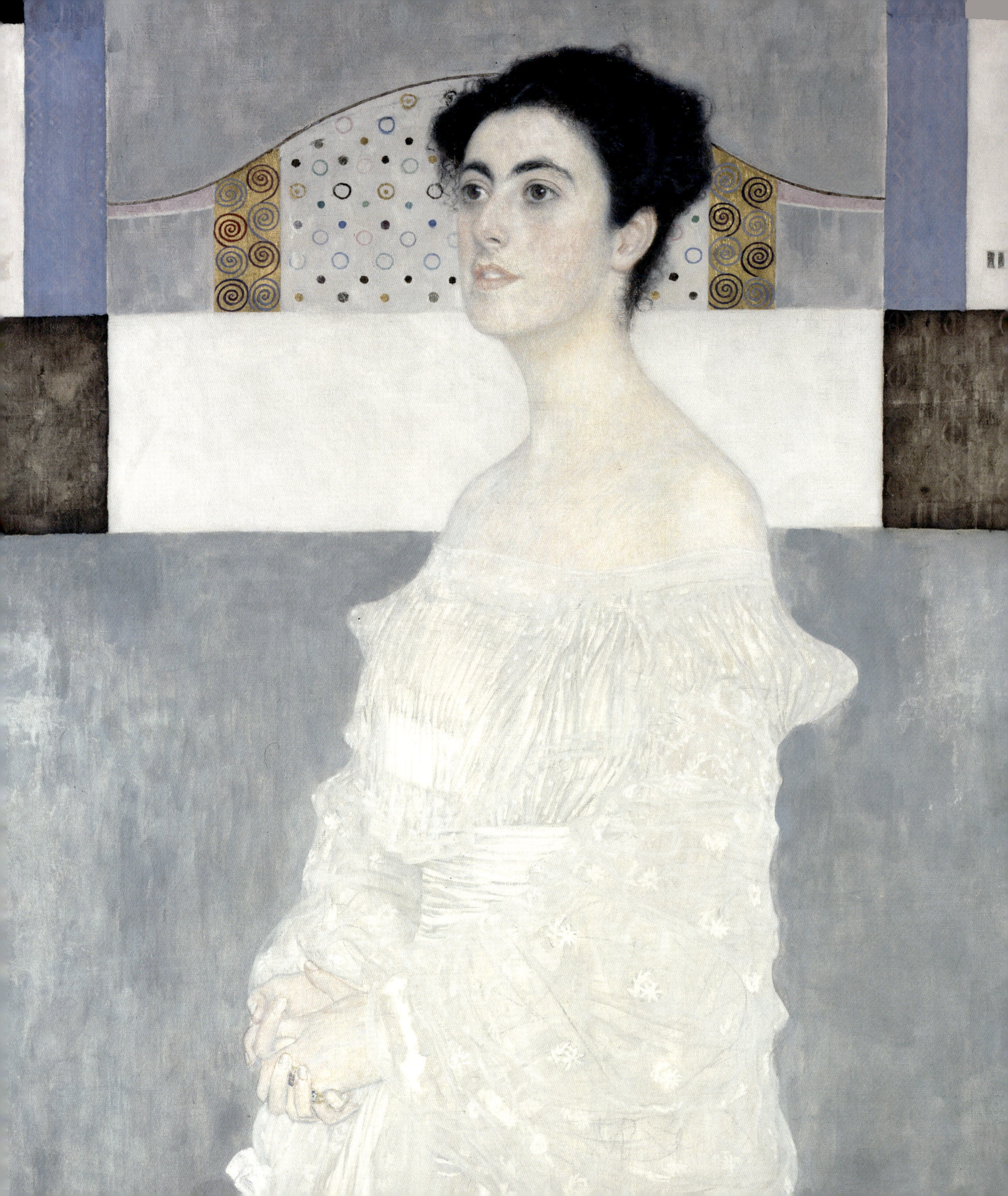

Chapter 8

The Allure of Nerves: Class, gender and neurasthenia in Klimt's society portraits

SABINE WIEBER

110 Gustav Klimt, *Margarethe Stonborough-Wittgenstein*, 1905, oil on canvas, 179.8 × 90.5 cm (70¾ × 35⅝ in). Bayerische Staatsgemäldesammlung, Neue Pinakothe, Munich 13074

In 1903, the Vienna Secession devoted its Eighteenth Exhibition to the work of Gustav Klimt (fig.99) and for two months (November–December) 48 of his paintings and 30 drawings were showcased in a modernist exhibition space designed by Josef Hoffmann and Koloman Moser (fig.100). Though famed for the display of Klimt's controversial *Faculty Paintings*, the exhibition also featured important examples of Klimt's portraits. These images of Vienna's leading society women take centre stage in this chapter. Klimt's society portraits have always played an important role in the artist's critical reception. In 2006 they entered the public imagination in spectacular ways when his *Adele Bloch-Bauer I* (fig.101) sold to the Neue Galerie in New York and Raoul Ruiz' biopic *Klimt* aired in cinemas across Europe and North America.[1] Art historians have traditionally divided Klimt's portraiture into three distinct phases – impressionistic (1898–1903), golden (1903–12) and ornamental (1912–18) – and been challenged by a certain sense of disjuncture, or *Doppelgleisigkeit*, in their interpretation.[2] Some have read Klimt's increasing use of ornament and abstraction as a visual retreat from the social, political and cultural realities of the

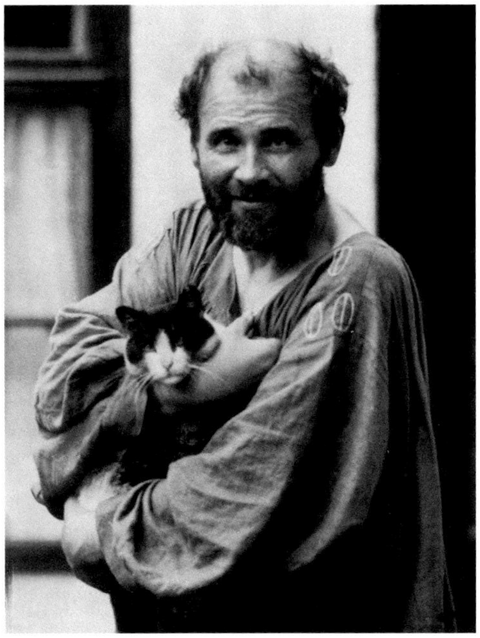

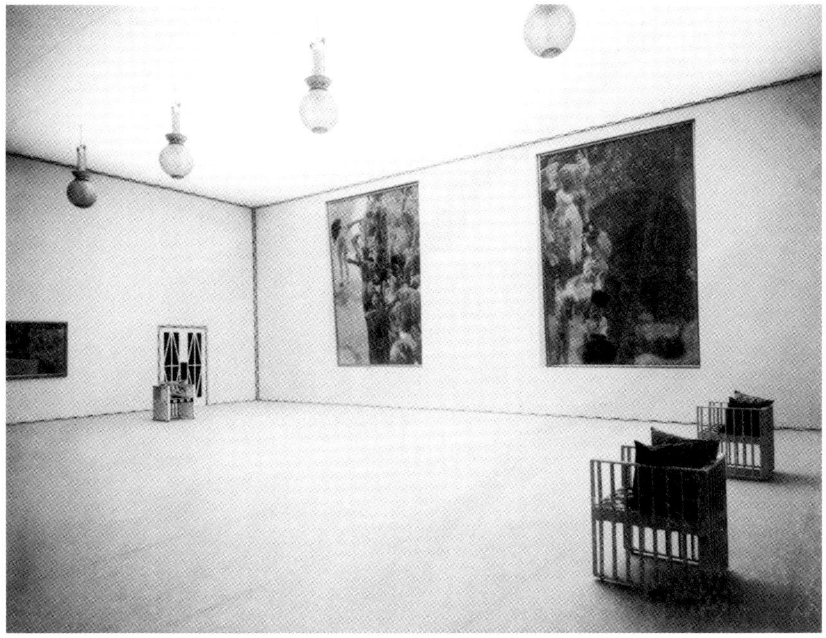

Habsburg Empire, while others propose that 'Klimt's ornate and suspended world view actually entered into a happy complicity with the current political trends of whitewashing social ills with an aesthetic façade akin to the Potemkinesque City'.[3] Without discarding either of these interpretative frameworks, this chapter offers a different approach to Klimt's early society portraits that (re)-connects the painter and his sitters to contemporary cultures and discourses of nerves within which these magnificent paintings emerged and conjured up meaning for producers and consumers of the progressive visual arts in Vienna 1900. This reintroduction of nerves and neurasthenia into the discussion of Klimt's Damenportraits also hopes to broaden the scope of Vienna 1900 studies which tend to focus on Sigmund Freud's psychoanalysis, hysteria and the mind.

Klimt's portrait section at the 1903 retrospective featured five important early portraits: *Sonja Knips* (1898), *Maria Henneberg* (1901–02), *Gertha Felsöványi* (1902), *Hermine Gallia* (1903–04) and a recent portrait of his lifelong companion *Emilie Flöge* (figs102–6). With the exception of Flöge, Klimt's sitters were members of Vienna's new urban financial elite, or *Geldadel*, characterised by their progressive artistic taste and keen desire to support avant-garde artists, architects and designers.[4] Christian Brandstätter saw Klimt as the 'court painter of a new social stratum … [populated by] upper middle-class ladies (mostly Jewish) of the turn-of-the-century, hyper-sensible, worldly and nervous …'.[5] From the moment Klimt's *Damenportraits* were first exhibited, Jewishness and nervousness were linked by critics and art historians alike. And yet, Tobias Natter shows that although Klimt's patrons often came from Jewish backgrounds, they (or their parents) had either converted to Christianity or assimilated.[6] This observation is borne out in three out of four

Above left:
99 Moritz Nähr, *Gustav Klimt in the Garden of his Studio*, 1912

Above right:
100 Koloman Moser, *Main Hall of the Eighteenth Secession Exhibition*, 1903

Opposite:
101 Gustav Klimt, *Adele Bloch-Bauer I*, 1907, oil, silver and gold on canvas, 138 × 138 cm (54⅜ × 54⅜ in). Neue Galerie, New York. This acquisition was made available in part through the generosity of the heirs of the Estates of Ferdinand and Adele Bloch-Bauer

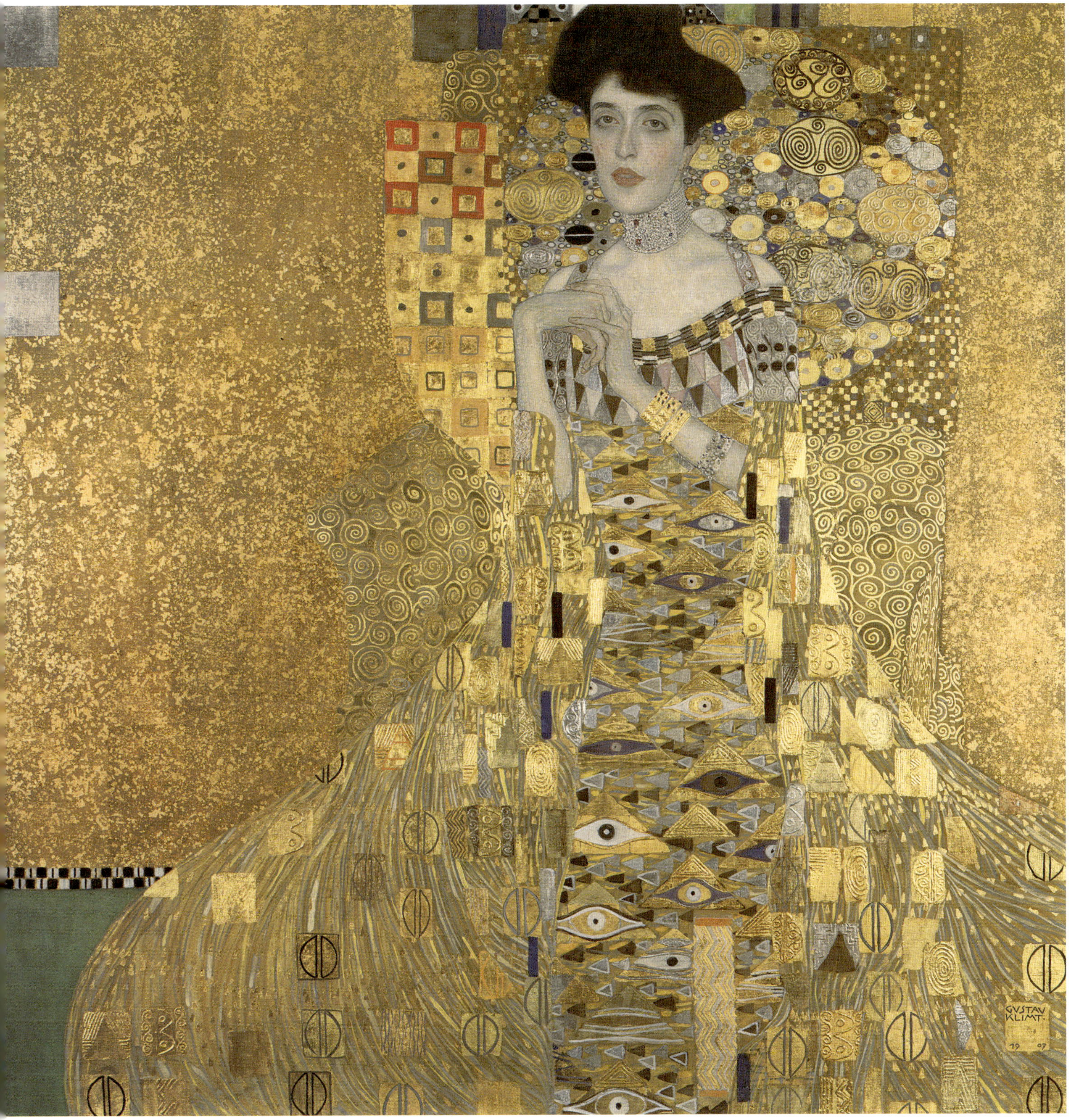
GUSTAV
KLIMT.
19 07

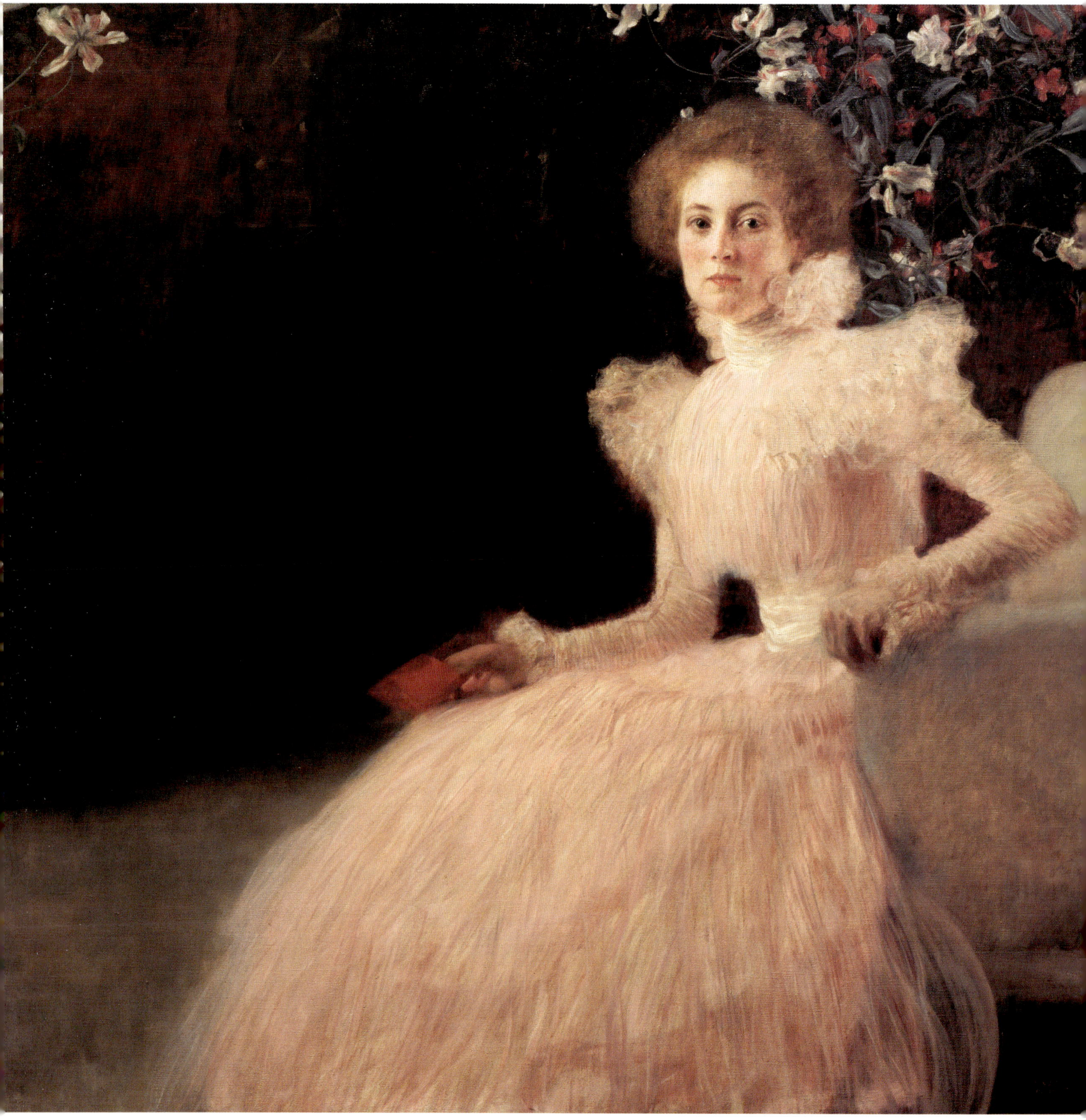

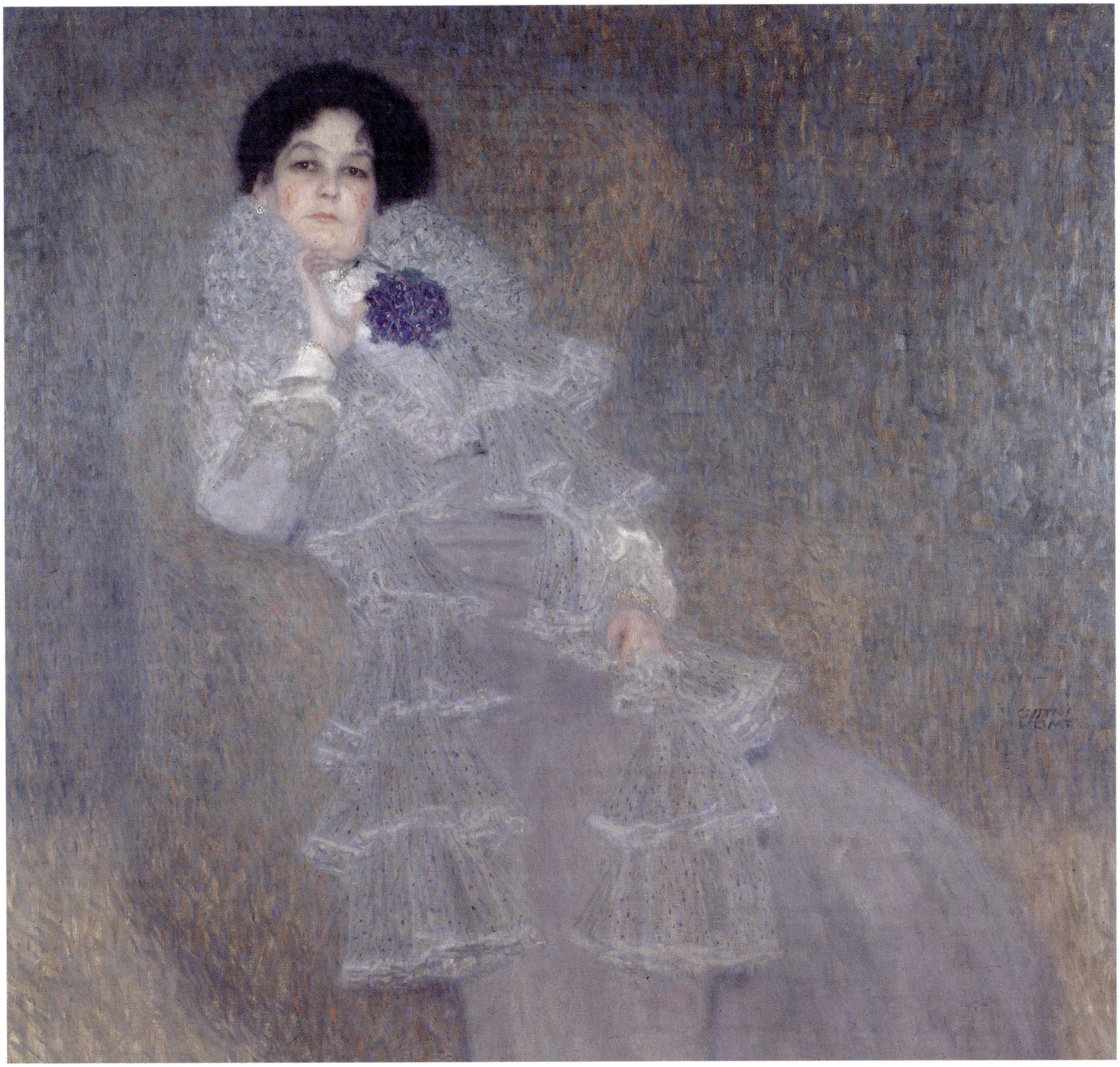

Opposite:
102 Gustav Klimt,
Sonja Knips, 1898, oil on canvas,
145 × 145 cm (57⅛ × 57⅛ in).
Belvedere, Vienna

103 Gustav Klimt,
Maria Henneberg, 1901–02,
oil on canvas,
140 × 140 cm (55⅛ × 55⅛ in).
Staatliche Galerie Moritzburg,
Landeskunstmuseum Sachsen-Anhalt

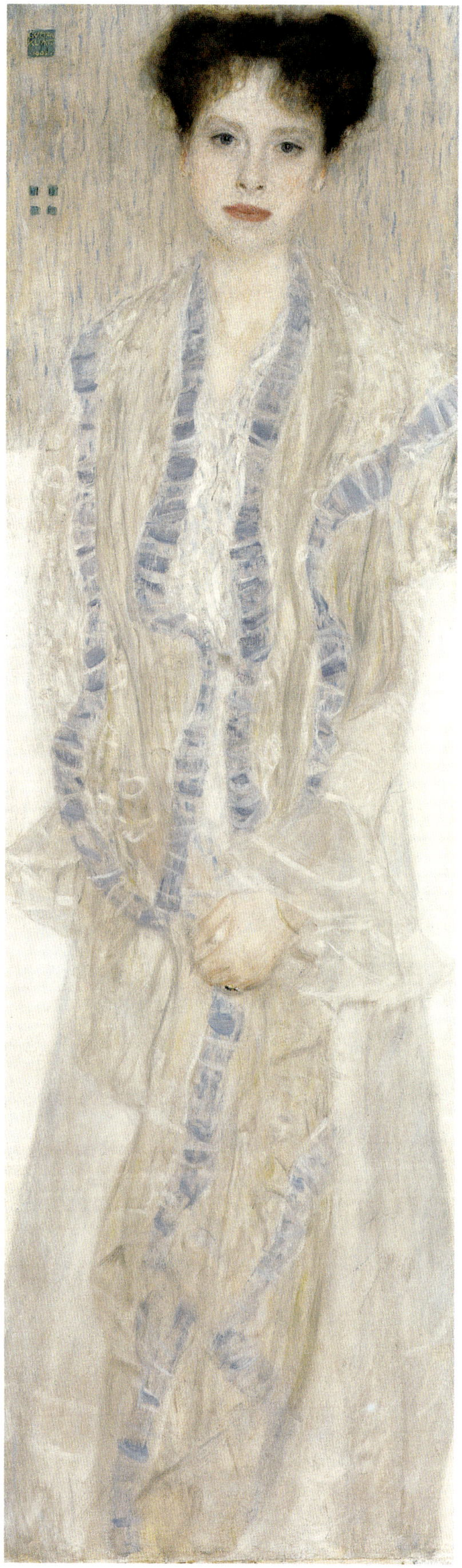

104 Gustav Klimt, *Gertha Felsövànyi* (Gertrud Low), 1902, oil on canvas, 150 × 45.5 cm (59 × 18 in). Private Collection

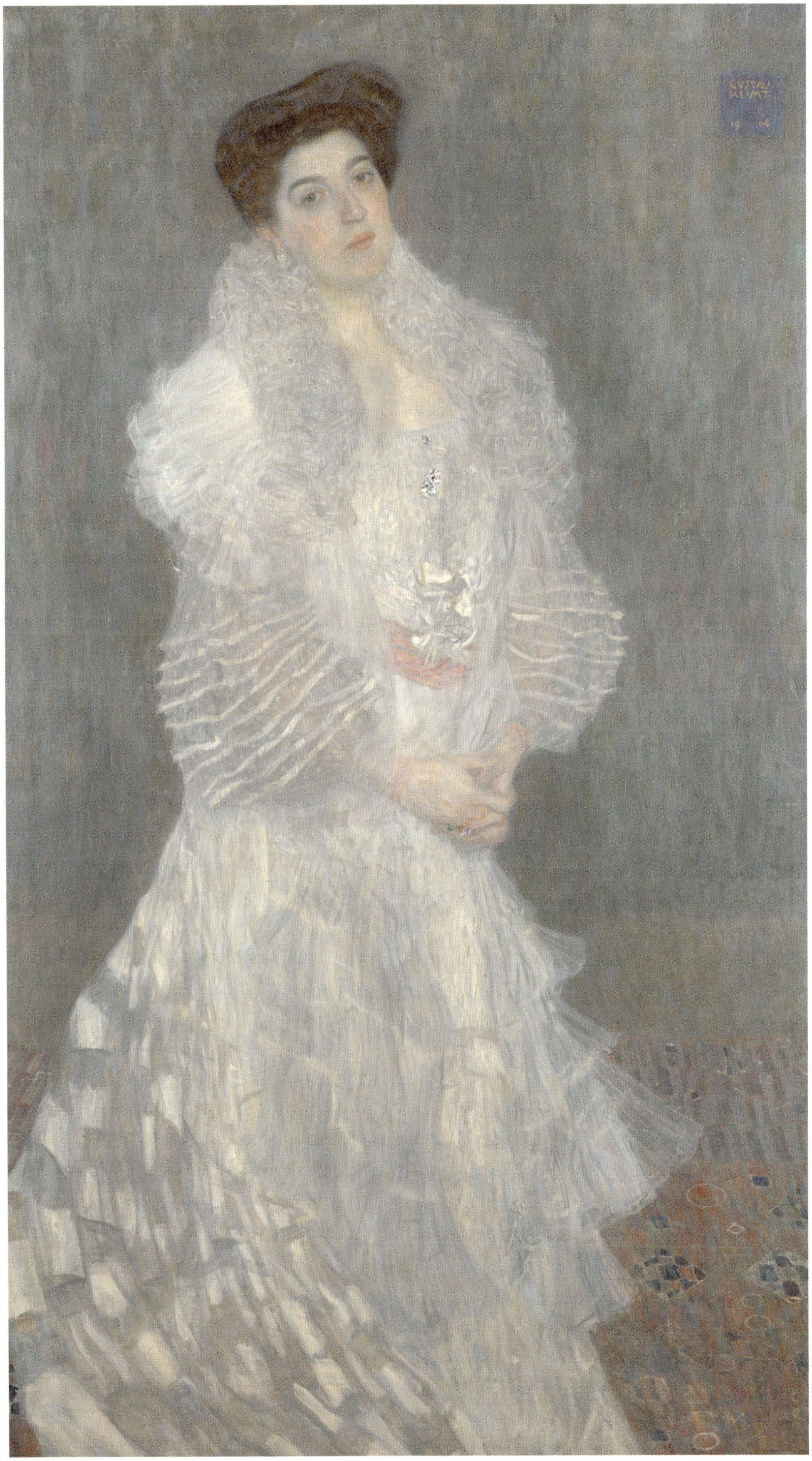

105 Gustav Klimt,
Hermine Gallia, 1903–4,
oil on canvas,
170 × 96 cm (67 × 37⅞ in).
The National Gallery, London

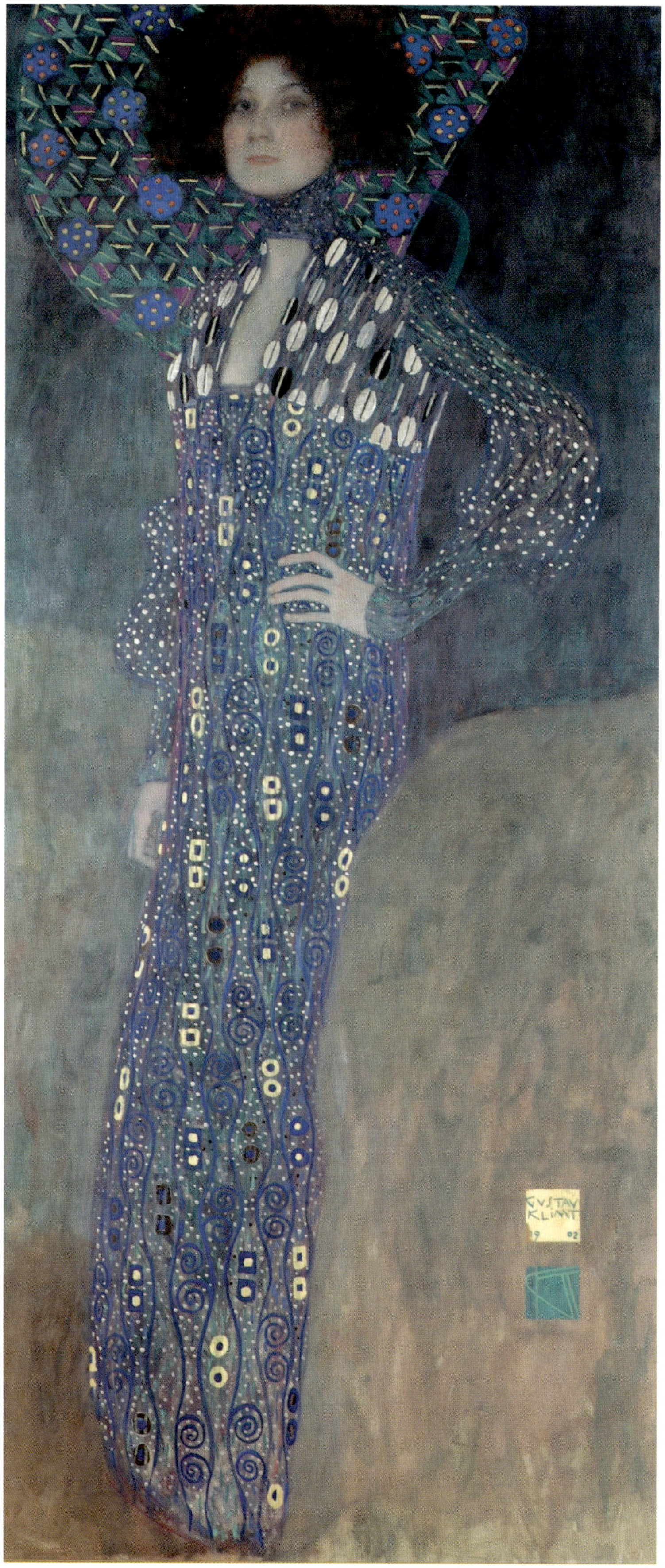

106 Gustav Klimt,
Emilie Flöge, 1902, oil on canvas,
181 × 84 cm (71 × 33 in).
Wien Museum

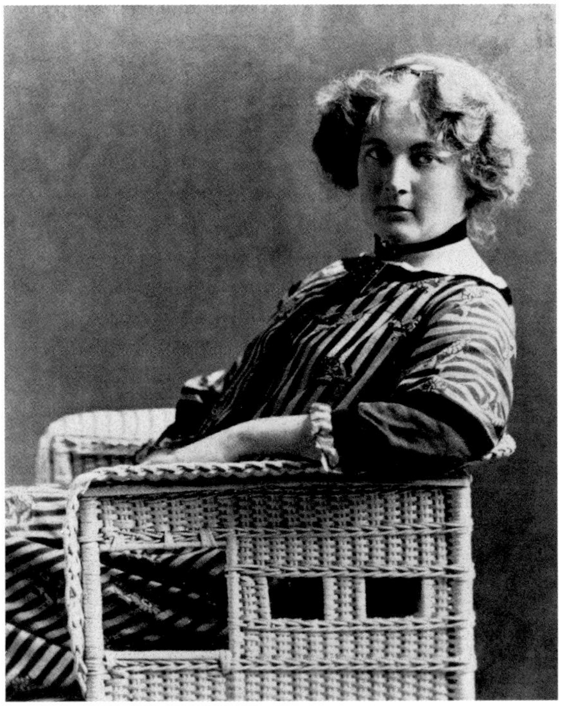

107 Sonja Knips in a Wiener Werkstätte dress designed by Eduard Josef Wimmer-Wisgrill, photographed c.1911

of Klimt's exhibited society portraits: Sonja Knips was Catholic, Maria Henneberg was Catholic but married her husband in a Protestant ceremony and Gertha Felsövänyi came from a family of assimilated Jews, which left Hermine Gallia as Klimt's only identifiably Jewish sitter.

Sonja Knips (figs102, 107) was Vienna's first society lady to sit for Klimt in 1898 and the painting clearly marked Klimt's transition from historicist academician to modern painter. She came from an aristocratic family, but married the industrialist Anton Knips in 1896. Throughout her life, Knips patronised the Flöge Sisters' Fashion House and the Wiener Werkstätte whose designers refurbished several of her domiciles.[7] In Klimt's portrait, Knips sits on the edge of an upholstered armchair, which is only vaguely indicated by soft brushwork and cut off by the frame of the painting. The setting is purposely ambiguous and much of the physical space around Knips disappears into Klimt's painterly brushstroke and dark palette. In her right hand, she holds a small red book, which has since been identified as one of Klimt's sketchbooks,[8] and with her left hand, she grasps the chair's arm-rest as if startled from her seat. Her direct gaze at the viewer emanates from a naturalistically painted, calm face which stands in a strange tension to the nervous energy conveyed by her posture and the pulsating ruffles, lines and fabric of her dress. When Berta Zuckerkandl, an ardent Secession supporter, renowned Salonnière, and astute correspondent for the *Wiener Allgemeine Zeitung*, first saw *Sonja Knips* exhibited at the Second Secession Exhibition in 1898, she considered her the 'sublimate extract of the modern woman'.[9] Vienna's progressive art critic, Ludwig Hevesi, also saw Klimt's portrait at this exhibition and pointed out that 'one should also pay attention to the rippling pink of the seated lady, his first portrait in this consciously modern [*neumodischen*] manner'.[10]

What makes Klimt's early society portraits such as *Sonja Knips* 'consciously modern' is further clarified in Hevesi's extended review of Klimt's portraits in the *Klimt Kollektive* of 1903, in which he wrote:

> ...He [Klimt] finds ever-new freedoms in his Damenportraits, each of which has a different colour-motif and is painted in a hand of changing moods. One should pay attention to the nervous, pronounced character of the woman in black which was painted several years ago in contrast to the very young white *Fräulein* [Felsövänyi] from this year, who appears airy with four pale-violet silk ribbons along her fragrant, wrinkled dress...[11]

Hevesi's poetic description of *Gertha Felsövanyi* tried to capture the physical and psychological delicacy, if not fragility, of Klimt's subject.[12] For Hevesi, as for Zuckerkandl,

Klimt's subtle painterly engagement with the psychological make-up of his sitter makes him a modern painter. This linkage of Klimt's early society portraits to psychology, nerves and delicate physiologies – both in terms of subject matter and mode of representation – pervaded Klimt's contemporary reception. Progressive critics considered these portraits utterly modern because, in their eyes, they were psychologically charged, allowing viewers to see and feel their subjects' agitation, restlessness and enervation.[13] By committing his sitters' nervous internal world onto the physical surface of the canvas, Klimt was seen to successfully dismantle the barrier between interior and exterior worlds – thus breaking with well-rehearsed conventions of nineteenth-century naturalism.

The interest of Vienna's cultural circles in the nervous body can be traced to the early 1890s, even before the Secession was founded. During this time, a general interest in nerves and nervous ailments gradually infiltrated popular discourse and progressive intellectuals started to embrace what Hugo von Hofmannsthal called in the early 1890s an 'ethic of modern nerves'.[14] Soon, the controversial Austrian author, playwright and cultural critic Hermann Bahr (1863–1934) became one of Vienna's most vocal advocates for a new type of art that took its cue from nerves, which he believed could finally free the visual arts from its 'enslavement' to naturalism. In his early writings, Bahr prophesised a subjective, inward-looking literature, but he also turned his rhetoric of 'nervous romanticism [*nervöse Romantik*]' and 'mysticism of nerves [*Mystik der Nerven*]', towards the arts in general.[15] In a diary entry about Klimt's *Gertha Felsövanyi*, for example, he poetically evokes this 'romanticism of nerves' when observing that 'Klimt now painted his [Dr. Löw's] daughter, white with a violet shimmer, so wonderfully floating and delicate that one has to cry'.[16] In his groundbreaking essay 'The Overcoming of Naturalism' (1891), Bahr advocated his nerve-art as a new idealism custom-tailored to the modern age:

> The new idealism expresses the new people. They are nerves; everything else died off, withered and scrawny. They only experience through nerves, they react solely from their nerves. [...] The content of the new idealism is nerves, nerves, nerves... Only if the nervous is completely liberated and individuals, but in particular artists, are able to dedicate themselves entirely to nerves, without reasonable or sensual consideration, only then does lost joy return into art.[17]

Despite Bahr's seductive rhetoric, it is important to remember that this language of nerves was not just a literary and/or painterly trope, but that nervousness and nervous ailments were very much part of concrete experience and psychiatric practices of the day.

In recent years, cultural and medical historians have increasingly turned their attention to nerves and nervous ailments as characteristically modern phenomena. Andreas Killen, for example, contended in his book *Berlin Electropolis* (2005) that by the turn of the last century, nervousness had become a mass phenomenon and a distinctly modern condition.[18] Although nervous individuals had populated medical discourse and practice throughout the nineteenth century, Killen argues that the diagnosis of nervous exhaustion as a distinctly modern condition was directly linked to the popularisation of the 'new disease construct of neurasthenia'[19] by the American physician and neurologist George M. Beard in 1869. Neurasthenia essentially means nerve-weakness and served as a 'catchall diagnosis applied to a syndrome with vague and variable symptoms'[20] such as anxiety and despair, eating disorders, insomnia, fatigue, fits of temper, mood swings and melancholic states of mind, migraines, phobias and sexual dysfunction. Despite these debilitating symptoms, no physiological cause could be found in their sufferers. At the turn of the last century, women, the upper classes and so-called 'brain workers', were seen as particularly susceptible to neurasthenia. Class and gender thus played key roles in the diagnosis and therapy of neurasthenia. In *Confessions of a Neurasthenic* (1908), William Taylor Marrs wrote that 'the best thing about neurasthenia is that it allows one to move in neurasthenic circles',[21] which clearly speaks to the perceived exclusivity of this diagnosis.

While psychiatrists saw nervous ailments as the alarming results of modernisation and industrialisation, progressive artists and cultural critics embraced the female neurasthenic as a powerful articulation of modern femininity. In the early society portraits exhibited in 1903, Klimt engaged with this nervous age by not only capturing the nervous mood of his sitter, but by trying to evoke an emotional-psychological response in the viewer at the same time. In this way, Klimt materialised in painting what Bahr had called for in literature: 'the sensation of nerves … are what one has to capture and fix and suggest to the others'.[22] In his later society portraits (1903–12), Klimt went even further by actually painting the physical signs of nervousness as inscribed on the body. Klimt first exhibited this new representational strategy at the 1908 *Kunstschau*, a momentous event in Viennese modernism. Conceived as a two-part event (in 1908 Austrian art was to be showcased and in 1909 international art), the *Kunstschau* featured over 176 of Austria's leading avant-garde practitioners. Rooms 22 and 23 were dedicated to the largest showing of Klimt's work to date and Peter Altenberg called these rooms a 'Klimt-church of modern art'.[23] Sixteen of Klimt's most famous paintings were shown (fig.108), among them *The Kiss* (1908) and three of Klimt's new society portraits, *Adele Bloch-Bauer I* (1907), *Fritza Riedler* (1906) and *Margarethe Stonborough-Wittgenstein* (1905) (figs.101, 109, 110). All three portraits exhibit Klimt's much-discussed move towards decoration and ornamentation, but in the context of the present discussion, it is important to note how

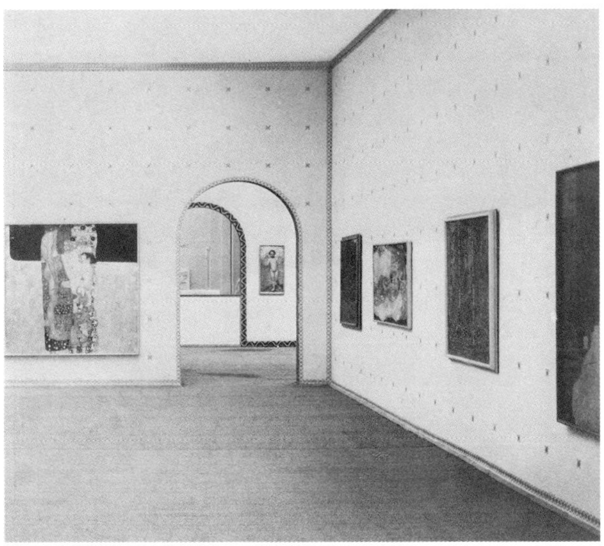

108 Room 22 (Klimt Room) at the Vienna Kunstschau, 1908

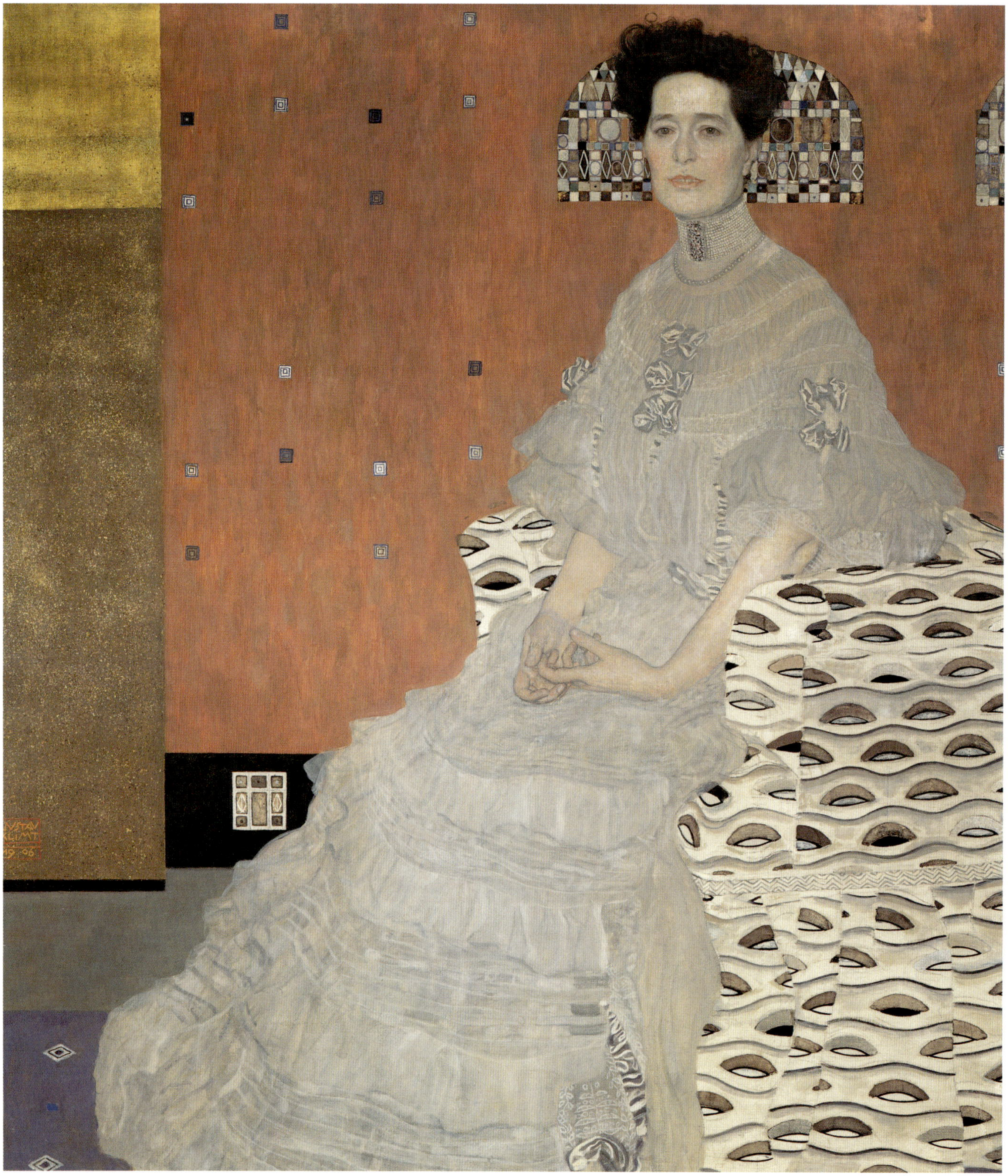
GUSTAV
KLIMT
19 06

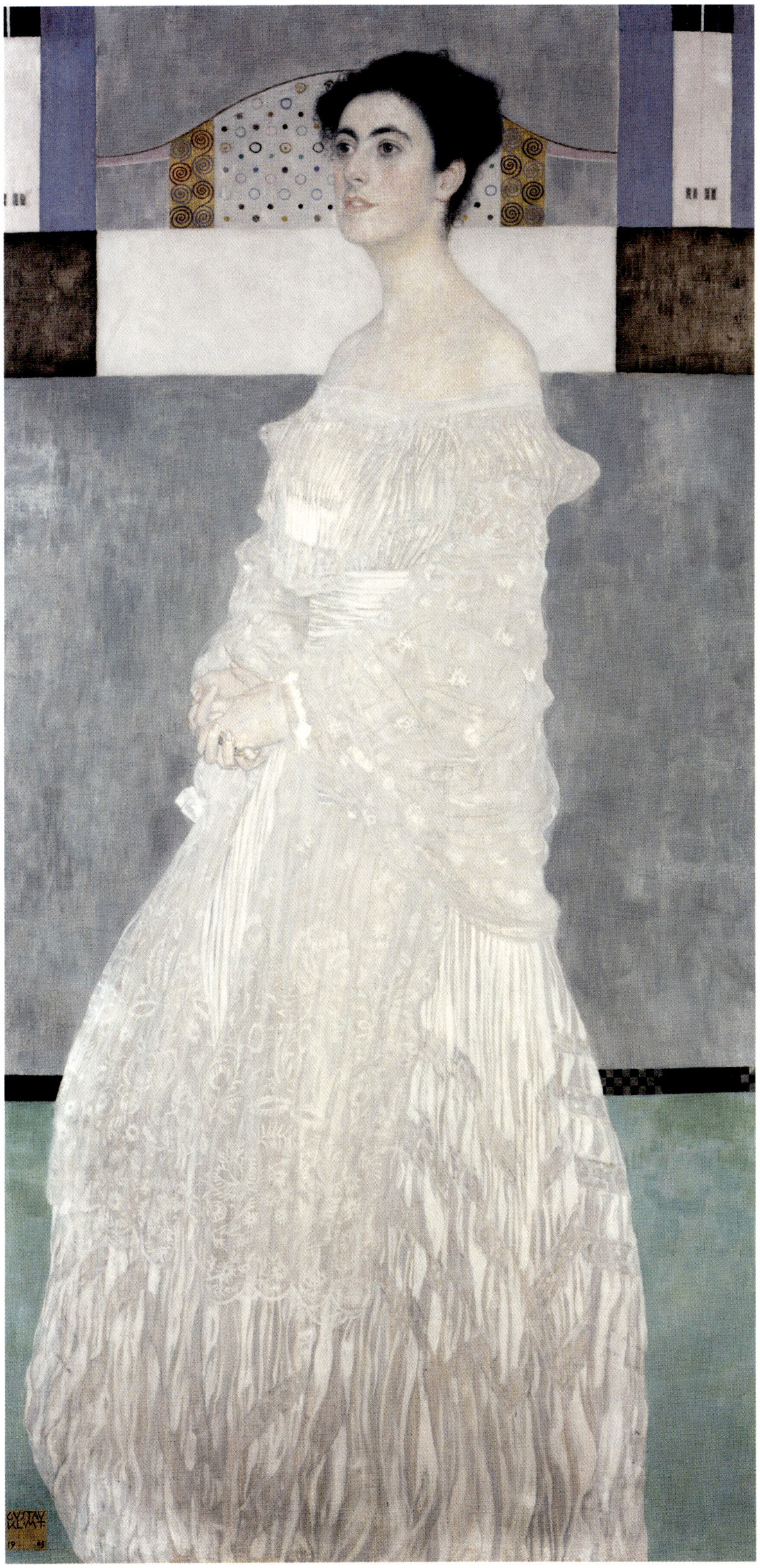

Opposite:
109 Gustav Klimt,
Fritza Riedler, 1906,
oil on canvas,
153 × 133 cm (60¼ × 52⅜ in).
Belvedere, Vienna

Right:
Opposite:
110 Gustav Klimt, *Margarethe Stonborough-Wittgenstein*, 1905,
oil on canvas, 179.8 × 90.5 cm
(70¾ × 35⅝ in). Bayerische
Staatsgemäldesammlung, Neue
Pinakothe, Munich 13074

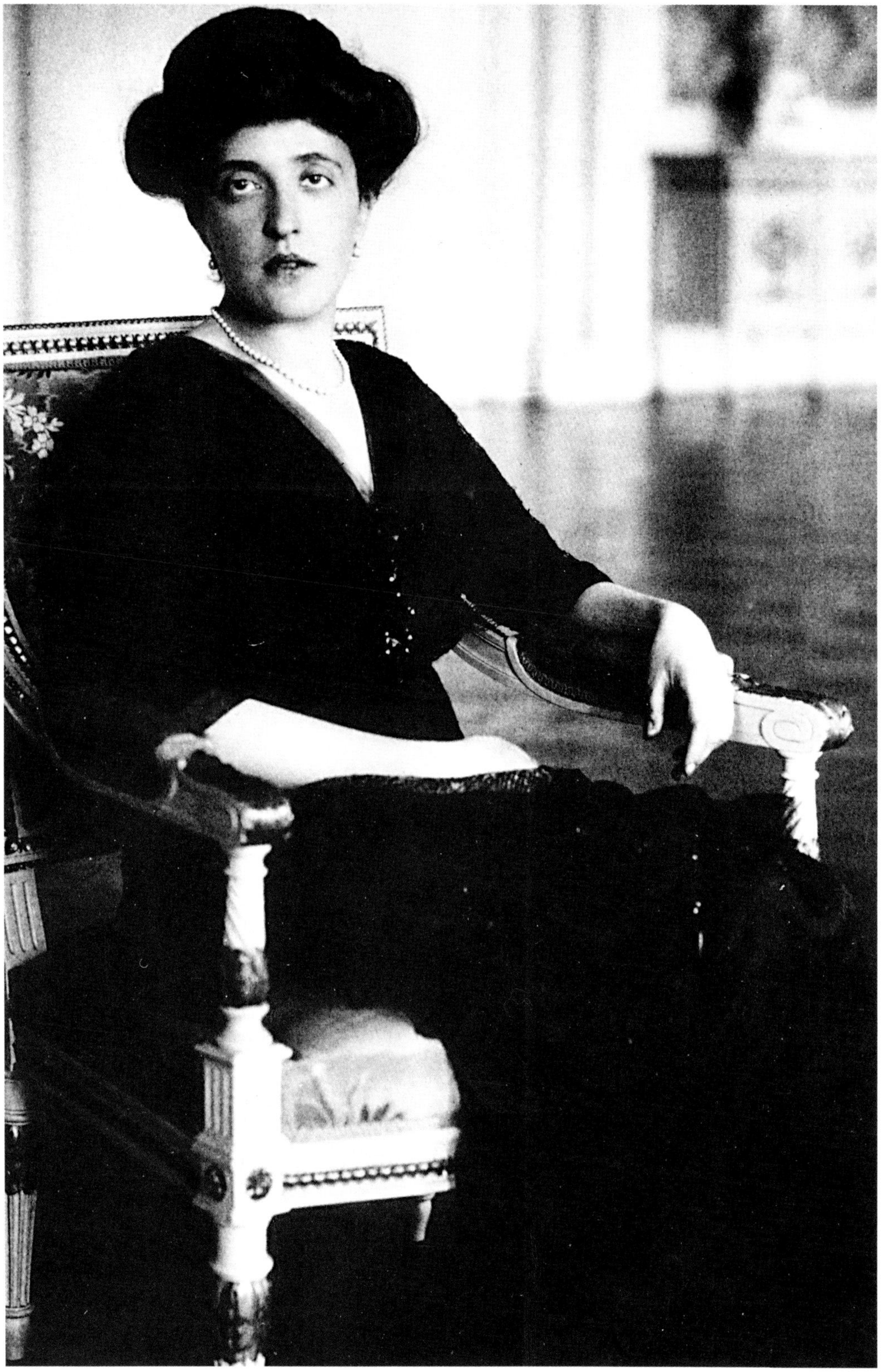

111 Photograph of Adele Bloch-Bauer, *c.*1910. Belvedere, Vienna

their naturalistic elements – in particular their hands – physically materialise the mental strains of the sitter's nervousness and neurasthenic state.

In 1931, Max Eisler, who wrote the first Klimt monograph in 1920, postulated a hypothetical scenario by which Vienna was erased from this planet:

> Let us embrace for a moment the adventurous thought that Vienna disappeared from the surface of this Earth. Nothing but Klimt's work survived, which is all future generations have to go by. What picture would … emerge from the sunken city at the hands of his oeuvre? Of the city's landscape and its inhabitants. Of their sophisticated tastes and their cultivated manners. Of their readily exited, overly sensitive nerves. Of their sensuous, richly decorated solemnity, the rhythmically ordered, paean sense of beauty. Of their exuberance and melancholy … Of the women, who walked on light feet, thin their bodies, small their shoulders, delicate their joints, trembling their skin, longing their mouths, flaming their dark eyes surrounded by secret, egregious airs.[24]

Eisler's description evokes the kind of femininity celebrated by Klimt's portraits of neurasthenic society ladies. Initially interested in conveying his sitter's psychology in his early Damenportraits and projecting their moods onto the viewer, Klimt's later society portraits concentrated his search for a modern language of nerves onto a few, yet absolutely crucial, pictorial details, such as the hands and the face. Surrounded, if not encased, by precious ornamentation, his subject's body has been literally effaced by sparkling gold 'amours' and all that was left is her highly expressive hands and beautiful, yet vacuous face. *Adele Bloch-Bauer*'s hands, for example, are those of an anxious, highly strung nervous person (fig.101). Klimt's pictorial representation of her fragile beauty matches her niece's description of Adele as 'suffering, always with a headache, smoking like a chimney, terribly fragile, dark, a cerebral face, thin, elegant and constantly in search of intellectual stimulation'.[25] While psychiatrists tried to manage neurasthenia with a series of therapies – ranging from water-therapy, to electro- and mechano-therapy, rest cures and diets – progressive artists such as Gustav Klimt celebrated its physical manifestations in the female body as a new and distinctly modern femininity. If, as Catherine M. Sousslof claims, a portrait is both a thing and an act, that is to say that 'portraits are … pictures particularly indicative not only of an individual, but also of kinship and social status',[26] then Klimt's society portraits need to be viewed from the historical context within which they were painted, exhibited and viewed. The context provided by this chapter links the visual articulation of 'kinship and social status' in Klimt's society portraits to the historically specific allure of nerves and neurasthenia.

NOTES

1. '$491 Million Sale Shatters Art Auction Record', *The New York Times*, 9 November 2006 http://www.nytimes.com/2006/11/09/arts/design/09christies.html [accessed 19 September 2008] and *Klimt*, dir. Raoul Ruiz (Koch Lorber Films, 2006).
2. Gerbert Frodl, 'Gustav Klimt – Maler zwischen den Zeiten', in *Klimt und die Frauen*, ed. Tobias G. Natter and Gerbert Frodl (Cologne: DuMont, 2000), pp 9–13.
3. Alessandra Comini, Review of *Gustav Klimt und die Wiener Jahrhundertwende*, Werner Hofmann, *Art in America* 61, 2 (1973), p. 116. For the view of Klimt's painterly practice as an inward-looking withdrawal from politics, see Carl Schorske's *Fin-de-Siècle Vienna: Politics and Culture* (New York: Random House, 1980).
4. See Tobias G. Natter, *Die Welt von Klimt, Schiele und Kokoschka: Sammler und Mäzene* (Cologne: DuMont, 2003), Natter, ed. (2000) and *Gustav Klimt: Painting, Design and Modern Life*, ed. Tobias G. Natter and Christoph Grunenberg, (London: Tate Publishing, 2008).
5. Christian Brandstätter, *Gustav Klimt und die Frauen* (Vienna: Brandstätter, 1994), p. 27.
6. Natter (2000), p. 67.
7. Manu von Miller, *Sonja Knips und die Wiener Moderne* (Vienna: Brandstätter, 2004).
8. Christian M. Nebehay, *Gustav Klimt: Das Skizzenbuch aus dem Besitz von Sonja Knips* (Vienna: Tusch, 1987).
9. Natter (2000), p. 84.
10. Ludwig Hevesi, *Acht Jahre Secession* (Vienna: Carl Konegen, 1906), p. 81.
11. Hevesi (1906), pp 451–2.
12. This description also calls up James McNeill Whistler's work – especially his Symphonies in White (1862–1873) – to which Klimt would have had access via *The Studio* (a very popular and highly coveted journal among members of the Secession). Whistler's impact on Klimt can also be seen in his choice of a fairly narrow and elongated format for *Marie Henneberg* and *Gertha Felsövànyi*. For a discussion of this link between Whistler and Klimt see Manu von Miller, 'Embracing Modernism: Gustav Klimt and Sonja Knips', in *Gustav Klimt: The Ronald S. Lauder and Serge Sabarsky Collections* (New York: Neue Galerie/Prestel, 2007), pp 188–211.
13. This reading of Klimt's early Damenportraits as psychological portraits plays a significant role in art historical interpretations of his work to this day. See for example, Michael Worbs, *Nervenkunst; Literatur und Psychoanalyse im Wien der Jahrhundertwende* (Frankfurt am Main: Europäische Verlags-Anstalt, 1983), Natter (2000) and *Sehnsucht nach Glück: Wiens Aufbruch in die Moderne*, ed. Sabine Schulze (Ostfildern-Ruit: G. Hatje, 1995).
14. Hugo von Hofmannsthal, 'Maurice Barrès (1891)', in *Die Wiener Moderne: Literatur, Kunst und Musik zwischen 1890 und 1910*, ed. Gotthard Wunberg (Stuttgart: Philipp Reclam Jr., 1982), p. 323.
15. Hermann Bahr, *Studien zur Kritik der Moderne* (Frankfurt: Rütten & Loening, 1894), p. 9.
16. Bahr quoted in Reinhard Farkas, *Hermann Bahr: Prophet der Moderne, Tagebücher 1888*–1904 (Vienna: Böhlau, 1987), p. 127.
17. Hermann Bahr, 'Die Überwindung des Naturalismus', in Wunberg, pp 204–5.
18. Andreas Killen, *Berlin Electropolis: Shock, Nerves, and German Modernity* (Berkeley: University of California Press, 2005). See also Joachim Radkau, *Das Zeitalter der Nervosität: Deutschland zwischen Bismarck und Hitler* (Munich: Hanser, 1998) and Andreas Steiner, *Das nervöse Zeitalter: Der Begriff der Nervösität bei Laien und Ärzten in Deutschland und Österreich um 1900* (Zurich: Juris, 1964).
19. Killen, p. 2.
20. Alfred M. Freedman, 'Introduction', in *Before Freud: Neurasthenia and the American Medical Community 1870–1910*, by Francis Gosling (Urbana: University of Illinois Press, 1987), p. 2.

21. William Taylor Marrs quoted in *Cultures of Neurasthenia from Beard to the First World War*, ed. Marijke Gijswijt-Hofstra and Roy Porter (Amsterdam/New York: Rodopi, 2001), p. 51.
22. Bahr quoted in Reinhard Farkas, *Hermann Bahr: Dynamik und Dilemma der Moderne.* (Vienna: Böhlau Verlag, 1989), p. 27.
23. Peter Altenberg quoted in Gottfried Fliedl, *Gustav Klimt: Die Welt in weiblicher Gestalt* (Cologne: Taschen, 1989), p. 159.
24. Max Eisler, 'Mit Leib und Seele', in Otto Beicha, *Gustav Klimt: Die Goldene Pforte* (Salzburg: Galerie Welz, 1978), p. 23.
25. Natter (2000), p. 70.
26. Catherine M. Soussloff, *The Subject in Art: Portraiture and the Birth of the Modern* (Durham: Duke University Press, 2006), p. 8.

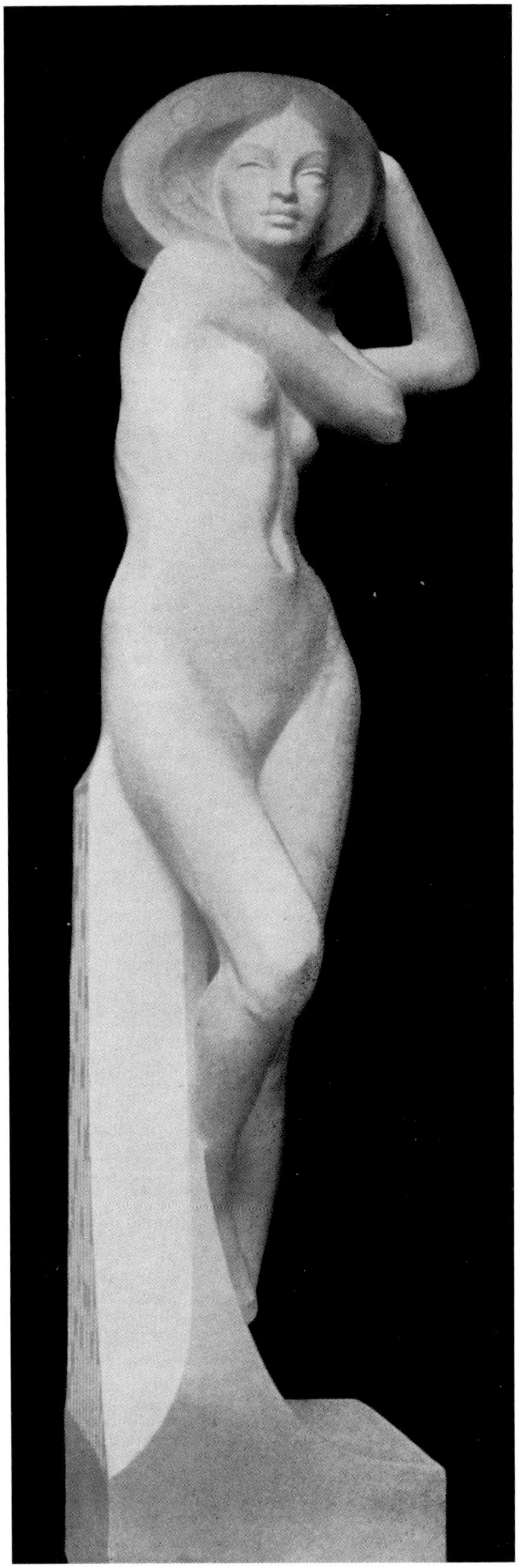

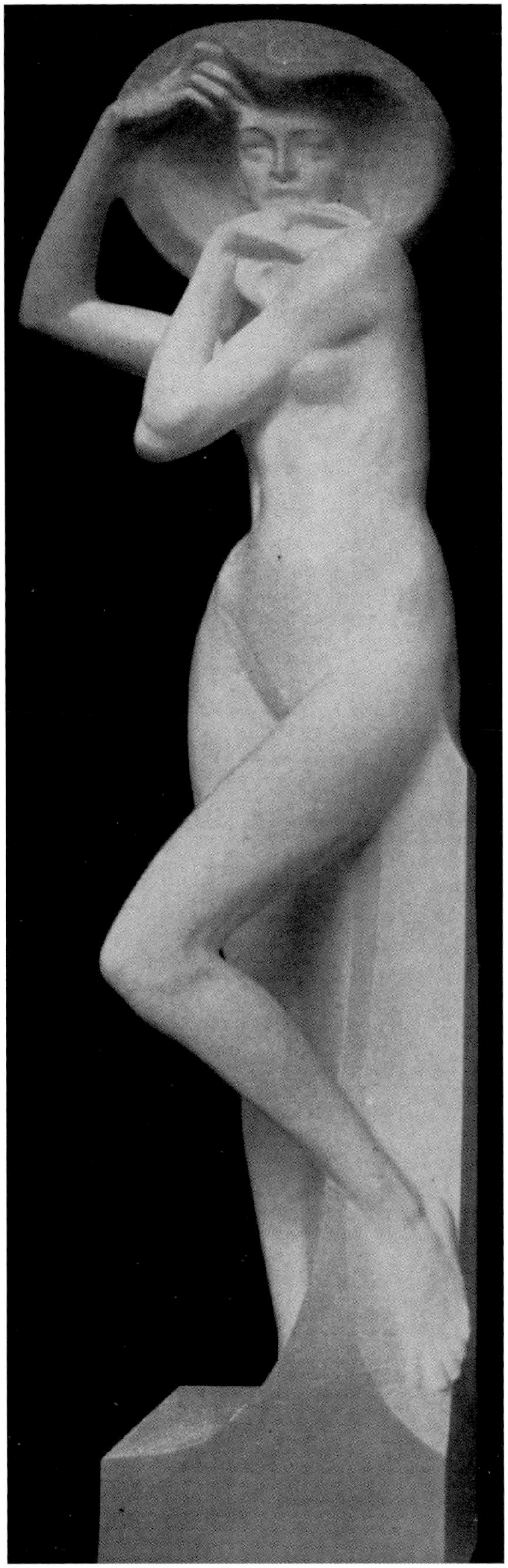

Chapter 9

Richard Luksch, Two Faience Figures for the Purkersdorf Sanatorium, 1905

SABINE WIEBER

In November of 1905, the progressive Viennese art critic Ludwig Hevesi published a feuilleton in the *Fremdenblatt* on the state of modern architecture in Vienna.[1] While complaining that the city was saturated with regressive historicist buildings, a short train journey into the Vienna Woods rewarded Hevesi with a perfect example of progressive architecture: Josef Hoffmann's recently completed social and therapeutic centre, the so-called *Kurhaus*, on the grounds of Victor Zuckerkandl's Purkersdorf Sanatorium (fig.114). For Hevesi, Hoffmann's flat-roofed, unadorned cube represented a quintessentially modern architectural vision of truth, clarity and 'simple harmony'.[2] During his visit, Hevesi was particularly struck by a set of sculptures that adorned the *Kurhaus*' western entrance: 'At the main entrances, the staircases in the front and above the driveway in the back, some sculptures (by Luksch) are displayed … in the back, [one finds] two blue-white faience figures, two meters tall, all in relation to the overall purpose of the building'.[3] The two sculptures 'in the back' also feature prominently in a photo essay published in the leading German design magazine *Deutsche Kunst und Dekoration*

112 Richard Luksch, *Entrance Figures for the Purkersdorf Sanatorium*, 1905. *Deutsche Kunst und Dekoration* 18 (1906), 423

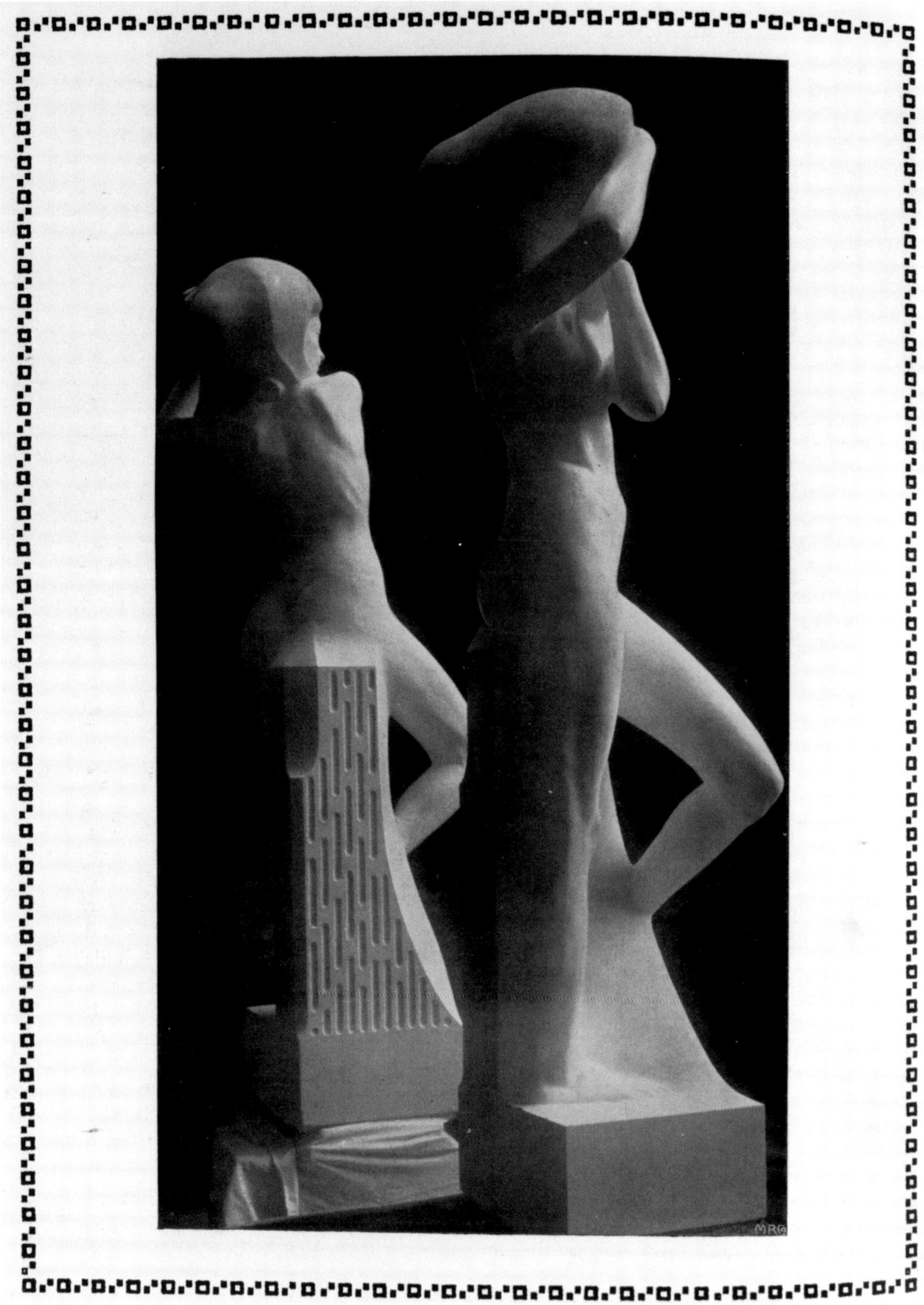

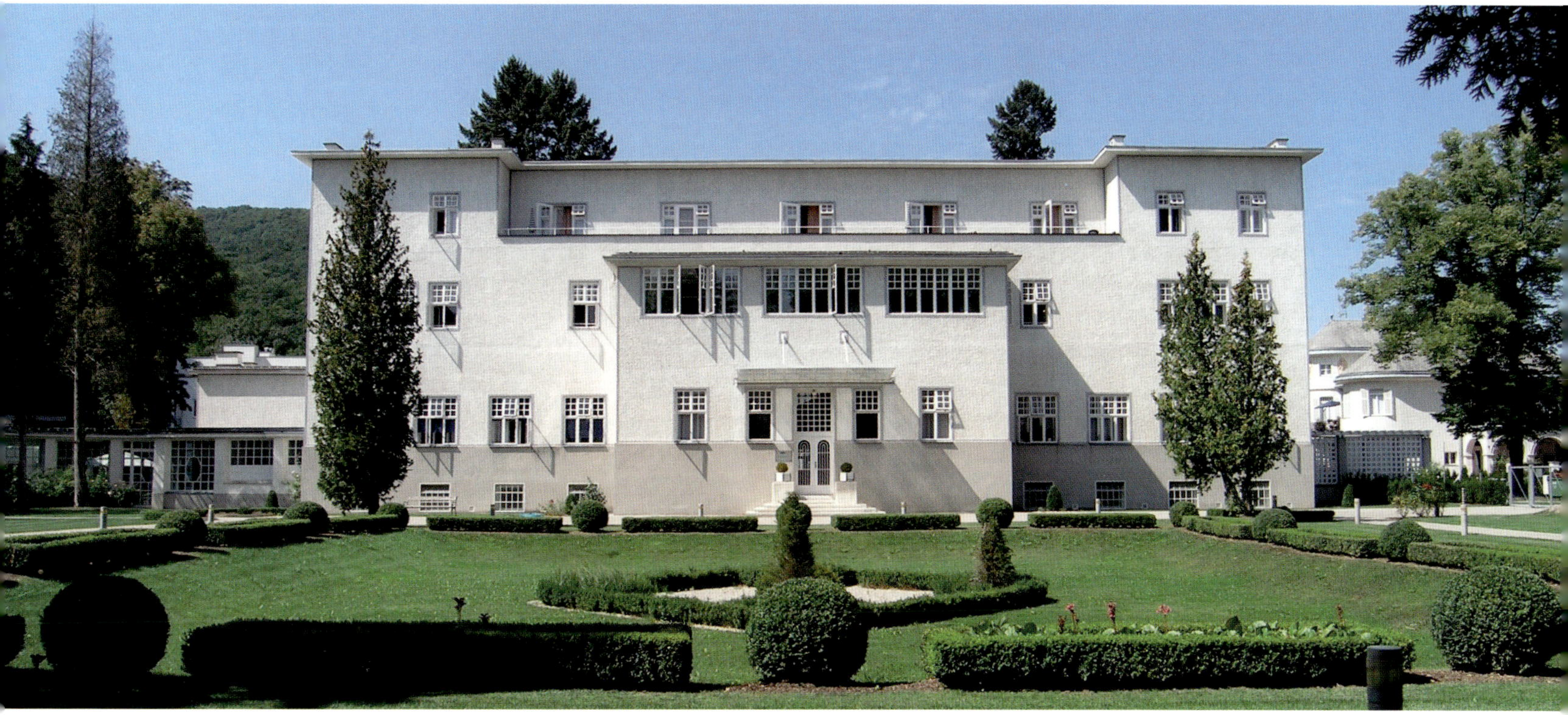

114 Josef Hoffmann, *Purkersdorf Sanatorium*, 1904–05

in 1906, where they appear in two dramatically lit photographs (figs. 112, 113). Unfortunately, these two photographs do not show the *Kurhaus* sculptures in situ and one has to rely on an architectural drawing to deduce their intended position on top of a ledge created by the recession of the central bay of the first and second floors. Facing outwards, this west façade represented the *Kurhaus*' public face and was the first point of contact between patients and the sanatorium. Placing two over-life-sized sculptures right above this entrance thus marked it as an important point of transition from everyday life into institutional life.[4]

Hevesi identified the maker of these two sculptures as Richard Luksch, a young German sculptor who after training at the Munich Academy moved to Vienna in 1900 with his wife, the artist Elena Makowsky. Upon their arrival, they both joined the Secession and Luksch exhibited regularly with this group of progressive artists. He was an early member of the Wiener Werkstätte and supported Gustav Klimt's withdrawal from the Secession in 1905. Although largely forgotten today, Luksch's sculptures bear witness to his close involvement in Vienna's progressive artistic circles. The *Kurhaus* figures are ceramics and stand virtually unprecedented within the wider context of modern Viennese sculpture. A closer inspection reveals that the figures are faiences, a term used to describe an earthenware ceramic body that has been covered with a tin glaze and fired at 1,100° Celsius or less. This firing process gives the kind of rich creamy surface effect of the glaze

Opposite:
113 Richard Luksch, *Entrance Figures for the Purkersdorf Sanatorium*, 1905. Deutsche Kunst und Dekoration 18 (1906), 422

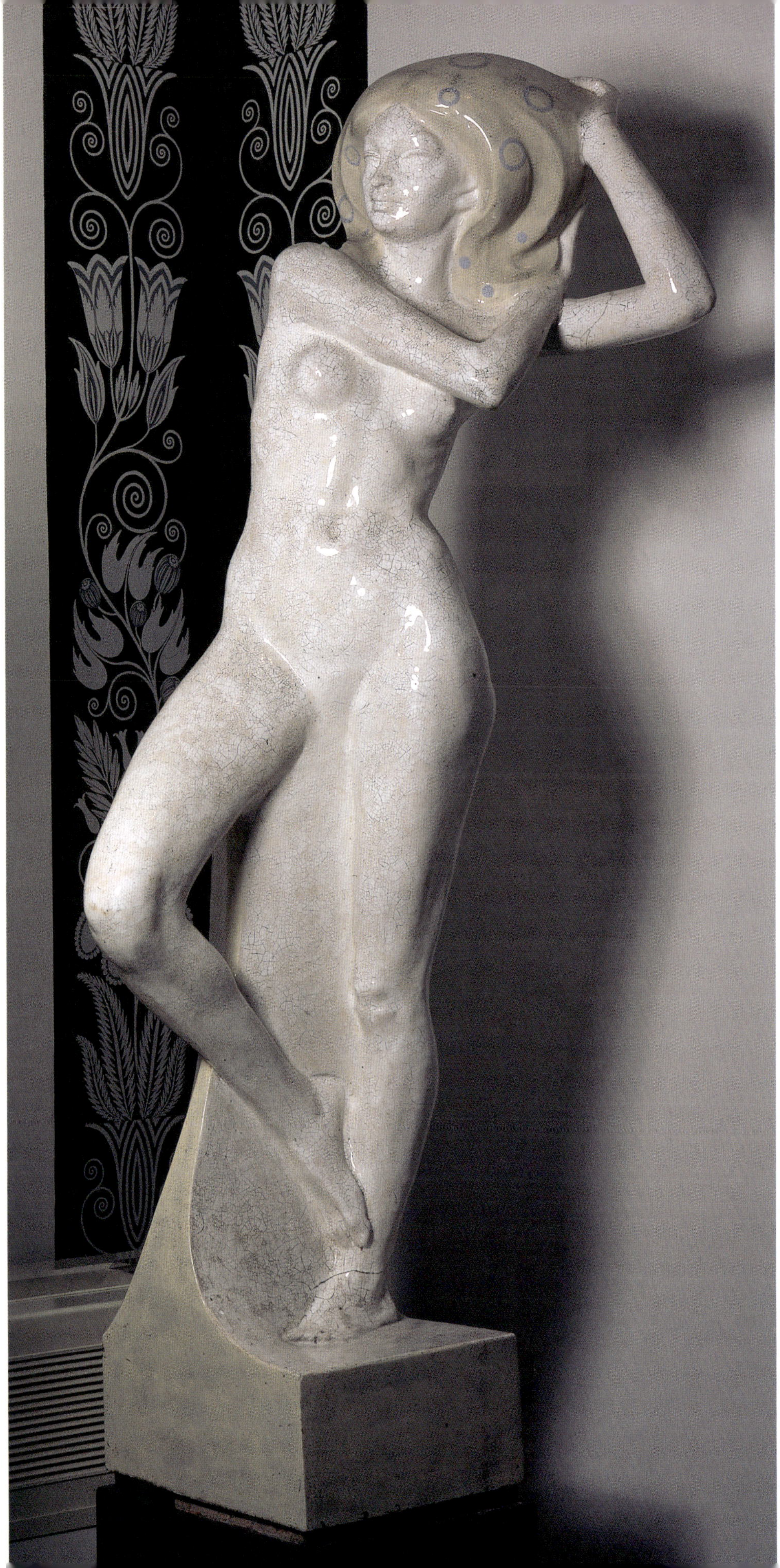

115 Richard Luksch,
Entrance Figures for the Purkersdorf Sanatorium, 1905,
Faience Ceramic,
202 × 64 cm (79½ × 25¼ in).
Museum für Kunst und Gewerbe, Hamburg

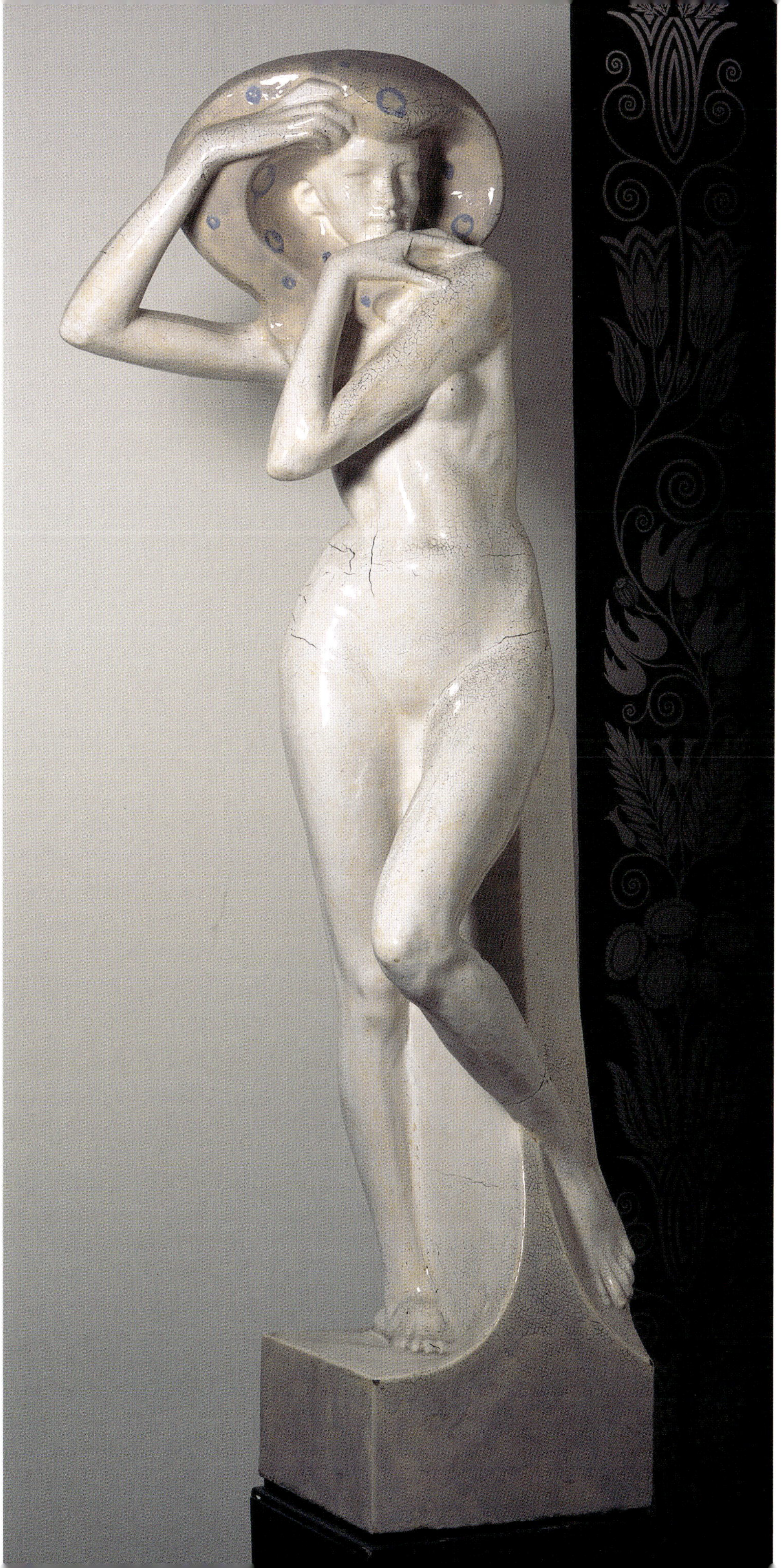

116 Richard Luksch,
Entrance Figures for the Purkersdorf Sanatorium, 1905,
Faience Ceramic,
200 × 62 cm (78¾ × 24⅜ in).
Museum für Kunst und Gewerbe, Hamburg

that makes the Kurhaus sculptures so attractive (figs 115, 116). And yet, to produce ceramic figures of this size posed a serious technical challenge, which is suggested by the two pillars from which the figures seem to emerge – they actually functioned as supporting structures during the firing process to prevent their collapse.

Technical virtuosity is signalled in the elongated bodies of the female figures, which curve sinuously around their centres of gravity. While facing one another, each figure is captured in a private moment of introspection. Despite an overall tendency towards abstraction, Luksch imbued each figure with individual facial features. Their bodies are thin if not emaciated – their shoulder bones stick out, their upper bodies are excessively lean and their ribs and hip bones protrude through their skin. And yet, as a result of the creamy glaze, they exude a sensuality that stands in disturbing contrast to their emaciated vulnerability. To further highlight the hair, Luksch added yellow pigment into the tin glaze and painted blue circles across the surface, possibly suggesting a link to water, both in reference to the Purkersdorf Sanatorium as a water-therapy clinic and to the modish popularity of this treatment. Luksch's faiences exhibit a curious tension between a deliberate aestheticisation of their fragile bodies and the fact that they were designed for the Sanatorium Purkersdorf's main entrance – a water-therapy clinic offering treatment for the very nervous disorders that gave rise to this idealised femininity in the first place.

The *Kurhaus* sculptures' representational language and their proposed location on the building's main entrance suggests that they were envisioned as crucial components in the marketing of the Purkersdorf Sanatorium to prospective patients who also supported avant-garde artists and who regularly visited Secession exhibitions.[5] Luksch's sculptures articulated a new type of femininity that was rooted in nerves and that celebrated the physical manifestations of nervous ailments in the female body as a beauty ideal perfectly suited for the modern age. The Kurhaus' overall design language, including its Wiener Werkstätte interiors and Luksch's stunning sculptures, was thus carefully crafted to resonate with progressive, upper-class patrons who themselves suffered from nervous ailments and who were steeped in the iconography of the nervous female body celebrated by the Vienna Secession.[6]

NOTES

1. Ludwig Hevesi, 'Neubauten von Josef Hoffmann', *Fremden-Blatt*, 8 November 1905, pp 13–14.
2. Hevesi, p. 13. On the currency of the notion of 'truth' in early twentieth-century Viennese architectural discourse, see Leslie Topp, *Architecture and Truth in Fin-de-Siècle Vienna* (Cambridge: Cambridge University Press, 2004).
3. Ibid.
4. There is reason to believe that Luksch's sculptures were never installed due to protracted financial disagreements between Zuckerkandl and the financial director of the Viennese Workshops, Fritz Waerndorfer. See Josef Hoffmann, 'Selbstbiographie', *Ver Sacrum: Neue Hefte für Kunst und Literatur*, 4 (1972), pp 104–23.
5. Although Hevesi implies in his essay in the *Fremden-Blatt* that he saw Luksch's sculptures in situ, it is not entirely clear if they were actually displayed at any point in time. Hoffmann stated in his above-mentioned autobiography that Zuckerkandl and Fritz Waerndorfer, the financial director of the Viennese Workshops, fought extensively over the cost of the *Kurhaus* and most likely, Luksch's figures were not installed. They re-surface in an exhibition at the Viennese Gallery Miethke in December of 1905 and end up being purchased by Adolphe Stoclet for his Palais in Brussels also designed by Hoffmann and furbished by the Viennese Workshops.
6. See chapter 8 and Sabine Wieber, 'Nervous Bodies and Femmes Fragile: Sculpting the Sanatorium in Vienna 1900', forthcoming.

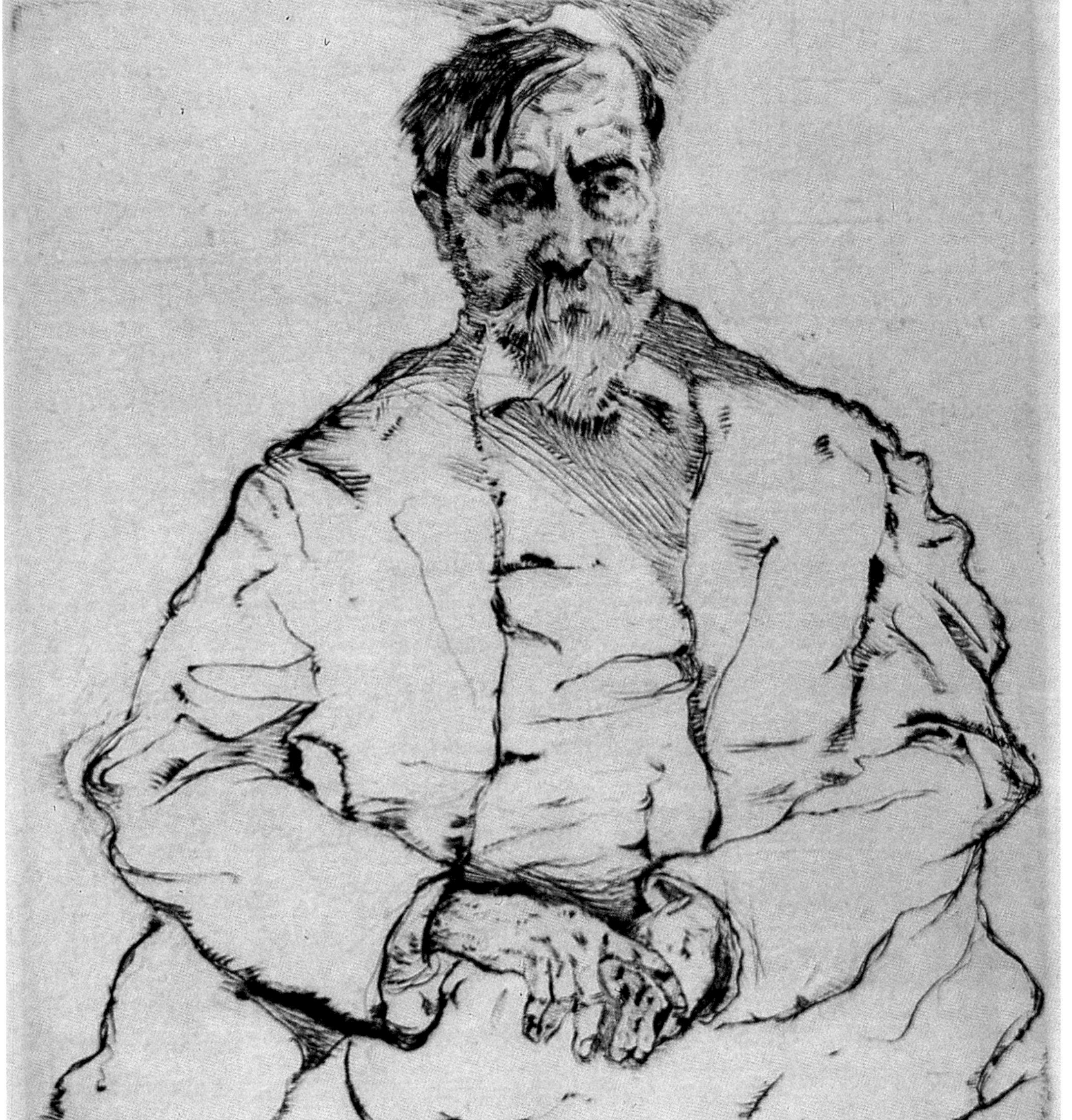

Chapter 10

Madness and Literature in Vienna 1900

GEOFFREY C. HOWES

In Austria, as in much of Europe, interest in madness grew with the ascent of modernism. After 1800 traditional definitions of madness as deficit – as lack of reason, lack of lucidity, lack of self-control – were gradually differentiated by more subtle readings that produced new classifications and nomenclatures, but were still based on a definition of madness as non-rational.[1] Friedrich Nietzsche's theorising of the Dionysian as the repressed substratum of western culture unleashed the cultural-critical force of delirium in its various guises. Anti-rationalists viewed madness as a possible ally in their opposition to reason and civilisation: it was unconventional, anti-bourgeois, and often outrageous. In the arts, it became a means for expanding the understanding of what is human beyond the social and ideological limitations of late nineteenth-century religion, capitalism, positivism and historicism. At times the arts also began to explore madness itself as a human experience viewed not only as negation but also on its own terms.

119 Max Oppenheimer, *Portrait sketch of Arthur Schnitzler*, 1912

After some background on the history and context of madness in Austrian literature before 1890, this chapter discusses vignettes by Peter Altenberg, who himself spent time in psychiatric care; mentally disturbed characters from the prose works of Arthur Schnitzler, one of the keenest observers of the Viennese psyche; and motifs from the rich imagery in the poetry of Georg Trakl. The chapter closes with a look towards post-1918 developments in the literary representation of madness in Vienna and Austria.

The Austrian and Viennese fascination with madness took on particular culturally determined forms, growing in part out of debates around the three main currents of Viennese psychiatry: the positivistic psychiatric research of the Second Vienna School of medicine at Vienna's General Hospital; the asylum-based psychiatry that had moved from restraint, to relief and management of symptoms, and even to attempts to cure; and an interest in nervous disorders that produced the psychoanalytic movement led by Sigmund Freud. Views of madness were also conditioned by the cultural pessimism of late Habsburg society. The descending fortunes of Austria in European politics, its internal struggles concerning class, nationality and anti-Semitism, and the contradictions and hypocrisies of middle-class existence contributed to a sort of apocalyptic melancholy. Concomitant neuroses and psychoses were registered by Freud in his case studies and theories, and by Arthur Schnitzler in his plays and prose. Breakdowns, dissociations, delusions, and suicides became standard material in both medical and artistic discourse.

Progress in the sciences and a celebration of the contemporary in the modernist arts converged with the general mood of melancholy and decadence to produce an excitement that was also unrest. This is an aspect of what David S. Luft calls the 'distinctive blend of scientific materialism and philosophical irrationalism that characterized liberal Vienna'.[2] Increasing understanding of psychopathology opened new prospects, but it also amplified anxiety in the face of the irrational, the subconscious and the insane. Madness fascinated but it also threatened; it disclosed both new territories and new terrors. It seemed to explain much of what was wrong in Austrian society, yet it was itself largely unexplainable.

Austrian writers' fascination with madness reaches back before the advent of modernism in the late nineteenth century. The Viennese popular dramatists Ferdinand Raimund (1790–1836) and Johann Nestroy (1801–62) both treated psychological disturbances. In *Der Alpenkönig und der Menschenfeind* (*The King of the Alps and the Misanthrope*, 1828), Raimund presents Herr Rappelkopf ('Mr. Crackbrain'), who in his natural generosity has been defrauded and therefore retreats into misanthropic melancholy. In a sort of proto-psychoanalysis, Astragalus, the King of the Alps, cures what we might now call depression in Rappelkopf by presenting him with a mirror image of himself. In *Der Zerrissene* (*A Man Full of Nothing*, 1844), Nestroy's Herr von Lips is a rich landowner whose excess leisure and wealth induce ennui and paranoia. Like Rappelkopf, he is cured of his malady when he sees himself through others' eyes.

Another Biedermeier author, Franz Grillparzer (1791–1872), describes what might now be diagnosed as an autistic disorder in his novella of 1848, *Der arme Spielmann* (*The Poor Fiddler*). An elderly street musician tells his story of social maladjustment and isolation. He makes his condition tolerable by obsessively playing music. The tale does

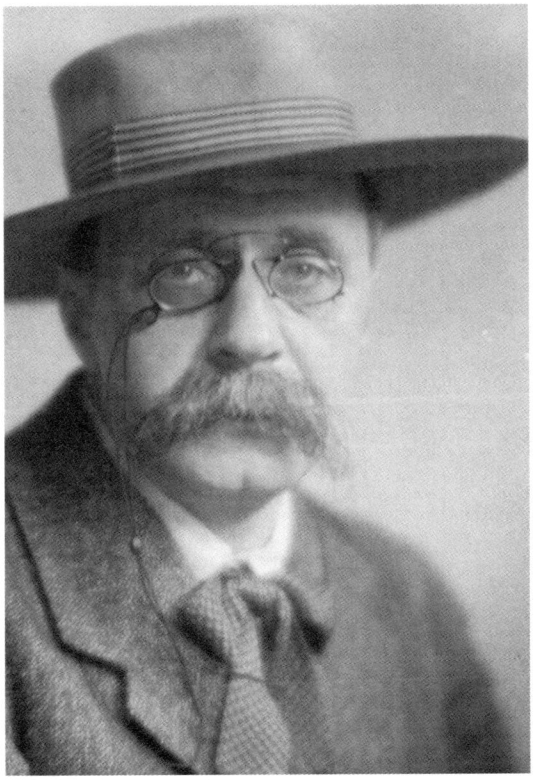

117 Portrait photograph of Peter Altenberg, n.d.

not present madness as psychosis, but it portrays a mind that cannot function within normal mores. Moreover, in contrast to the therapeutic successes in Raimund and Nestroy, it is an instance of Viennese pessimism: the fiddler does not overcome his condition.

A further example of literary melancholy is found in the lyric poems of Nikolaus Lenau (1802–50), who himself suffered from depression and occasional derangement and died in the asylum at Oberdöbling near Vienna. Another well-known name in this regard is Leopold von Sacher-Masoch (1836–95), whose prolific oeuvre includes treatments of misogyny, fetishism, and the psychological urge that bears his name, most notably in his famous *Venus im Pelz* (*Venus in Furs*, 1871). Like Lenau, Sacher-Masoch spent the end of his life in psychiatric care. An additional psychological ballast in the Austrian literary tradition is the fact that several important authors – Raimund, the novelist Adalbert Stifter (1805–68) and the novella writer Ferdinand von Saar (1833–1906) – committed suicide.

Thus the problems of psychopathology were not new to the Viennese literary scene as it entered the 1890s and produced *Jung-Wien* (*Young Vienna*), a group of writers that included Hermann Bahr, Schnitzler and Hugo von Hofmannsthal (1874–1929). This movement was associated with literary *Jugendstil* (art nouveau), which encompassed Symbolism and Impressionism and explored the psychological dimensions of human experience. According to Michael Worbs, there was a general Austrian literary interest in psychiatry with its accounts of pathologies like hysteria, neurasthenia and sexual perversions. Worbs relates this interest to such non-Austrian predecessors as Emile Zola (1840–1902), Joris-Karl Huysmans (1848–1907), Henrik Ibsen (1828–1906) and Gerhart Hauptmann (1862–1946).[3] Scientific, philosophical, and aesthetic discourses were merging in a general turn toward a psychological conception of human identity, but it was the borders of normality that gave this identity its shape.

Peter Altenberg, perhaps the best known of the 'coffeehouse literati' of Vienna, lived his life as the insider's outsider (fig.117). Championed by such luminaries as Adolf Loos and Karl Kraus, he produced delicate literary vignettes.[4] Constitutionally incapable of conforming to bourgeois social demands, Altenberg suffered from depression, indulged in self-medication with alcohol and sleeping pills, and spent time in several psychiatric clinics, including Inzersdorf and Steinhof (fig.118). He was acutely aware of the ostracism that sickness brings, and wrote in 'Krankheit' (Illness, 1911) that a sick person is good for nothing, and is allowed to stay alive out of shame and because of the possibility that 'among the millions of idiots there might be one who sees through the whole maneuver'.[5] Altenberg saw himself in this perspicacious role, and he viewed his dislocation from normal life as a source of creativity: 'If the experiences of the sick man had benefited the healthy

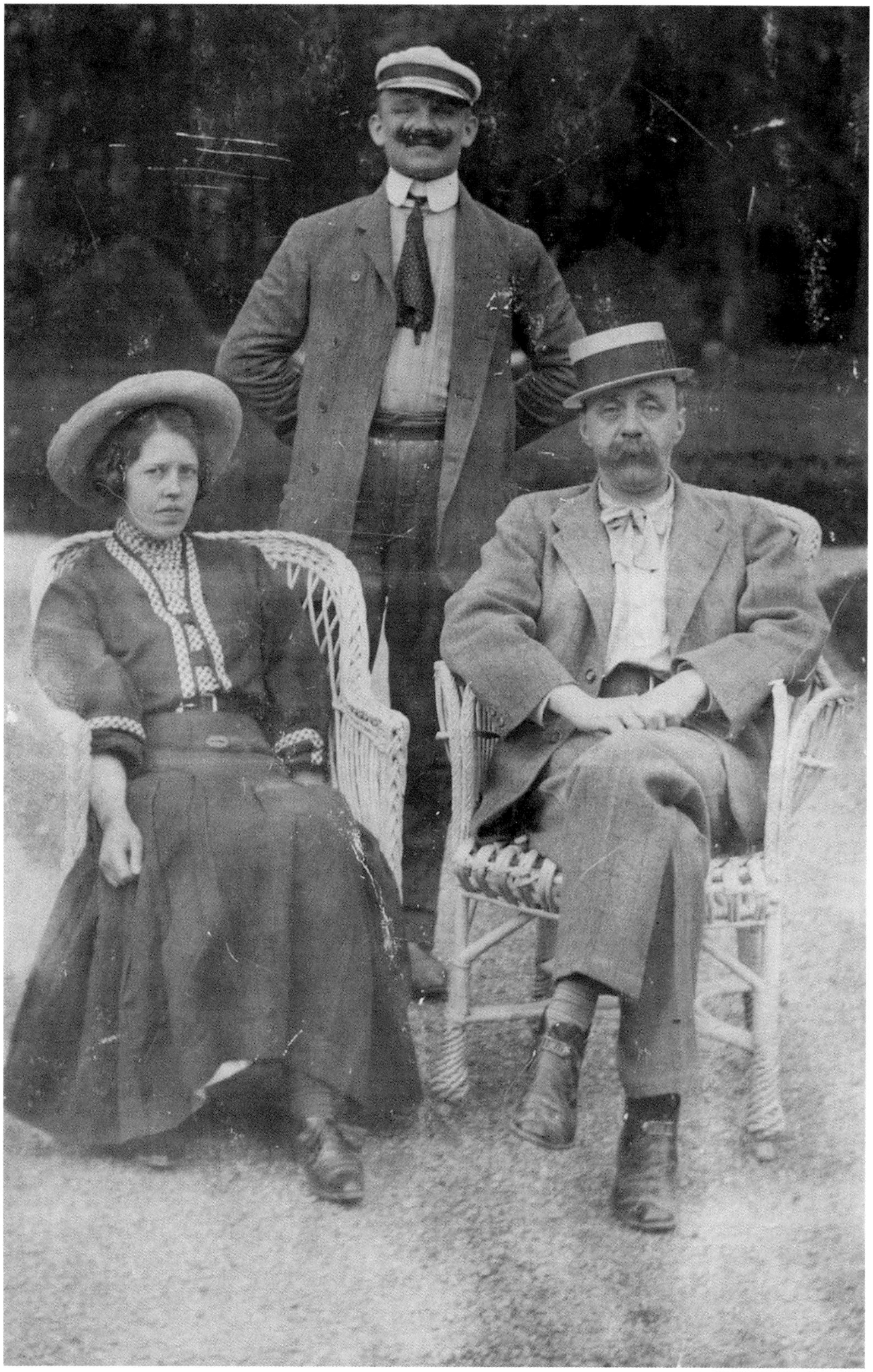

118 Peter Altenberg (bottom right) with Helga Malmberg and Mr Spatzek, attendant, at Sanatorium Dr Fries, Inszersdorf (near Vienna), 1910. Wien Museum

man, he would have become almost a genius in the art of living', but instead he is the victim of the 'lie of life', the idea that the strength to stay alive is not something precious. The sick man knows that it is, and lives his life undistracted by petty cares.[6]

Such witty bitterness about the fate of the mental patient surfaces many times in Altenberg's prose. In 'Sanatorien' (Sanatoria), published after his death, he decries the treatment of patients as objects when they are not allowed to participate in their own cures. He complains that he has been denied his 'holy laxative', the 'primordial spring of my poetic powers' – 'I immediately went insane'. When the care-givers (a term he doubts) respond by sedating him with opium, he goes 'three times as insane'.[7] A perhaps understandable paranoia shows through when he accuses everyone of being against his chance to get well.

From this patient's point of view, there is a vicious cycle in psychiatric treatment: the conditions of the asylum, the objectifying of the patient and the medications themselves lead to a loss of personal agency, to which Altenberg responded with more self-medication. In the text 'Sanatorium für Nervenkranke' ('Sanatorium for Nervous Disorders', 1913) Altenberg expresses the sense that the patient is being not helped, but accused and punished: the doctor at his morning consultation looks like a district attorney. The patient thus becomes the 'delinquent'.[8] In the ensuing dialogue Altenberg asserts his taste for coffee against the doctor's wish that he drink tea instead. When he mentions that his breakfast consists only of coffee, the doctor objects that he should eat something solid. Upon his response that he has had this breakfast for 30 years, the doctor questions where this has got him. Thus what should have been a medical consultation turns into a battle of wits, with Altenberg's insistence on his idiosyncrasies winning out (in his own account, of course) over the doctor's shallow attempts at depth psychology. Later, when the doctor asks whose empty bottles are under the patient's bed, it turns out that most of the alcoholic patients are bribing the staff to get alcohol. Called to account, one of the employees says that if they had not been providing drink 'every one of them would've flown the coop after three days and we'd have an empty asylum!'[9] In this one sentence, Altenberg exposes the hypocrisy of the institution: the patients' need to take control and be cured of the cure, as well as the asylum's economic dependence on keeping the patients. He thus gives us a glimpse into how difficult it is to live with mental problems in a society whose duplicities are made only more glaring when one does not cooperate with them.

Not as a participant like Altenberg, but as an observer, Arthur Schnitzler showed again and again in his fiction and his plays how social conformism makes psychopathology even worse when it applies moral judgment rather than psychological understanding to the afflicted (fig.119). In a comprehensive analysis, Robert Weiss found a high incidence in Schnitzler's works not only of neuroses, but also of psychoses, ranging from psychotic breaks to schizophrenia to paranoid conditions to constitutional psychopathy.[10] Weiss concluded that Schnitzler's 'concept and understanding of the dynamics of the psychoses were entirely correct in the light of modern knowledge, as well as amazingly advanced in comparison with the general status of psychiatric knowledge in his own time.'[11] This chapter looks at two short stories from the first decade of the twentieth century as concentrated examples of Schnitzler's astute grasp of mental illness: *Die Fremde* (*The Unknown Woman*, 1902) and *Andreas Thameyers letzter Brief* (*Andreas Thameyer's Last Letter*, 1900).

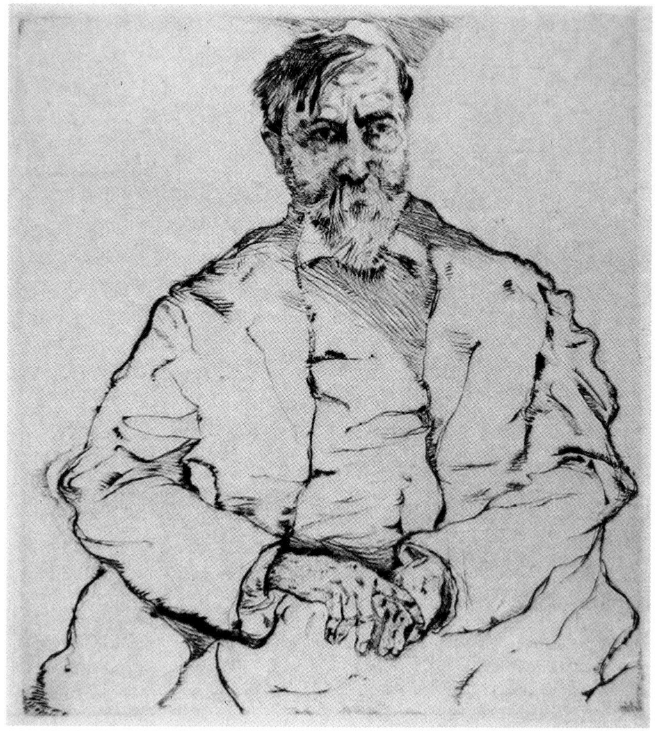

119 Max Oppenheimer, *Portrait sketch of Arthur Schnitzler*, 1912

In *Die Fremde* Albert awakes on his honeymoon in Innsbruck to find a note from his bride Katharina saying she may not return. Albert's recollections, which comprise most of the subsequent narrative, explain why this comes as no surprise to him. Her father was killed in battle, and her brother ran through the family fortune and then shot himself, whereupon Katharina's fiancé abandoned her. She began to show immediate and passionate attachments to men she hardly knew, as well as 'signs of a mental disorder that gradually increased to the point of the deepest depression'.[12] But her mother resisted the doctors' wishes to institutionalise her. After Katharina seemingly recovered, Albert met her and fell deeply in love. He recalls instance after instance in which she strayed from him to unknown men, and became obsessed even with artistic images. Finally he realised that he meant no more to her than these casual but passionate affections. Still, they married, though she remained as unknown to him as on the day they met.[13] When she leaves him on their honeymoon, Albert kills himself. In the last paragraph we read that Katharina is pregnant by a man she casually encountered in Innsbruck, from whom she never hears again. This is a tale of two pathologies – Katharina's obsession with strange men and Albert's obsession with the unknown woman. His deluded love causes him to compensate for and forgive her disorder, but he cannot live with it, and so he becomes its victim as well.

In *Andreas Thameyers letzter Brief* the epistolary form allows a first-person account of a 'mentally deranged' person[14] who is about to commit suicide. The letter's paradoxical purpose is to convince posterity that he will kill himself not because his wife has been unfaithful, but to prove that she has not been. Thameyer, a modest man whose sense of humility – and humiliation – is similar to Albert's in *Die Fremde*, cites a number of authorities, including Martin Luther, to 'prove' the folk belief that traumatic experiences can cause pregnant women to bear offspring with unusual traits related to the trauma. What becomes clear through his arguments is admitted toward the letter's end: his wife has given birth to a black child. Rather than entertain the idea that she had a liaison with one of a group of Africans on 'display' at the zoo, he believes her story that she was frightened by these exotic men. He states that if he tried to convince those who are whispering around him 'scientifically' that his wife was not unfaithful, they would only laugh and mock him behind his back, or even say 'Thameyer is insane'.[15] In his mind, then, the only way he can vouch for his wife is by taking his life. Thameyer's rewriting of reality requires so much self-delusion that it is indeed insane and, unable to bear the contradiction between his inner conviction and the outward truth, he ends his life. Although minor works, these early short texts show Schnitzler's intensive interest in psychopathology, which he was to weave into many of his major plays and stories. They are also precursors to two important later narratives, *Fräulein Else* (1924) and *Flucht in die Finsternis* (Flight into Darkness, 1931), which concentrate on the inner disorders of protagonists who are driven by social expectations and the obtuseness of family and acquaintances to the point of psychotic break.

Georg Trakl wrote some of the most compelling yet enigmatic poetry in the German

Below:
120 Georg Trakl, photograph from 1914

Below right:
121 Max von Esterle, caricature of Georg Trakl, *Brenner-Jahrbuch*, 1913

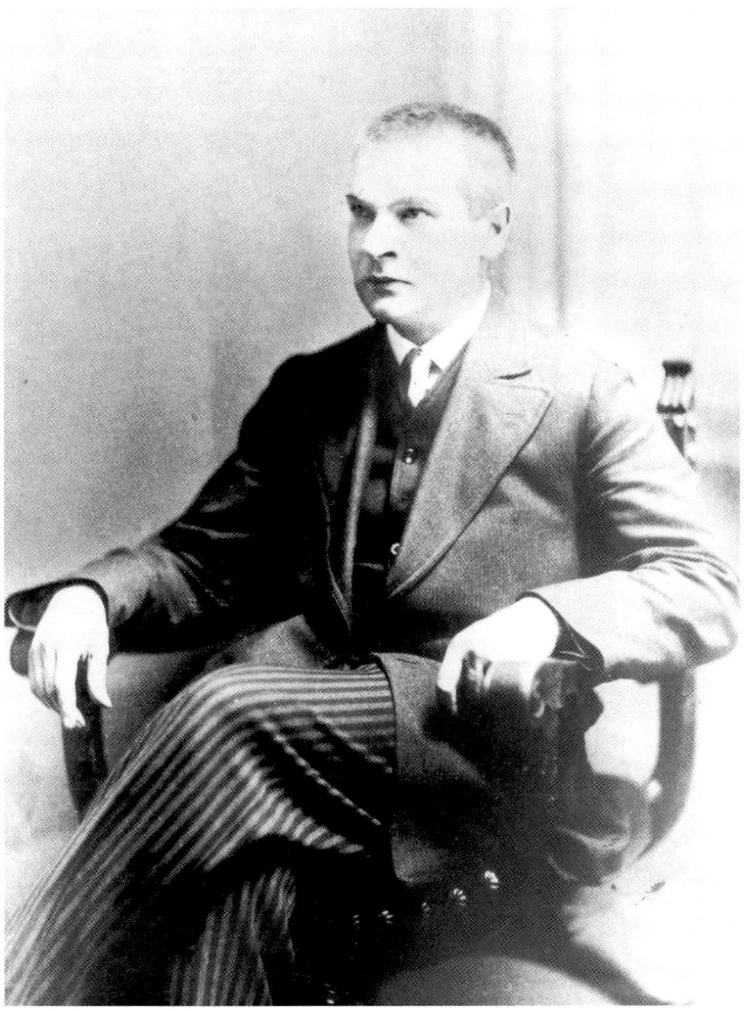

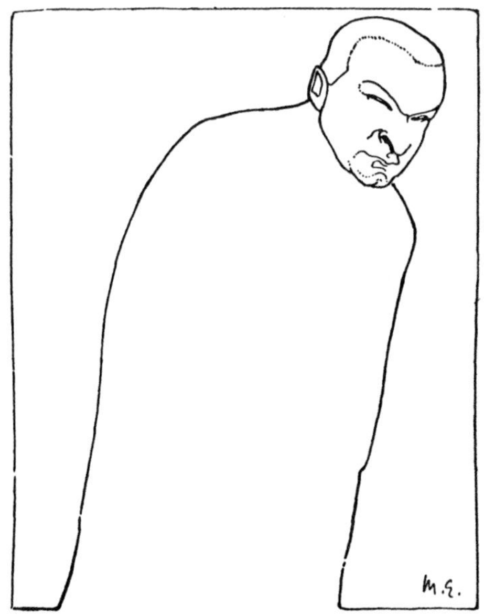

language (figs 120, 121). It is difficult not to connect the dark and lonely imagery of his poems to his life, through which 'drug addiction, madness, and suicide threats … ran like leitmotifs'.[16] Although the madness in Trakl's poetry 'resists capture or exhaustion by the conceptual framework of psychiatry',[17] it can, like the madness in Altenberg's and Schnitzler's texts, contribute to our understanding of extraordinary mental states outside of that framework. Unlike the cases already considered, however, madness in Trakl is not primarily an expression of the individual experience of psychopathology or its social repercussions, and so the connection to the biography is oblique and suggestive rather than direct. It is the power of madness as metaphor that characterises Trakl's images. Yet this is not analogy or simile; rather, madness seems to be embedded in the relationship between the poetic voice and the images and locales it evokes. It is an edge toward which Trakl's world constantly tends, as in the image of the city in 'An die Verstummten' (To Those who Fell Silent, 1915): 'Oh, the madness of the great city, when at evening / By a black wall crippled trees are staring / From a silver mask gazes the spirit of evil'.[18] This madness threatens when the limits of human suffering are reached, in a stillbirth, or on the 'brow of a man obsessed'.[19] In 'Gesang des Abgeschiedenen' (Song of the Departed One, 1915), the quiet that sets in as evening falls is fraught with impending departure from the consolations of society: 'For ever more radiant awakes from black minutes of madness / The patient one at the petrified threshold'.[20] Here madness seems to be not a permanent condition, but the moment of separation, which insinuates itself first in brief impulses ('black minutes'). Madness is thus a sort of liberation, the pain at the threshold of release. This is only a tiny sampling of Trakl's direct use of the concept of *Wahnsinn* or madness. His oeuvre wanders both sides of the border between clarity and delusion, whether madness is mentioned explicitly or not.

Altenberg, Schnitzler and Trakl represent three literary modes of madness in fin de siècle Vienna: personal accounts, fictional representations and madness as metaphor and expression. Many more examples from turn-of-the-century literature, theatre and opera could be cited. The interest of Austrian creative writers in madness only grew after the First World War. Robert Musil, for instance, portrays the social, legal and psychiatric dimensions of madness in his magnum opus *Der Mann ohne Eigenschaften* (*The Man without Qualities*, 1930), especially in the figures of the schizophrenic murderer Moosbrugger and the Nietzsche adherent Clarisse. We have seen that Schnitzler's fascination with psychological disorders continued into the 1920s and 30s. The names of other authors who wrote about madness read like a *Who's Who* of Austrian literature in the twentieth century: Franz Kafka, Joseph Roth, Elias Canetti, Hermann Broch, Heimito von Doderer, Ingeborg Bachmann, Elfriede Jelinek, Peter Handke, Thomas Bernhard, Gerhard Roth, and many others. Indeed, the story of Austrian literature of the fin de siècle and beyond cannot be told without addressing the question of madness.

NOTES

1. Louis A. Sass, *Madness and Modernism: Insanity in the Light of Modern Art, Literature, and Thought* (London: Basic Books, 1992), pp 4–5.
2. David S. Luft, *Eros and Inwardness in Vienna: Weininger, Musil, Doderer* (University of Chicago Press, Chicago), 2003, p. 35.
3. Michael Worbs, *Nervenkunst: Literatur und Psychoanalyse im Wien der Jahrhundertwende* (Frankfurt am Main: Europäische Verlagsanstalt 1983), p. 57.
4. See chapters 3 and 4.
5. Peter Altenberg, *Auswahl aus seinen Büchern*, ed. by Karl Kraus (Zurich: Atlantis Verlag, 1963), p. 248. Translations from the German by the author except where indicated.
6. Altenberg, p. 248.
7. Altenberg, p. 484.
8. Altenberg, p. 269. Translation from Peter Altenberg, *Telegrams of the Soul: Selected Prose of Peter Altenberg*, trans. by Peter Wortsman (Brooklyn, NY: Archipelago Books, 2005), p. 130.
9. Altenberg, *Auswahl*, p. 272. Translation from Altenberg, Telegrams, p. 132.
10. Robert O. Weiss, 'The Psychoses in the Works of Arthur Schnitzler', *The German Quarterly* (1968), pp. 377–400.
11. Weiss, pp 398–9.
12. Arthur Schnitzler, *Die erzählenden Schriften*, 2 vols (Frankfurt am Main: S. Fischer Verlag, 1961), 1, p. 552.
13. Schnitzler, 1, p. 556.
14. Maja D. Reid, '"Andreas Thameyers letzter Brief" and "Der letzte Brief eines Literaten": Two Neglected Schnitzler Stories', *The German Quarterly* (1972), p. 443
15. Reid, p. 519.
16. Francis Michael Sharp, *The Poet's Madness: A Reading of Georg Trakl* (Ithaca: Cornell University Press, 1981), p. 17.
17. Sharp, p. 40.
18. Georg Trakl, *Dichtungen und Briefe* (Salzburg: Otto Müller Verlag, 1969), p. 124.
19. Trakl, p. 124.
20. Trakl, p. 144.

Bibliography

'Atelier für Moulage (Provisorisch)', *Jahrbuch der Wiener K. k. Krankenanstalten*, 2, (1893), 474–8; 3 (1894), 734–8; 5 (1896), 142–6; 6 (1897), 114–7

'Karl Henning' in *Biographische Enzyklopädie Deutschsprachiger Mediziner*, Dietrich von Engelhardt (ed.), (Munich: K. G. Saur, 2002), i, p. 270

'Karl Henning' in *Historisches Lexikon Wien*, Felix Czeike (ed.), (Vienna: Kremayr and Scheriau/Orac, 2004), iii, p. 143

'Karl Henning' in *Österreichisches Biographisches Lexikon* (Vienna: Verlag der österreichischen Akademie der Wissenschaften, 1994), ii, p. 274

Altenberg, Peter, *Auswahl aus seinen Büchern*, Karl Kraus (ed.), (Zürich: Atlantis Verlag, 1963)

Altenberg, Peter, *Telegrams of the Soul: Selected Prose of Peter Altenberg*, trans. by Peter Wortsman (New York: Archipelago Books, 2005)

Aschenbeck, Nils, *Die Moderne, die aus den Sanatorien kam: Reformarchitektur und Reformkultur um 1900* (Delmenhorst: Aschenbeck & Holstein, 1998)

Bahr, Hermann, *Gegen Klimt* (Vienna: Eisenstein, 1903)

Bahr, Hermann, *Studien zur Kritik der Moderne* (Frankfurt: Rütten & Loening, 1894)

Barker, Andrew, *Telegrams from the Soul: Peter Altenberg and the Culture of Fin-de-Siècle Vienna* (Columbia: Camden House, 1996)

Beicha, Otto, *Gustav Klimt: Die Goldene Pforte* (Salzburg: Verlag Galerie Welz, 1978)

Berze, Josef, 'Bauliche Beschreibung und Geschichte der alten Anstalt', *Psychiatrisch-Neurologische Wochenschrift*, 9 (1907), 221–6

Beyer, Ernst, 'Nervenheilstätte, Sanatorium und Irrenanstalt', *Psychiatrisch-Neurologische Wochenschrift*, 12 (1910), 229–32

Beyer, Ernst, 'Zum allgemeinen Bauprogramm der Nervenheilstätten', *Psychiatrisch-Neurologische Wochenschrift*, 6 (1904), 236–8

Blackshaw, Gemma 'The Pathological Body: Modernist Strategising in Egon Schiele's Self-Portraiture', *Oxford Art Journal*, 30 (2007), 377–401

Brandstätter, Christian, *Gustav Klimt und die Frauen* (Vienna: Verlag Christian Brandstätter, 1994)

Bresler, Johannes, 'Die deutschen Volksnervenheilstätten im Jahre 1913', *Psychiatrisch-Neurologische Wochenschrift*, 15(1913), 353–66 and continued in 15 (1914), 375–84

Bresler, Johannes. 'Zur Eröffnung der Niederösterreichischen Landes – Heil – und Pflege – Anstalten für Geistes – und Nervenkranke "Am Steinhof" in Wien XIII.' *Psychiatrisch-Neurologische Wochenschrift* 9, no. 27–28 (1907), 213–15

Cernuschi, Claude, *Re/Casting Kokoschka: Ethics and Aesthetics, Epistemology and Politics in Fin-de-Siècle Vienna* (London: Associated University Presses, 2002)

Clegg, Elizabeth, *Art, Design and Architecture in Central Europe 1890–1920* (New Haven: Yale University Press, 2006)

Comini, Alessandra, *Egon Schiele's Portraits* (Los Angeles: University of California Press, 1974)

Farkas, Reinhard, *Hermann Bahr: Dynamik und Dilemma der Moderne* (Vienna/Cologne: Böhlau Verlage, 1989)

Fliedl, Gottfried, *Gustav Klimt: Die Welt in weiblicher Gestalt* (Cologne: Taschen, 1989)

Foucault, Michel, *History of Madness*. transl. Jonathan Murphy and Jean Khalfa (London: Routledge, 2006)

Gerényi, Fédor, 'Die Entwicklung der Irrenpflege in Niederösterreich', *Psychiatrisch-Neurologische Wochenschrift*, 9 (1907), 216–21.

Gerényi, Fédor, 'Irrenpflege und Verwaltung', *Dritter internationaler Kongress für Irrenfürsorge in Wien vom 7–11, Oktober 1908* (Vienna: Franz Doll, 1909)

Gijswijt-Hofstra, Marijke and Roy Porter (eds.), *Cultures of Neurasthenia from Beard to the First World War* (Amsterdam/New York: Rodopi, 2001)

Gosling, Francis, *Before Freud: Neurasthenia and the American Medical Community 1870–1910*, by Francis Gosling (Urbana: University of Illinois Press, 1987)

Graf, Otto Antonia. *Otto Wagner*. 7 vols. Vol. 1, Das Werk des Architekten, 1860-1902, *Schriften des Instituts für Kunstgeschichte, Akademie der Bildenden Künste, Wien* (Vienna: Böhlau, 1985)

Grillparzer, Franz, *The Poor Fiddler*, transl. Alexander and Elizabeth Henderson (New York: Frederick Ungar, 1967)

Gronberg, Tag, *Vienna: City of Modernity 1890–1914* (Bern: Peter Lang, 2007)

Heighton, Luke, 'Exhibiting Madness, Art and the Asylum: The Creation and Exhibition of Images by Psychiatric Hospital Patients in Vienna, 1890-1914' (unpublished doctoral thesis, University of London, Birkbeck College, 2008)

Hevesi, Ludwig, *Acht Jahre Secession* (Vienna: Carl Konegen, 1906)

Hevesi, Ludwig, *Altkunst – Neukunst* (Vienna: Carl Konegen, 1909)

Hofmokl, Eugen, *Wiener Heilanstalten. Darstellung deren baulichen Anlage und Einrichtung* (Vienna: Alfred Hölder, 1910)

Holub, Edmund, 'N.Oe.Landes – Heil – und Pflegeanstalten für Geistes – und Nervenkranke "Am Steinhof" in Wien, XIII' in *Die Irrenpflege in Österreich in Wort und Bild*, ed. by Heinrich Schlöss (Halle: Carl Marhold, 1912), pp 178–89

Holub, [Edmund], 'Wir und die Öffentlichkeit!' in *Psychiatrisch-Neurologische Wochenschrift*, 9 (1907), 357–61

Hrase, Johann 'Die königlich böhmische Landes-Anstalt für Geisteskranke in Bohnitz bei Prag' in *Irrenpflege in Österreich in Wort und Bild*, Heinrich Schlöss (ed.), (Halle: Carl Marhold, 1912), pp 9–32

Imrie, Nicola J., 'The Architecture and Culture of Sanatoria for Nervous Ailments in the Austro-Hungarian Empire, 1890–1914' (unpublished doctoral thesis, University of London, Birkbeck College, 2008)

Keintzel, Brigitte and Eberhard Gabriel, eds., *Gründe der Seele: Die Wiener Psychiatrie im 20. Jahrhundert* (Vienna: Picus,1999)

Killen, Andreas, *Berlin Electropolis: Shock, Nerves, and German Modernity* (Berkeley: University of California Press, 2005)

Koblizek, Ruth and Gernot Schnaberth, *Neurologie Rosenhügel Rothschild-Stiftung* (Vienna: Eigenverlag Verein MEMO, 2002)

Kolb, G[ustav] (ed.), *Sammel-Atlas für den Bau von Irrenanstalten: Ein Handbuch für Behörden, Psychiater und Baubeamte*, 2 vols (Halle: Carl Marhold, 1907)

Krafft-Ebing, Richard von, *Nervosität und neurasthenische Zustände*, 2nd edn (Vienna: Alfred Hölder, 1903)

Krafft-Ebing, Richard von, *Über gesunde und kranke Nerven*, 5th edn (Tübingen: Verlag der H. Laupp'schen Buchhandlung,1903)

Lachmayer, Herbert, Christian Gargerle & Géza Hajós, transl. Pamela Johnston, 'The Grand Hotel', *AA Files*, 22 (1991), 33–41

Lesky, Erna, *The Vienna Medical School of the 19th Century* (Baltimore: Johns Hopkins University Press, 1976)

Linhardt, Marion, *Residenzstadt und Metropole: Zu einer kulturellen Topographie des Wiener Unterhaltungstheaters (1858–1918)* (Tübingen: Max Niemeyer Verlag, 2006)

Luft, David S., *Eros and Inwardness in Vienna: Weininger, Musil, Doderer* (Chicago: University of Chicago Press, 2003)

Lunzer, Heinz, *Peter Altenberg: Extracte des Lebens* (Vienna: Residenz Verlag, 2003)

Meier-Graefe, Julius, *Modern Art: being a contribution to a new system of aesthetics* (London: Heinemann, 1908)

Miller, Manu von, *Sonja Knips und die Wiener Moderne* (Vienna: Christian Brandstätter, 2004)

Möbius, Paul Julius, *Ueber die Behandlung von Nervenkranken und die Errichtung von Nervenheilstätten* (Berlin: S. Karger Verlag, 1896)

Musil, Robert, *The Man without Qualities*, transl. Sophie Wilkins, (New York: Knopf, 1995)

Natter, Tobias and Christoph Grunenberg, (eds.), *Gustav Klimt: Painting, Design and Modern Life* (London: Tate Publishing, 2008)

Natter, Tobias and Gerbert, Frodl (eds.), *Klimt und die Frauen*, (Cologne: DuMont Buchverlag, 2000)

Natter, Tobias G., *Die Welt von Klimt, Schiele und Kokoschka: Sammler und Mäzene* (Cologne: DuMont, 2003)

Natter, Tobias, (ed.), *Oskar Kokoschka: Early Portraits from Vienna and Berlin*, exhibition catalogue (New York: Neue Galerie; New Haven: Yale University Press, 2002)

Navratil, Leo, *Josef Karl Rädler (1844–1917)* (Vienna: Niederösterreichisches Landesmuseum, 1994)

Nebehay, Christian Michael, *Gustav Klimt: Dokumentation* (Wien: Nebehay, 1969)

Nestroy, Johann, 'A Man Full of Nothing', in *Three comedies*, transl. Max Knight and Joseph Fabry, Foreword by Thornton Wilder (New York: Frederick Ungar, 1967), pp 29–93

Nouvelle Iconographie de la Salpêtrière: Clinique des Maladies du Système Nerveux, Paris, 1888–1918

Paetz, Albrecht, *Die Kolonisirung der Geisteskranken in Verbindung mit dem Offen-Thür-System, ihre historische Entwickelung und die Art ihrer Ausführung auf Rittergut Alt-Scherbitz* (Berlin: Julius Springer, 1893)

Pilcz, Alexander, *Die Irrenbehandlung Einst und Jetzt* (Vienna: Nieder-Österreichische Landesausschusse, 1898)

Portele, Karl A., *Die Moulagensammlung des Pathologisch-anatomischen Museums in Wien*, 1 (1977)

Price, Renee, (ed.), *Gustav Klimt: The Ronald S. Lauder and Serge Sabarsky Collections* (New York: Neue Galerie/Prestel, 2007)

Raimund, Ferdinand, *The King of the Alps: a romantic drama in three acts*, transl. John Baldwin Buckstone (London: T.H. Lacy, 1831)

Reid, Maja D, '"Andreas Thameyers letzter Brief" and "Der letzte Brief eines Literaten": Two Neglected Schnitzler Stories', *The German Quarterly* 45 (1972), 443-460

Rukschcio, Burkhard and Roland Schachel, *Adolf Loos: Leben und Werk* (Salzburg: Residenz Verlag, 1982)

Sass, Louis A., *Madness and Modernism: Insanity in the Light of Modern Art, Literature, and Thought* (London: Basic Books, 1992)

Schalk, Franz, 'Sanatorium Dr Schalk' in *Feschrift zum 60. Geburtstag des Prof. J Glax*, (ed.) J. Cohn, G. Fodor et al (Abbazia, 1906), pp 171–180

Schalke, Thomas, *Diseases in Wax*, transl. by Kathy Spatschek (Chicago: Quintessence Publishing, 1995)

Schlöss, Heinrich, 'Demonstration zweier mikrocephaler Idioten', *Wiener klinische Wochenschrift*, 23 (1895), p. 425

Schlöss, Heinrich, (ed.), *Die Irrenpflege in Österreich in Wort und Bild* (Halle: Carl Marhold, 1912)

Schlöss, Heinrich, *Einführung in die Psychiatrie für weitere Kreise*, second, revised and expanded edition (Berlin: Herdersche Verlagshandlung, 1919)

Schnitzler, Arthur, *Die erzählenden Schriften*. vol. 1 (Frankfurt am Main: S. Fischer Verlag, 1961)

Schorske, Carl, *Fin-de-Siècle Vienna: Politics and Culture* (New York: Random House, 1980)

Schulze, Sabine, (ed.), *Sehnsucht nach Glück: Wiens Aufbruch in die Moderne* (Ostfildern-Ruit: G. Hatje, 1995)

Schweiger, Werner, *Der Junge Kokoschka: Leben und Werk 1904–1914* (Vienna: Brandstätter, 1983)

Scull, Andrew, *The Most Solitary of Afflictions: Madness and Society in Britain, 1700–1900* (New Haven: Yale University Press, 1993)

Sharp, Francis Michael, *The Poet's Madness: A Reading of Georg Trakl* (Ithaca: Cornell University Press, 1981)

Shorter, Edward, 'Private clinics in central Europe, 1850–1933', *Social History of Medicine*, 3 (1990), pp 159–95

Soussloff, Catherine M., *The Subject in Art: Portraiture and the Birth of the Modern* (Durham: Duke University Press, 2006)

Stein, Ludwig, *Jahresbericht des Sanatoriums Purkersdorf bei Wien für das Jahr 1911 nebst literarischem Anhang* (Vienna: Franz Doll, 1912)

Stewart, Janet, *Fashioning Vienna: Adolf Loos's Cultural Criticism* (London: Routledge, 2000)

Stohl, Alfred, *Der Narrenturm oder die dunkle Seite der Wissenschaft* (Vienna: Böhlau, 2000)

Topp, Leslie, *Architecture and Truth in Fin-de-Siècle Vienna* (Cambridge: Cambridge University Press, 2004)

Topp, Leslie, 'Psychiatric Institutions, Their Architecture and the Politics of Regional Autonomy in the Austro-Hungarian Monarchy', *Studies in the History and Philosophy of the Biological and Biomedical Sciences* 38 (2007), pp 733–755

Topp, Leslie, 'The Modern Mental Hospital in Late Nineteenth-Century Germany and Austria: Psychiatric Space and Images of Freedom and Control', in *Madness, Architecture and the Built Environment: Psychiatric Spaces in Historical Context*, Leslie Topp, James Moran and Jonathan Andrews (eds.), (New York and London: Routledge, 2007), pp 241–262

Topp, Leslie, 'Otto Wagner's Steinhof Psychiatric Hospital: Architecture as Misunderstanding', *Art Bulletin*, 87 (2005), pp 130–56

Trakl, Georg, *Dichtungen und Briefe*, (Salzburg: Otto Müller, 1969)

Vitochová, Marie, Jindřich Kejř and Jiří V?etečka, transl. by Ruth and Jiří Kuča, *Prag und der Jugendstil* (Prague: V Ráji, 1993)

Von Puttkamer, Marie-Agnes, *Max Oppenheimer – MOPP (1885–1954) Leben und malerisches Werk mit einem Werkverzeichnis der Gemälde* (Vienna: Böhlau, 1999)

Wagner, Otto, *Modern Architecture: A Guidebook to his Students to this Field of Art*, transl. Harry Francis Mallgrave (Santa Monica: Getty Center for History of Art and the Humanities, 1988)

Wagner-Jauregg, Julius, 'Die Anfänge der Nathaniel Freiherrn v. Rothschild'schen Stiftung für Nervenkranke', *Wiener Medizinische Wochenschrift*, 78 (1938), 113–5

Weiss, Robert O., 'The Psychoses in the Works of Arthur Schnitzler' *The German Quarterly* 41 (1968), pp 377-400

Wieber, Sabine, 'Nervous Bodies and Femmes Fragile: Sculpting the Sanatorium in Vienna 1900', forthcoming

Witt-Dörring, Christian, 'Der therapeutische Innenraum' in *Josef Hoffman's Sanatorium Purkersdorf bei Wien*, (ed.) kunst.buwog.at & Bundesministerium für Wissenschaft und Kultur (Vienna: Agens, 2003), pp 28–34

Worbs, Michael, *Nervenkunst: Literatur und Psychoanalyse im Wien der Jahrhundertwende* (Frankfurt am Main: Europäische Verlags-Anstalt, 1983)

Wunberg, Gotthard, (ed.), *Die Wiener Moderne: Literatur, Kunst und Musik zwischen 1890 und 1910* (Stuttgart: Philipp Reclam Jr., 1982)

Object Checklist

This list reflects the loans secured for the exhibition at the time this book went to press.

Section 1 – The Tower of Fools: A Prehistory

Franz-Xaver Messerschmidt
Character Head
(Die Einfalt im höchsten Grade)
After 1770
Alabaster
Height: 41.5 cm (16⅜ in)
Wien Museum, Vienna, Inv no. 67.137

Franz-Xaver Messerschmidt
Character Head
(Ein wolllüstig abgehärmter Geck)
After 1770
Plaster cast after original in private collection
Height: 42 cm (16½ in)
Belvedere Vienna, Inv. no. 5668

Franz-Xaver Messerschmidt
Character Head (Ein Hippochondrist)
After 1770
Plaster cast, after original in Museum of Fine Arts, Boston
Height: 42 cm (16½ in)
Belvedere Vienna, Inv. no. 5688

Franz-Xaver Messerschmidt
Character Head (Ein Erzbösewicht)
After 1770
Plaster cast from an original in Belvedere Vienna
Height: 40 cm (15¾ in)
Belvedere Vienna, Inv no. 5701
a2-prix.com, Vienna

Architectural model of the Narrenturm, Vienna
2005
63 × 63 × 44 cm (24⅞ × 24⅞ × 17⅜ in)
Technisches Museum, Vienna,
Inv. no. 72045
(replica of older, undated model in Niederösterreichisches Landesmuseum)
Fig. 68

Section 2 – The Modernist Mental Hospital

Erwin Pendl (studio)
Model of Lower Austrian Provincial Institution for the Cure and Care of the Mentally and Nervously Ill 'am Steinhof', scale 1:640
c.1907,
247 × 154 × 138 cm (97¼ × 60⅝ × 54⅜ in)
Technisches Museum, Vienna ,
Inv. No. 13167
Figs 85, 86

Architectural model, St Leopold's Church, Lower Austrian Provincial Institution for the Cure and Care of the Mentally and Nervously Ill 'am Steinhof', scale 1:50
c.1930
Otto-Wagner-Spital und Pflegezentrum

Otto Wagner
Presentation drawings for St Leopold's Church, Lower Austrian Provincial Institution for the Cure and Care of the Mentally and Nervously Ill 'am Steinhof'

1. First design, main facade,
Coloured pencil, ink, drawing paper on canvas
55.9 × 48.3 cm (22 × 19 in)
Wien Museum, Inv. no. 96011/5

2. First design, colour section from N to S in front of altar
Coloured pencil, ink, drawing paper on canvas
55.7 × 48.3 cm (22 × 19 in)
Wien Museum, Inv. no 96011/8
Fig. 90

3. Final design, view and site plan, with pavilions
Pencil, ink, coloured pencil, drawing paper on card
71.3 × 43cm (28 × 17 in)
Wien Museum, Inv. no. 96011/30

4. Final design, side facade
Pencil, ink, watercolour, drawing paper on card
68 × 49.9 cm (26¾ × 19⅝ in)
Wien Museum, Inv. no. 96011/16
Fig. 91

5. Final design, section (C–D)
Pencil, ink, watercolour, drawing paper on card
68 × 49.9 cm (26¾ × 19⅝ in)
Wien Museum, Inv. no. 96011/18

6. Final design, section (A–B)
Pencil, ink, watercolour, drawing paper on card
68 × 49.9 cm (26¾ × 19⅝ in)
Wien Museum Inv. no. 96011/19

7. Final design, floor plan
Pencil, ink, watercolour, drawing paper on card
68 × 49.9 cm (26¾ × 19⅝ in)
Wien Museum Inv. no. 96011/20

Erwin Dom Osen
Two portraits of Steinhof patients, Oskar Loewg and Karl Kalnik
Oskar Loewg, admitted to Steinhof in 1911, patient no. 1963
Karl Kalnik, admitted to Steinhof in 1913, patient no. 1802
1913 (both)
Tempera on cardboard (both)
35 × 50 cm (13¾ × 19⅝ in) (both)
Raiffeisen Bank, Schladming, Austria
Figs 29, 30

Karl Henning
Portrait busts of two brothers with Microcephaly
1897–8
Wax
Height: (approx) 40 cm (15¾ in) (both)
Pathologisch-Anatomisches Bundesmuseum (Narrenturm), Vienna, Inv. no. 22.001 and 22.002
Figs 9, 32, 35, 36, 38, 39

Door from isolation cell, pavilion 15, Lower Austrian Provincial Institution for the Cure and Care of the Mentally and Nervously Ill 'am Steinhof'
234 × 122 × 12 cm (92 × 48 × 4¾ in)
Otto-Wagner-Spital und Pflegezentrum, Vienna

Poster advertising Sanatorium section of Lower Austrian Provincial Institution for the Cure and Care of the Mentally and Nervously Ill 'am Steinhof' with watercolours by Erwin Pendl
94 × 63 cm (37 × 24¾ in)
Otto-Wagner-Spital und Pflegezentrum, Vienna
Fig. 75

Section 3 – Nerves: The Therapeutic Spectrum

Koloman Moser, Armchair, 1903
used in the entrance hall of the Purkersdorf Sanatorium
white enamelled beech with black and white woven cane seat
70 × 65 × 63.1 cm (27½ × 25½ × 24⅞ in)
Neue Galerie New York

Josef Hoffmann, manufactured by J&J Kohn
Dining Room Chair, Purkersdorf Sanatorium
1904
Bentwood, beech with replacement upholstery in red leather
99 × 43 × 44.5cm (39 × 17 × 17½ in)
Victoria and Albert Museum, London, Inv no. Circ.289 – 1967
Fig. 6

Josef Hoffmann
Wall sconce from dining room, Purkersdorf Sanatorium
1904
Black metal Gitterwerk light fixture, rectangular mirror with white wooden frame and bell-shaped black hammered metal flower basket
75 × 20 cm (29½ × 7⅞ in)
Ernst Ploil, Vienna

Josef Hoffmann
Ashtray from waiting room, Purkersdorf Sanatorium
1904
Silver-plated brass
19 × 5 cm (7½ × 2 in)
Ernst Ploil, Vienna

Josef Hoffmann
Wall lamp, Purkersdorf Sanatorium
1903
Nickel-plated brass
19 × 13.5 cm (7½ × 5⅜ in)
Ernst Ploil, Vienna

Josef Hoffmann
Wall lamp, Purkersdorf Sanatorium
1903
30 × 30 cm (11⅞ × 11⅞ in)
Ernst Ploil, Vienna

Josef Hoffmann
Wooden chair with diamond pattern in back, Purkersdorf Sanatorium
1904
Soft wood painted white
45 × 40 × 98 cm (17¾ × 15¾ × 38½ in)
Ernst Ploil, Vienna

Rossel, Schwarz & Company of Wiesbaden, Germany
Exercise (Mechanotherapy) chair
c.1901–05
180 × 108 × 70 cm (70⅞ × 42½ × 27½ in)
Science Museum, London, Inv. 1979–136
Fig. 3

Richard Heller, Paris
D'Arsonval Electrotherapeutic Cage
c.1890–1910
180 × 88 cm (70⅞ × 34⅝ in)
Science Museum, London, Inv. A182649
A. Malaquin, Paris
Electrotherapy control panel
c.1895–1910
Science Museum, London, Inv. A639435

Der Felsentempel von Abu Simbel
[The Rock Temple at Abu Simbel]
Reproduction of watercolour by Ernst Koerner (1846–1927), by Hanfstaengl
1906 (print published 1907)
Owned by Sigmund Freud and displayed in his office and residence at Berggasse 19, Vienna
95 × 68 cm (37⅜ × 26¾ in)
Freud Museum London, Inv. no, 3980

Lithograph of André Brouillet
Une Lécon Clinique à la Salpêtrière
Late 19th century
Engraved by E. Pirodon
59 × 45.5 cm (24¼ × 18 in)
Owned by Sigmund Freud and displayed in his office and residence at Berggasse 19, Vienna
Freud Museum London, Inv. no. 4378

Persian Rug – Qashqa'i
19th century
wool
277 × 165 cm (109 × 65 in)
Owned by Sigmund Freud and used to cover his pschoanalytic couch
Freud Museum London, Inv. no, 6410

Baboon of Thoth, Egyptian
c. 30 BC–AD 395
Marble
22.5 × 9.5 × 10.5 cm (8⅞ × 3¾ × 4¼ in)
Owned by Sigmund Freud and displayed in his office and residence at Berggasse 19, Vienna, before 1914
Freud Museum London, Inv. no. 3133

Warrior, Italic, Umbrian
c. 500–450 BC
Bronze
Height: 20.8 cm (8¼ in)
Owned by Sigmund Freud and displayed in his office and residence at Berggasse 19, Vienna, before 1914
Freud Museum London, Inv. no. 3135

Head of Osiris, Egyptian
1075–716 BC or later
Bronze
Height: 18 cm (7 in)
Owned by Sigmund Freud and displayed in his office and residence at Berggasse 19, Vienna, before 1914
Freud Museum London, Inv. no. 3128

Bes, Egyptian
c.600 BC
Bronze
Height: 16.5 cm (6½ in)
Owned by Sigmund Freud and displayed in his office and residence at Berggasse 19, Vienna, before 1914
Freud Museum London, Inv. no. 3485

Figure of goddess Neith, Egyptian
Late Period
Copper alloy (solid cast)
33 × 7.3 × 10 cm (13 × 2 ⅞ × 4 in)
Owned by Sigmund Freud and displayed in his office and residence at Berggasse 19, Vienna, before 1914
Freud Museum London, Inv. no. 3134

Finial – Figure of Centaur holding rock above head, Roman
Bronze
19.3 × 4.7 × 6.7 cm (7 ⅝ × 1 ⅞ × 2 ⅝ in)
Owned by Sigmund Freud and displayed in his office and residence at Berggasse 19, Vienna, before 1914
Freud Museum London, Inv. no. 3137

Figure of god Osiris standing on block with hieroglyphs, Egyptian
Late Period
Copper alloy
23 × 5 × 4.4 cm (9 × 2 × 1 ? in)
Owned by Sigmund Freud and displayed in his office and residence at Berggasse 19, Vienna, before 1914
Freud Museum London, Inv. no. 3136

Figure of Head of Bearded Man
Owned by Sigmund Freud and displayed in his office and residence at Berggasse 19, Vienna, probably before 1908
Private collection of Ida Fairbairn

Josef Hoffmann and Joh. Backhausen & Söhne
Reproductions of fabric 'Sehnsucht' designed for Purkersdorf Sanatorium, 1904
Backhausen, Vienna

Section 4 – The Pathological Artist

Egon Schiele
Male Nude (Self-Portrait)
1912
Lithograph
42 × 21.5 cm (16½ × 8½ in)
Galerie St Etienne, New York

Egon Schiele
Male Torso (Body and Arm)
1911
Gouache, watercolour and crayon,
43.2 × 29.2 cm (17 × 11½ in)
Private Collection
Courtesy of Richard Nagy, London
Fig. 5

Egon Schiele
FACSIMILE Male Nude in Profile Facing Left (Self-Portrait)
1910
Gouache, watercolour and black crayon with white heightening
Dimensions of original:
43 × 27.5 cm (17½ × 10⅞ in)
Graphische Sammlung Albertina, Vienna, Inv. no. 23.599

Egon Schiele
FACSIMILE Self-Portrait with Hand to Cheek
1910
Gouache, watercolour and charcoal
Dimensions of original:
44 × 30.5 cm (17⅜ × 23⅞ in)
Graphische Sammlung Albertina, Vienna, Inv. no. 30.395

Egon Schiele
FACSIMILE Nude Self-Portrait, Grimacing
1910
Gouache, watercolour and pencil with white heightening
Dimensions of original:
55.8 × 36.9 cm (21¾ × 14½ in)
Graphische Sammlung Albertina, Vienna, Inv. no. 30.766
Fig. 20

Egon Schiele
FACSIMILE Shouting Man (Self-Portrait)
1911
Gouache, watercolour and pencil
Dimensions of original:
48.3 × 31.8 cm (19 × 12½ in)
Graphische Sammlung Albertina, Vienna, Inv. no. 39.930

Egon Schiele
FACSIMILE Semi-Nude Self-Portrait in Black Cloak
1911
Pencil, watercolour on Japanese Vellum
Dimensions of original:
47.9 × 32.1 cm (18⅞ × 12⅝ in)
Graphische Sammlung Albertina, Vienna, Inv. no. 31.159

Section 5 – The Pathological Patron

Max Oppenheimer
Portrait of Sigmund Freud
1909
Oil on canvas
97 × 87.5 cm (38⅛ × 34½ in)
New York Psychoanalytic Society
and Institute
Fig. 31

Max Oppenheimer
Portrait of Heinrich Mann
1910
Oil on Canvas
88 × 80 cm (34 ⅝ × 31½ in)
Wien Museum

Gustav Jagerspacher
Portrait of Peter Altenberg
1909
Watercolour and pastel applied wet on
woven cream paper applied to board.
Maximum dimensions (of secondary
support), 39.8 × 32.9 cm (15⅝ × 13 in)
Neue Galerie, New York
Inscribed recto in pen and black ink at
bottom edge of secondary support: 'Are we
not all only caricatures from the truly and
ideal wishes, which God and Nature made
with our souls and our bodies?!?'
Fig. 54

Gustav Jagerspacher,
Portrait of Peter Altenberg
1909?
Pencil on paper
19.5 × 24 cm (7¾ × 9½ in)
Wien Museum, Inv no. 94.705

Oskar Kokoschka
Portrait of Lotte Franzos
1910
Oil on canvas
115 × 79.5 cm (45¼ × 31¼ in)
Phillips Collection, Washington DC,
Inv. no. 1062
Fig. 45

Oskar Kokoschka
Portrait of Karin Michaelis
1911
Ink on paper
36 × 23 cm (14⅛ × 9 in)
Museum Stiftung Oskar Reinhart

Egon Schiele
FACSIMILE Portrait of Eduard Kosmack
1910
Black chalk, watercolour, opaque white on
brown paper
43 × 30.5 cm (17 × 12 in)
Albertina, Vienna, Inv. no. 31170r

Egon Schiele
FACSIMILE The Painter Max
Oppenheimer
1910
Black chalk, India ink, watercolour on
brown paper
44 × 31.7 cm (17⅜ × 12½ in)
Albertina, Vienna, Inv. no. 31.176

Section 6 – The Patient Artist

Frau St Collage, made in Ober-Döbling
clinic, Vienna
c.1890
Newspaper scraps
25 × 270 cm (9⅞ × 106⅜ in)
Sammlung Prinzhorn, University of
Heidelberg, Inv. no. 3417
Figs 11, 12

Josef Karl Rädler
Half figure of a man standing before a dark
green wall with a window
1902
Verso: Portrait of an old man sitting on a
bench smoking a pipe
1911–12.
Watercolour and opaque pigment
39.5 × 29.5 cm (15½ × 11⅝ in)
Christian M. Nebehay Antiquariat und
Kunsthandlung, Vienna, JKR 5
Fig. 94

Josef Karl Rädler
Portrait of a group of five men
1905
Verso: Handwritten texts
1912
Watercolour and opaque pigment
31.3 × 23.6 cm (12⅜ × 9⅜ in)
Christian M. Nebehay Antiquariat und
Kunsthandlung, Vienna, JKR 17
Fig. 97

Josef Karl Rädler
Half figure of a man in a brown coat before
a wooden bench
1906
Verso: In the garden before a house a sitting
man and a reclining man, a standing man,
trees in the background, evening sky
1912
Watercolour and opaque pigment
36 × 26 cm (14⅛ × 10¼ in)
Christian M. Nebehay Antiquariat und
Kunsthandlung, Vienna, JKR 22

Josef Karl Rädler
Half figure of a man sitting on a bench
1906
Verso: Birds in the branches of an oak tree
No date
Watercolour and opaque pigment
36.6 × 25.5 cm (14⅜ × 10 in)
Christian M. Nebehay Antiquariat und
Kunsthandlung, Vienna, JKR 23

Josef Karl Rädler
Half figure of a man sitting
1906
Verso: Handwritten texts and ornamental
frame
1908/1911
Watercolour and opaque pigment
31.2 × 23.4 cm (12¼ × 9¼ in)
Christian M. Nebehay Antiquariat und
Kunsthandlung, Vienna, JKR 26
Fig. 96 (recto), 98 (verso)

Josef Karl Rädler
A room in the asylum
1906
Watercolour and opaque pigment
Verso: Bird among branches with red berries
No date
Watercolour
26.1 × 35.8 cm (10¼ × 14 in)
Christian M. Nebehay Antiquariat und Kunsthandlung, Vienna, JKR 38

Josef Karl Rädler
Busts of a young man and a slightly older, bearded man
1908
Verso: Handwritten texts
1908/1916
Watercolour and opaque pigment
29 × 21.3 cm (11½ × 8⅜ in)
Christian M. Nebehay Antiquariat und Kunsthandlung, Vienna, JKR 46

Josef Karl Rädler
Bust of a woman with a head scarf
1909
Verso: Handwritten texts
1910
Watercolour and opaque pigment
30.1 × 21.7 cm (11⅞ × 8½ in)
Christian M. Nebehay Antiquariat und Kunsthandlung, Vienna, JKR 51

Josef Karl Rädler
Half figure of a sitting young man knitting
1909
Verso: Handwritten texts
1912/1913
Watercolour and opaque pigment
30.1 × 21.7 cm (11⅞ × 8½ in)
Christian M. Nebehay Antiquariat und Kunsthandlung, Vienna, JKR 53
Fig. 4

Josef Karl Rädler
Bust, en face, of a man with white hair
1909
Verso: handwritten texts
1910/1912
Watercolour and opaque pigment
31.8 × 25.4 cm (12½ × 10 in)
Christian M. Nebehay Antiquariat und Kunsthandlung, Vienna, JKR 55

Josef Karl Rädler
A woman sitting on the ground in the foreground, left
1910
Watercolour and opaque pigment
Verso: Four birds among branches; handwritten texts
1911/1913
Watercolour
25.8 × 36.2 cm (10⅛ × 14¼ in)
Christian M. Nebehay Antiquariat und Kunsthandlung, Vienna, JKR 58

Josef Karl Rädler
Three men at the window
1912
collection: Christian M. Nebehay Antiquariat und Kunsthandlung, Vienna, JKR 71

Josef Karl Rädler
In the asylum garden
1912
Verso: Two men on telegraph poles with a forest behind; handwritten text
No date
Watercolour and opaque pigment
24.9 × 35.6 cm (9⅞ × 14 in)
Christian M. Nebehay Antiquariat und Kunsthandlung, Vienna, JKR 75

Josef Karl Rädler
Self-Portrait
1913
Verso: Handwritten texts
No date
Watercolour and opaque pigment
39.5 × 29.8 cm (15½ × 11¾ in)
Christian M. Nebehay Antiquariat und Kunsthandlung, Vienna, JKR 78
Fig. 93

Josef Karl Rädler
In the dormitory at Mauer Öhling asylum
1913
Verso: Handwritten texts
1913
Watercolour and opaque pigment
25.7 × 31.8 cm (10⅛ × 12½ in)
Christian M. Nebehay Antiquariat und Kunsthandlung, Vienna, JKR 79
Fig. 95

Josef Karl Rädler
In a room at Mauer Öhling asylum
1914
Verso: Birds among branches, four men, negro; handwritten texts
1914
Watercolour and opaque pigment
31.8 × 25.7 cm (12½ × 10⅛ in)
Christian M. Nebehay Antiquariat und Kunsthandlung, Vienna, JKR 88

Josef Karl Rädler
Five men standing
1915
Verso: A clock with four apples; handwritten texts
1915
Watercolour and opaque pigment
25.6 × 31.9 cm (10½ × 12½ in)
Christian M. Nebehay Antiquariat und Kunsthandlung, Vienna, JKR 113

Josef Karl Rädler
Half figure of a woman standing
1915
Verso: A fruit tree in the foreground with a bird house
1915
Watercolour and opaque pigment
31.2 × 25 cm (12½ × 9⅞ in)
Christian M. Nebehay Antiquariat und Kunsthandlung, Vienna, JKR 116

Josef Karl Rädler
Numerous promenaders/strollers in the garden
1916
Verso: Landscape with houses and a church
1916
Watercolour and opaque pigment
26.2 × 33.6 cm (10⅜ × 13¼ in)
Christian M. Nebehay Antiquariat und Kunsthandlung, Vienna, JKR 137

Josef Karl Rädler
Birds
1905
Verso: Bust of a grey-haired, bearded man
1910
Watercolour and opaque pigment
35.8 × 25.8 cm (14 × 10⅛ in)
Christian M. Nebehay Antiquariat und Kunsthandlung, Vienna, JKR 211

Picture Credits

Austrian National Library Vienna, Picture Archive: figs 41, 43, 48, 49, 62, 64, 71, 99, 117

Francis D. Baudry, MD (photography by): fig. 31

David Bickerstaff, 2008 (photography by): figs 66, 67, 89

Bildersammlung, Sammlungen der MUW: figs 16, 63, 69, 78

bpk / Bayerische Staatsgemäldesammlungen – Neue Pinakothek München (photography by): fig. 110

bpk / Nationalgalerie, Staatliche Museen zu Berlin. Jörg P. Anders (photography by). © Fondation Oskar Kokoschka/ 2009 DACS

© Fondation Oskar Kokoschka / 2009 DACS: frontispiece and figs 27, 42, 44, 45, 47

Galerie St Etienne (photograph courtesy of): fig. 23

I. Harkanyi. © Wien Museum (photography by): fig. 61

IMAGNO/Austrian Archive © Fondation Oskar Kokoschka / 2009 DACS: fig. 46

IMAGNO/Austrian Archives: figs 15, 40, 60, 100, 107, 108, 119, 120, 121

IMAGNO/Manfred Horvath: fig. 56

IMAGNO/Sigmund Freud Privatstiftung: fig. 8

Nicola Imrie (photography by): figs 36, 79, 81, 82

© MUMOK, Museum Moderner Kunst Stiftung Ludwig Wien: fig. 52

© National Gallery in Prague 2008: fig. 18

Nieder-Österreichische Landesbibliothek: figs 1, 87, 88

Otto-Wagner-Spital, Vienna (courtesy of): fig. 24

Stadtmuseum Purkersdorf (courtesy of): fig. 25

Leslie Topp (photography by): figs 35, 38, 39

UCL Institute of Neurology (photograph courtesy of): figs 21, 22

© V&A Images / Victoria and Albert Museum, London: figs 6, 112, 113

Michael Wabb (photography by): figs 19, 65, 70, 76, 77

Sabine Wieber (photography by): figs 9, 10, 32, 80, 114

© Wien Museum: figs 2, 51, 55, 57, 59, 90, 91, 106, 118

Index